Journal of the Fantastic in the Arts
Volume 35 Number 2

JFA

Journal of the Fantastic in the Arts
Volume 35/ Number 2

FAVIAN PRESS

A FAVIAN PRESS PAPERBACK

© Copyright 2024
JFA

The right of JFA to be identified as author of this work has been asserted in accordance with the Copyright, Designs and Patents Act 1988

All Rights Reserved

No reproduction, copy or transmission of the publication may be made without written permission. No paragraph of this publication may be reproduced, copied or transmitted save with the written permission of the publisher, or in accordance with the provisions of the Copyright Act 1956 (as amended).

Any person who does any unauthorised act in relation to this publication may be liable to criminal prosecution and civil claims for damages.

ISBN 978 1 78695 898 3

Published by Favian Press
an imprint of Fiction4All
www.fiction4all.com

This edition published 2024

Journal of the Fantastic in the Arts
—The Fantastic is the Allegory of the Actual—

Volume 35/ Number 2
Whole Number 120
Supported by the
International Association for the Fantastic in the Arts.

Editors-in-Chief	Jude Wright *Managing*
	Cat Ashton *Production*
	Novella Brooks de Vita *Acquisitions and Reviews*
Senior Submissions and Reviews Editor	Farah Mendlesohn
Submissions Editor	Tedd Hawks
Peer Review Editor	Ida Yoshinaga
Copy Editor	Cat Ashton
Accessibility & Sensitivity Coordinator	Alexis Brooks de Vita
Regional Submissions, Accessibility, Sensitivity & Reviews Editors	Taryne Taylor Sang-Keun Yoo
Editor-at-Large	Dale Knickerbocker
Editorial Advisory Board	Michelle Anya Anjirbag Cristina Bacchilega Kyle William Bishop Jim Casey

Ian Campbell
Bodhisattva Chattopadhyay
F. Brett Cox
Mame Bougouma Diene
Grace Dillon
Tananarive Due
Neil Gaiman
John Garrison
Mads Haahr
Regina Hansen
Rachel Haywood
Kathryn Hume
Aaron Kashtan
Brooks Landon
Isiah Lavender III
Roger Luckhurst
Rob Maslen
Cheryl Morgan
James Morrow
Alec Nevala-Lee
Joy Sanchez-Taylor
Wole Talabi
Sherryl Vint
Gary K. Wolfe

COVER ART
A Tourist on Mt. Helicon, by Jean Lorrah

GENERAL INQUIRIES
Inquiries and other editorial correspondence should be directed to journal@fantastic-arts.org.

SUBMISSIONS

Like the International Conference on the Fantastic in the Arts, *JFA* welcomes papers on all aspects of the fantastic in world literatures and media, as well as interdisciplinary approaches including African/Diaspora Studies, anthropology, area studies, critical game studies, disability studies, future studies, gender studies, history, Indigenous studies, music, philosophy, political science, postcolonial studies, psychology, queer studies, religious studies, science and technology studies, and sociology. All papers are made available in English and fully refereed. The journal is indexed in the MLA Bibliography.

Submissions should contain a more in-depth discussion than a conference-length paper and demonstrate a grasp of current scholarship on the subject. The length of articles generally varies from 3,500-9,000 words and ranges from 15-35 pages.

All submissions are peer-reviewed in accordance with our peer review statement, the *Submission, Accessibility and Sensitivity Review Handbook*, and the BIPOC Anti-Racist Statement on Scholarly Reviewing Practices. If submissions are flagged at any point of the review process for the risk of promulgating potentially misrepresentative, stereotypical, ableist, or racist views, contributors will be asked to address these problems before the review process can continue.

Since the refereeing process is anonymous, the author's name should not appear anywhere on the text file itself, including the notes. No title page is needed. However, an abstract of 100-150 words must be inserted at the beginning of each submission, clearly stating what contribution the essay makes to the study of the fantastic.

Please ensure that all citations and the Works Cited entries are in current MLA style. Please do not use automatically generated notes; end notes (only) must be entered manually. A paper that doesn't meet our printing parameters can take many hours to adjust. To avoid needless changes and delays, it is best to use our guidelines from the start. For complete guidelines, please refer to the *Submission, Accessibility and Sensitivity*

Review Handbook and the JFA In-House Style Guide. In case of conflicting instructions, defer to the Submission, Accessibility and Sensitivity Review Handbook and the JFA In-House Style Guide. Contributors are responsible for acquiring all permissions to quote and/or use illustrations that accompany their article, and for paying (or arranging to have their institutions pay) all usage fees, including copyright.

Due to the need to provide the journal in multiple formats, the journal does not currently publish images/illustrations in articles.

Scholarly articles should be directed to the JFA's Acquisitions and Reviews team (under Editor-in-Chief Novella Brooks de Vita at jfa.acquisitions@fantastic-arts.org). Please send your anonymized submission to the Submissions Editor, Tedd Hawks, at journal@fantastic-arts.org and include "ATTN: JFA Article Submission" at the start of your subject line. Allow thirty days for confirmation of receipt before querying.

BOOK REVIEWS

JFA also publishes reviews of scholarly works addressing the fantastic, broadly construed. Reviews of fiction are limited to reissues of speculative works with new introductions and scholarly apparatuses, and speculative works with the potential to impact scholarship in the genre. Books and other media received are advertised on the IAFA discussion list (which can be subscribed to through the IAFA homepage at www.iafa.org), and IAFA members are encouraged to suggest titles for review.

To mail book copies for review and for queries or reviews of English-language publications, please contact the JFA at journal@fantastic-arts.org.

Contents

Latinx Young Adult Fantasy as Guides through Portals: A Potential Framework for Portals as Sites for Agency and Identity — 8
    Jordan Alves-Foss

Time Travel as the Displacement of the Fantastic: The Shifting Temporal Paradigms of Genre and Narratology in the *Outlander* Television Drama — 40
    Michael Unger

The Ekphrastic Narrative of the Silmarils: The Prevalence of Ekphrasis in J. R. R. Tolkien's *The Silmarillion* — 63
    Patrícia Sá

Creative Think Piece: A Gift From Pegasus — 90
    Jean Lorrah

David G. Hartwell Award Winner, 2024
"The Beauty of the House is Immeasurable": Susanna Clarke's *Piranesi* on the Uses of Speculative Fiction for Escape During the Covid Pandemic — 101
    Liz Busby

David G. Hartwell Award Winner, 2024
Toxic Tales: The Craft of Enchantment in Fiction and Memoir — 113
    Sasha Bailyn

Walter James Miller Memorial Award Winner, 2024
Resurrecting Indigenous Sciences from the Prehistoric Myths of Chinese Ancestral Tribes: The Whimsical Cosmographer in Weiyu's *Great Fable* Tetralogy — 125
    Yuheng Ko

Analyzing Works Of James Baldwin, Toni Morrison, and Octavia E. Butler As Prophetic Literature In American Society — 150

Stevens Orozco

Map Before Territory: Cartography and Ecology in Erik
Granström's *Svavelvinter*   173
   Svante Landgraf

REVIEWS

Anastasio, Matteo, Margot Brink, Lisa Dauth, Andrew Erickson,
Isabelle Leitloff, and Jan Rhein's (eds.) *Transnationale
Literaturen und Literaturtransfer im 20. und 21.
Jarhrhundert: Plurilinguale und interdisziplinare
Perspektiven*   198
   Rev. by Alexis Brooks de Vita

Kimberly Cleveland's *Africanfuturism: African Imaginings of
Other Times, Spaces, and Worlds*   209
   Rev. by Olawale Oladokun

Antonio Córdoba and Emily A. Maguire's *Posthumanism and
Latin(x) American Science Fiction*   215
   Rev. by Cailey Poirier

Abstracts

Jordan Alves-Foss
Latinx Young Adult Fantasy as Guides through Portals: A Potential Framework for Portals as Sites for Agency and Identity

This essay proposes a new overarching framework, portals as sites for agency and identity, for analyzing portals within fantasy as a potential way to analyze a character's agency and identity. Under this larger framework, this essay proposes five different types of portals: Exploration, Intrusion, Agency/Transformation, Destruction, and the Portal not Traveled. By looking at how characters move across these different portals and how these portals are presented, readers and theorists can analyze characters' levels of agency and the shaping of their identity. This analysis can reveal larger implications of what identities are protected, valued or sacrificed, and thus reveal more extensive commentaries about the world at large. Finally, this essay puts forth an argument that Latinx Critical Theory should be included in future fantasy work, as it provides a powerful analysis into what it means to be a person trapped between two worlds. While the case is made for all fantasy works, examples are specifically made with Zoraida Córdova's *Labyrinth Lost*, Aiden Thomas's *The Sunbearer Trials*, and, briefly, Louis Sachar's *Holes*.

Michael Unger
Time Travel as the Displacement of the Fantastic: The Shifting Temporal Paradigms of Genre and Narratology in the *Outlander* Television Drama

The critically acclaimed television drama *Outlander* (Starz: 2014-present) in its first two seasons challenged the ontological flexibility and narrative pleasures of time travel by presenting it initially as an earthbound fantasy in Season 1 and then as an explicated facet of a science fiction rationality in Season 2. This essay examines how the first two seasons of *Outlander* constitute what I term "the displacement of the fantastic": an ongoing structural segue of what Tzvetan Todorov categorizes as a literary construct of the fantastic marvelous in which a narrative's protagonist, and by extension the reader, move from the fantastic as a duration of uncertainty in the narrative to the marvelous, in which the supernatural entity or phenomenon is accepted and explained. The displacement of the fantastic thus allows for the viewer to experience two time-travel pleasures and premises: the fantasy of the paradoxical time loop where causality is void and the standing stones operate as a temporal glitch in *Outlander's* first season, and then as a science fiction theorization of the multiverse in Season 2. The formation of chronology of the closed causal time loop in Season 1 transforms into multiple timelines that contain different narrative paradoxes, making the narrative of Claire's relationships across time and history itself become more complex through fantastical portals. As Claire tries to correct the wrongs of her past and history writ large, the narrative of time travel appeals to the viewer's fantasy to go back in time, addressing thematic issues of time and memory and historical revisionism, engaging the viewer by raising questions about his/her own experiences. How does the past influence the present? Can one correct the wrongs of the past?

Patrícia Sá
The Ekphrastic Narrative of the Silmarils: The Prevalence of Ekphrasis in J. R. R. Tolkien's *The Silmarillion*

The current understanding of ekphrasis is of a verbal recreation of a visual representation and is quite different from ekphrasis as it was understood in Classical Antiquity, when it pertained to imaginary objects, people, places, time periods, and events. Ancient ekphrasis is description animated by narrative, to make a subject stand out as crucial. As Page duBois claims in her 1982 study *History, Rhetorical Description, and the Epic: From Homer to Spenser*, ekphrasis operates as a significant turning point in the epic, the mark of a change in the narrative. Examples similar to its ancient use can still be found in the present day. This paper investigates the uses of ekphrasis in Tolkien's fantasy world in the *The Silmarillion*, demonstrating that the descriptions of the Silmarils are not merely ornamental but crucial to the overall narrative, and are thus examples of ancient ekphrasis. It is not

3 • Abstracts

simply description of a decorative object, a fragment of the text; ekphrasis speaks of how the object looks, how it comes to be, and what sort of feelings it inspires, thereby creating a vivid representation in the reader's imagination. Tolkien creates vivid images of the Silmarils so that they feel like living things. Their imaginary quality allows for an infinite number of representations, as each reader is thus able to invent their own Silmarils. Readers may be moved by the characters who lust for the Silmarils because they know that an inevitable, tragic destiny shadows them. On the other hand, characters who handle the Silmarils with noble purpose revive the reader's hope in the triumph of good over evil, Tolkien's eucatastrophe. This evokes Ruth Webb's assertion that ekphrasis, in its ancient understanding, hinges on its impact on an audience ("*Ekphrasis* Ancient and Modern" 12). Thus, readers become a part of the literary process. With the exploration of these ideas, I add to the conversation regarding the ancient use of ekphrasis in Tolkien's fiction and lend weight to the argument that despite its distance in time, ekphrasis in its primordial understanding still has a place in contemporary texts, not only in poetry, but narrative fiction as well, and would therefore benefit from further discussion.

Liz Busby
David G. Hartwell Award Winner, 2024
"The Beauty of the House is Immeasurable": Susanna Clarke's *Piranesi* on the Uses of Speculative Fiction for Escape During the Covid Pandemic

When Susanna Clarke wrote her novel *Piranesi*, she could not have predicted that it would be published during a global pandemic. The book's narrative of being trapped alone in an infinite interior space resonates with the enforced social isolation during the Covid-19 pandemic. Piranesi copes with his isolation through his study of the symbolic statues that line the halls of the House: their stories become a lifeline, enabling his survival in otherwise insufferable circumstances. Perhaps one of the most unique things about reading *Piranesi* during the pandemic is its reframing of a quiet life confined to an interior space as tranquil and beautiful rather than constricting and claustrophobic. This perspective on abiding in a work of art echoes a formalist appreciation of story: story doesn't need to mean anything or have any practical application in the world to be valuable.

Sasha Bailyn
David G. Hartwell Award Winner, 2024
Toxic Tales: The Craft of Enchantment in Fiction and Memoir

Enchantment is not a genre in and of itself, falling somewhere between speculative and magical realism. It's a craft approach that takes the reader out of a linear, logical experience of reality, while highlighting and exploring the complexities of life. What distinguishes enchanted storytelling is its form, which references or directly imitates classic European fairy tales. Enchantment is a perspective, a slanted look at reality. It asks readers to let go of expectations and whisks them out of the ordinary, away from linear, logical lives. But to be convincing, enchantment must occur in the day-to-day, with a sense of depth and purpose—reflection, as opposed to pure escape. This is not a study of enchantment as genre, but as craft device: what are its uses in prose, and how is it deployed in both fiction and creative nonfiction? This essay explores how *Gingerbread*, a fairy tale rewrite novel by Helen Oyeyemi, and the fairy tale-like memoir *In the Dream House* by Carmen Maria Machado, are alike or different in their enchanted prose.

Yuheng Ko
Walter James Miller Memorial Award Winner, 2024
Resurrecting Indigenous Sciences from the Prehistoric Myths of Chinese Ancestral Tribes: The Whimsical Cosmographer in Weiyu's *Great Fable* Tetralogy

This article proposes to read the speculative aesthetics of Weiyu's *Great Fable* tetralogy as an example of indigenous Chinese science fiction based on its appropriation of the motif of cosmographical collection from Chinese *zhiguai*, or strange tales, and its rationalization of Chinese origin mythology and folklore through a whimsical rhetoric that appeals to modern scientific discourse while simultaneously questioning its

5 • Abstracts

epistemological foundation. This reading of Indigenous Chinese science fiction underscores the close ties between internet literature, science fiction, and the modernity discourse of the Chinese literary establishment since May Fourth, particularly in relation to key issues such as vernacular language, anti-orthodox innovation, and critical reflection on scientific reasoning. Through an analysis of the central whimsical figure, the *shengun* or godly trickster, I will demonstrate how Weiyu develops a distinctive strategy of mythological rationalization—one that both inherits and subverts the approach of her May Fourth predecessors, shaped by the emergent whimsical paradigm in internet literature.

Stevens Orozco
Analyzing Works Of James Baldwin, Toni Morrison, and Octavia E. Butler As Prophetic Literature In American Society

In exploring the connections between the literary arts and the history of society, this study points to the existence of a prophetic element within the proposed formula by French historian Hippolyte Taine when analyzing works of African American writers James Baldwin, Toni Morrison and Octavia E. Butler. By tracing the history of society through a linear path of published and canonized works, this essay argues in support of Taine's theory that the molding of society throughout history is a result of the manipulation of identities and narratives that have established the foundation for the historically dominant culture in a multicultural society in literature, philosophy, and government. The importance of the human element of the writer cannot be overstated for this formula to be successful. It is the writer who lives the shared experiences of the society they inhabit. The sense of identity of the writer depends on the systemic beliefs of their homeland in regards to race, ethnicity, and faith. These systemic beliefs shape the social conditions, the political environment, and the power dynamics that exist between the social classes of people. The tension of the social climate is influenced by how these sub-elements interact with and react to one another. The success of Taine's formula relies upon the passage of time and technological advancement for writers to develop a sharper literary lens for predicting future trends and civilizations. Historical narratives expose the society's victims and resistors within the margins of its neglected storylines. This has led to moments in which the morality of a nation is confronted and the threat of a collapse looms larger as the balance between social classes becomes overburdened by greed, selfishness, and hatred. Taine did not live long enough to witness the possibilities for massive data collection and historical documentation created by the information age. In response to this new potential for narrative manipulation, this essay demonstrates that the twentieth-century works of Baldwin, Morrison, and Butler have executed a practice of radical imagination that succeeds in reclaiming their community's identity, narrative, and history. Mirroring the years leading to the Civil War, as well as the years leading to the Civil Rights and Black Power Movements, this current moment has been constructed by the same oppositional forces and narratives that have plagued the nation since its founding. Whether analyzing through the Hegelian historical cycles or the prophetic writings of Baldwin, Morrison, and Butler, this moment had been foreseen and has arrived. This practice of radical imagination produces a forward vision consciousness that transparently addresses the status of postcolonial society and proposes attitudes and approaches to confront obstacles that still lie ahead.

Svante Landgraf
Map Before Territory: Cartography and Ecology in Erik Granström's *Svavelvinter*

This article analyzes the maps in the Svavelvinter series of novels and role-playing games by Swedish author Erik Granström. The maps activate readers, turning them into players of the game. These cases are examples of how the fantastic is intimately tied to a transgression of material boundaries: between reader and textworld, between map and territory, and between narrative levels in the text. This essay studies how different maps are represented in texts, how the reader is activated in different ways so that the distinction between text and game becomes blurred, and how the fantastic allows for a convergence of metaphor, theme and form. I further highlight the transgression of material boundaries in the fantastic aesthetic object: between reader and

7 • Abstracts

textworld as the reader interprets maps in the book, between map and textworld territory as the map can magically affect the space it depicts, and between narrative levels in the text by metafictional leaps. This convergence is accomplished by employing tools and strategies connected to the field of general ecology, encompassing themes such as the dissolution of boundaries between human and nonhuman actors, between living and nonliving matter, between nature and culture, and decentralizing the place of humanity in the world. The fantastic mode affords specific methods for blurring form and content, for example, when the map occurs as metaphor, theme and form. This hybrid nature of the fantastic aesthetic object reveals ecological themes in the texts and contributes to making the reader a co-creator of the aesthetic experience. This transgressive property of the fantastic shows the importance of studying that form of literature in this age of increasing ecologization of space, of reconfigurations and renegotiations: migration and globalization simultaneously transcend and highlight issues of physical borders and of places blending into each other; technological developments in augmented reality and online communications blur the lines between virtual and actual space; the concept of the Anthropocene highlights how humanity is reshaping the physical world. In the fantastic, these aspects of the world are made especially visible; the metaphors can take on literal meanings, bringing light to how nature and technology, science and culture, human and non-human interact and intertwine.

Latinx Young Adult Fantasy as Guides Through Portals: A Potential Framework for Portals as Sites for Agency and Identity

Jordan Alves-Foss

I ARGUE FOR A NEW FRAMEWORK, portals as sites for agency and identity, to utilize portals as points for analysis to help identify elements of identity and agency within fantastic texts, which is especially pertinent in the case of Young Adult (hereinafter referred to as YA) fantasy. This new framework reconstructs Farah Mendlesohn's previous *Rhetorics of Fantasy* as a series of five portals to identify sites of agency and identity. I also draw on Lori Campbell's thoughts on portals in *Portals of Power*, on the Latinx Critical Theories in Gloria Anzaldúa's *Borderlands/La Frontera*, and on Dorthy Holland's et al., Emma Upichard's, and Richard Flynn's thoughts on identities as being fluid, developing and defined by space. Portals as sites for agency and identity is an argument for the need and benefit of including Latinx Critical Theories in fantasy theorization. The framework can be described as asking two essential questions: Do characters have the opportunity to make an informed choice about whether they cross a portal? How are character identities highlighted, centered, navigated, or sacrificed in the world where the characters live before they interact with the portal, as they are interacting with the portal, and after they pass through or close the portal? By asking and finding the answers to these questions, I propose that a reader can utilize portals as sites for analyzing questions of agency and identity in regard to the characters, as well as reach larger understandings or implications of the real and fantastical worlds. I walk through the theoretical background that forms the elements for this framework, and then delve into a brief overview of the framework and texts I utilize to highlight different portals presented within the framework. Finally, I go into an overview of each portal, with an analysis of a text to showcase how these portals interact with the text and reader. The purpose of this approach is to build an understanding of the framework from a theoretical approach to an actual application.

As a brief note on the term Latinx, I utilize the term Latinx throughout this paper as do other contemporary scholars in the field. I acknowledge the complexities and general flattening that may occur with such a sweeping term. I also acknowledge this term may prove outdated in time. As a self-identified Latinx scholar, I choose to use this term as it is the one I most closely identify with, and I utilize terms such as "we" and "us" as well when discussing such terminologies.

Theoretical Framework

Anzaldúa's *Borderlands/La Frontera* puts forth a cultural study to theorize the identity of a specific group of Latinx people, whom she calls the mestiza, living on the border between the U.S. and Mexico. Anzaldúa argues that mestizaje do not belong to either location, but rather live in an in-between space: the borderlands. Borders are more than just a physical divide, but a historical, social, cultural, and psychic terrain that the mestizaje inhabit, and that inhabits us. This borderland informs the mestizaje's ever-shifting and multitudinous identities; to keep a single identity intact is similar to "trying to swim in a new element" (Anzaldúa 19). As such, mestizaje often experience a "fear of going home" (42), that we will be rejected from our "mother/culture" because there is something "fundamentally wrong with us" (67); yet we carry our cultures and homes with us wherever we go like a "turtle" (43). Mestizaje straddle multiple cultures and ways of being, and we "continually walk out of one culture and into another" (90). Anzaldúa notes this feeling of being torn between two worlds in *Light in the Dark/Luz en lo Oscuro* as "Nepantla," a space of transition located between two worlds (2-3); though notably Marcos de Artuna pushes back on this definition, noting that the Aztec did not use Nepantla as such and instead presents the Aztec term "malinalli" instead as a transformative space. Regardless, the framework of the borderlands exists as a rejection of a singular identity. The borderlands act as a call to accept all parts of oneself. The identity markers that Anzaldúa argues are inherently mestiza can be seen within a larger scope of Latinx identity, especially within Latinx identities that reside in the U.S. and within Latinx characters in U.S. commercial publication. I will continue to utilize the term Latinx when describing the characters and texts below as that term more accurately describes them than the specific mestiza identity and, as mentioned above, follows in the footsteps of contemporary scholars in the field.

Borderlands, while not an exact match (nor do I intend to imply it to be), applies well to YA fantasy. The YA fantasy genre is wholly concerned with movement between worlds: the real or known world (whether the character's real fictional world or the reader's real actual world) and the fantastic world. Rosemary Jackson in *Fantasy: The Literature of Subversion* argues that fantasy is movement or expression of cultural unease and unconscious drives; Kathryn Hume in *Fantasy and Mimesis* looks at fantasy rhetorically, as a movement or a reflection both from the author's perceived world of reality and the reader's; and Mendlesohn in *Rhetorics of Fantasy* argues for a framework of fantasy to look at how characters and readers move through fantastical worlds. The real world and the fantastic world seep into one another, influencing characters (L. Campbell introduction; Mackley 1), readers and authors, (Hume 10), or, holistically, the other world.

YA literature as a whole deals with navigating transition points between childhood and adulthood, and provides avenues for characters and readers to "put on" and perform different identities (Polleck 140). Children and young adults are both "being and becoming" (Uprichard 1-2) social actors, thus flitting between worlds of childhood and adulthood. Therefore, YA fantasy literature, focusing on and looking at young adults, is a more thorough examination of in-betweenness as characters navigate the borderlands. This navigation centers, highlights, formulates, or erases identities, for example, forcing children to abandon their childhood (Chowdhury 107), cure their disabilities (Stemp), slay a Dark Other (Thomas 23), or remove other outside identities.

When it comes to identity, theorists may confine identity to a series of cultural identifiers, or major structural features, such as race, class, genders, sexual orientation, disability, or nationality (Holland et al. 7). While these are relevant aspects of identity, Holland et al. in *Identity and Agency in Cultural Worlds* expand the understanding of identity to include a form of self-understanding that is fluid and influenced by social, historical, personal and outside events (7). Holland et al. argue that identity is constructed through self-definition in the social or imagined/figured worlds in which one exists, how one is positioned within these worlds, how one self-describes, and how one remakes these worlds. This allows for other identity roles to be analyzed, such as romantic notions of self: nerd, jock, goth, hero, beauty.

Utilizing Holland et al.'s understanding of identity, then, how do characters situate themselves, and define themselves and their world? This question is answered through examining a character's agency. Agency can be defined as "the ability to act" (Flynn 255). However, Holland et al. utilize Inden's definition of agency from *Imagining India*:

> the realized capacity of people to act upon their world and not only to know about or give personal or intersubjective significance to it. That capacity is the power of people to act purposively and reflectively, in more or less complex interrelationships with one another, to reiterate and remake the world in which they live, in circumstances where they may not consider different courses of actions possible and desirable, though not necessarily from the same point of view. (42)

This definition expands the idea of "the ability to act" to include having knowledge in a way that allows for significant and purposeful change in one's world, even when actions do not seem possible or desirable. The significance between these two definitions is stark as the questions of portals is a question of fantasy and the unknown, thus querying the ability to act with knowledge and agency, which will be addressed in the next section. This definition, which includes acting with knowledge and agency, allows for a further examination into the concept of children as social actors, and whether they are fully able to manipulate the world around them (Flynn 262; Lee 468-470) or whether their agency, and thus their identity, evolve as a state of "being and becoming" (Uprichard 1-2).

The Framework of Portals as Sites for Agency and Identity

Portals have often been regarded as a physical object granting passage from the real or physical world into the fantastic world, such as the looking glass in *Alice in Wonderland* (Caroll), the wardrobe to Narnia (Lewis), or the train to Hogwarts (Rowling). However, portals comprise a much larger part of fantasy. Mendlesohn argues, "We commonly assume that the portal is from 'our' world into the fantastic, but the portal fantasy is about entry, transition, and negotiation" (xix). As Mendlesohn notes, portals can exist as a transition point in any world, even in high fantasies—for example, Bilbo's walking through a door and down a path, to the world outside the Shire, in *The Hobbit* (Tolkien). Advancing Mendlesohn's ideas, Lori Campbell's *Portals of Power* "proposes a more expansive definition of the portal to include not only the concrete doorway like Alice's mirror, but *all those living beings, places, and magical objects that act as agents for a hero(ine) to travel between worlds and/or to access higher planes of consciousness*" (6, Italics original). The portal is reconceptualized as all agents that allow the character or reader to move through fantastical worlds or "access higher planes of consciousness" (6), which in turn reconfigures the idea of a portal as a transformative instance and matter of movement, whether physically or psychologically.

While Lori Campbell does significant work expanding Mendlesohn's framework, her theory does not examine the agency and the identities surrounding the portals. The movement described within L. Campbell's and Mendlesohn's work revolves around framing the portal as movement of the character; yet, these theories do not fully engage with the movement of identities, cultures, or values surrounding these portals. Indeed, questions about how the characters, and thus the readers, interact with these portals (if at all), and perhaps just as importantly, how characters and readers are positioned in relation to the portal, need to be asked. Looking at portals primarily as tools of mobility through which fantastical elements or characters can cross, the framework of portals as sites of agency and identity can be considered broadly as looking at moments of *where* there is a crossing of fantastical elements and *how* the identity and agency of characters thereby changes.

Broadly speaking, viewing portals as sites of agency and identity not only creates a way to identify portals within a fantasy world, but also marks a clear difference in characters' agency and identity before and after their interactions with the portal. Portals thereby help delineate a sense of a character's normal world, and the identities valued in that world, as separate from or bordering the fantastic world and the identities valued therein. At the instant the character crosses, they begin formulating and authoring new identities. One identity is that of a traveler from the non-fantastic world and another is as a tourist or traveler in the fantastic world.

The context of whether a character has agency in choosing to cross the portal is therefore crucial, as such agency helps define whether the character understands what transitioning through the portal implies. If a character understands that an identity is highlighted or centered within a fantastic world before they cross through or over a portal, the character is utilizing the portal to help formulate that specific identity, or to perform that identity. The portal can be broadly seen as a form of power granting the character the agency to formulate this identity. On the other hand, if a character has no knowledge of identities centered or highlighted in the realms of the fantastic, the portal can then be seen as a way of suppressing their agency and their ability to form their own identities, especially if they are forced over or through the portal, whether physically or situationally. For example, Julia Pond in "A Story of the Exceptional: Fate and Free Will in the Harry Potter Series" describes in detail how Harry is not given a choice throughout the Harry Potter series because he is repeatedly forced to go through magical portals, whether he is willing to do so or not.

Thus the framework of portals as sites for agency and identity looks broadly at these issues and interrogates them. However, the framework can be broken down or analyzed further through an understanding of how specific portals appear or operate within a text. Specifically, I coin the following list that will be discussed in support of this argument:

- Portal of exploration
- Portal of intrusion
- Portal of agency/transformation
- Portal of destruction
- Portal not traveled

The portals in question will be discussed theoretically and then their application demonstrated through a series of three texts: Zoraida Córdova's *Labyrinth Lost*, Aiden Thomas's *The Sunbearer Trials*, and Louis Sachar's *Holes*.

Briefly, I will summarize the texts to be discussed in this analysis: Córdova's *Labyrinth Lost* follows Alejandra (Alex) Martin, a Latinx high school girl, as she struggles to be a bruja—meaning a healer, seer or witch—in modern Brooklyn. Notably at the beginning of the novel, Alex grapples with the issue of having magic in a world that shuns magic as abnormal, different, or non-existent. She fears magic and what it has done to her family: magic killed her aunt, made her father disappear, and caused their family to be hunted by denizens of the magical world. It comes as little surprise that Alex is determined to get rid of her magic and makes a plan to denounce her ancestors' blessing of magic on her Deathday, which is a celebration to increase her powers and, at the same time, make them easier to control. A brujo named Nova hints at a way for Alex to reject her Deathday ceremony, and Alex attempts to do just that. However, she instead accidentally opens a portal to Los Lagos, a magical island that acts as an in-between space bordering the land of the living and the dead, and all her ancestors and living family members are banished to the island. Worst of all, her magic is still with her. Determinedly, Alex opens a new portal with Nova, and she goes through in an attempt to save her family.

Aiden Thomas's *The Sunbearer Trials* follows Teo, a trans boy, as he competes in the Sunbearer trials with nine other teen demigods. The trials determine who will be the next sunbearer: a champion tasked with refilling Sol's sunstone with sunlight in order to prevent the Obsidian gods from returning and destroying their world. The only catch is that to fill the sunstone, one of the competitors must be sacrificed. Teo and Xio, a thirteen-year-old boy, are the only two Jade demigods, meaning the offspring of Jade gods, who have not competed in the trials in a very long time. The Gold demigods, offspring of Gold gods, possess greater powers, abilities, and training. Teo is determined to save himself, Xio, and his gold demigod friend Niya from being sacrificed, but inadvertently ends up as Sol's chosen champion. When Teo is told to sacrifice Auristela, his crush and Aurelio's twin sister, Teo is not able to do so. The obsidian gods come back into the world and leave it in chaos.

Portal of Exploration

The portal of exploration acts as the intermediate point between the character's known world and the unknown world. The portal of exploration's most notable feature is that it is tangible, and the character literally walks, falls or is pushed through the portal to the other world. This tendency is marked, as L. Campbell argues, by an internal movement of the character's understanding of the world at large (4); but understanding this portal as a physically tangible doorway, so to speak, differentiates it clearly from a portal of agency and transformation, which will be discussed below. In many ways, a portal of exploration presents often within fantasy, such as in the Caroll and Lewis examples cited above as well as the portal to Los Lagos in *Labyrinth Lost* by Córdova, but it can also present as a more abstract doorway, as in Bilbo's green front door in Tolkien's *The Hobbit*, Diagon Alley in *Harry Potter*, and crossing past the tree and through the barrier to Camp Half-Blood in Riordan's *Percy Jackson*.

There are clear moments in which to look for a portal of exploration. This portal usually comes near the beginning of what is often referred to as the Hero's journey, specifically at the moment of "crossing the first threshold" (Joseph Campbell 71). The portal of exploration represents the physical movement of the character from their known world to the unknown, which J. Campbell notes in *The Hero's Journey* is a movement caused when "old concepts, ideas and emotional patterns no longer fit" (47). Other areas of J. Campbell's Hero's Journey also indicate plot points for portals of exploration such as death and rebirth as well as return and change.

However, while the character moves through portals of exploration, their agency—their willingness, knowledge, and ability to shape their world and cross through the portal—are put into question. This framework deliberately asks whether a character intentionally crosses through the portal of exploration, and, if they do, if they understand what crossing through the portal means. A character who intentionally stumbles or walks through a portal but does not understand what is on the other side, such as Alice in *Alice in Wonderland* or Lucy in *The Lion, the Witch, and The Wardrobe*, can be seen as participating in a form of escapism from their society and the identities, and restrictions of their lives in the known world, escapism being a characteristic often attributed to children's and YA fantasy (Hintz and Tribunella 365). These characters' agency is limited, as they do not know about the fantastic world, but the portal of exploration acts as a sort of catalyst for them to reconfigure their identities in a new world. Characters who move through the portal with purpose and some understanding of the other world, such as Sierra in Daniel Jose Older's *Shadowshaper*, move deliberately towards a culture or set of identities found in the fantastic world. This is especially poignant in the cases of Latinx speculative YA, where characters deliberately subvert systems or explore their identities outside of their known world, or as Ashley Pérez argues is the case in Older's texts, where characters can learn about themselves.

Regardless of intentions, the effect is then one of shifting and playing of identities. Characters navigate contradicting and conflicting identities between the known world and that of the fantastic. For one reason or another, the character is unable to remain in the known world any longer.

Zoraida Córdova's *Labyrinth Lost* is an example with a clearly defined portal of exploration, which is the second physical portal Alex opens to Los Lagos. Notably, the first portal Alex opens to Los Lagos banishes her family to the island. In terms of agency, this particular portal of exploration is a bit complex. Alex is aware of the portal beforehand, and, after talking to Nova, gains knowledge of the fantastic on the other side. It is important to note Nova is lying to Alex to get her to cross through the portal. He needs her to cross over due to a deal he made with a demon on the island. Alex's power is needed to open the portal in the first place, and this therefore places agency in Alex's hands. However, Nova is the expert in magic, at least in comparison to Alex, who tells herself, "Nova will know what to do" (Córdova 82). While there is arguably a moral obligation for Alex to rescue her family—she thinks, "I owe my family my life. I owe them everything I am" (89)—this obligation ensnares her in a socially and historically constructed world, limiting her agency and authoring her identity as first and foremost a family member and dutiful daughter. While such obligation can be read as love, it also presents a problematic issue: when Alex makes mistakes trying to author herself by opening the first portal, she is seen as being required to sacrifice her life and "everything I am" (89) to fix her mistakes, relegating her to disposability. To complicate the issue of agency further, Nova is the one who shoves Alex into the portal after it has been created (97), thus allowing her neither full agency to author her own world nor free will in making her choice.

In terms of identity, the portal of exploration can be read, through Nancy Lesko's concept in *Act Your Age*, as a presumable characterization of coming of age. Alex, by crossing through the portal, is coming of age and stepping into her society's role. One could further extrapolate Alex's resolve to cross the portal of exploration as a moment of her accepting her Latinx identity and associated magic as essential parts of herself. Alex's creation of the portal, regardless of the complications of agency, can be read as a moment of self-realization, when she understands that she cannot imagine herself as an individual without her family. Alex notes that she owes her family "everything I am" (Córdova 89). She therefore sacrifices her childhood for the greater good, something that, as Chowdhury argues in "A Chosen Sacrifice," many YA protagonists do (107). Alex also sacrifices her bodily autonomy, as she notes: "My body isn't my own, like something greater is wrapping its arms around me and pulling me into the black hole" (Córdova 96-97). The "something greater" here can be read as the Devourer, the demon interested in Alex's Encantrix magical power, but it can also be read as a transformational catalytic moment as argued by L. Campbell, when Alex transcends into the Encantrix. The greater force can be read as her fate—or the heroic journey—taking Alex's control and agency away, to meld her into the story. However, Alex moves towards her new identity through the portal of exploration through the use of her own power, which marks a further acceptance of herself.

Portal of Intrusion

The next two portals are derived from Mendlesohn's thoughts on intrusion fantasy. Mendlesohn notes that an intrusion fantasy is defined as a refusal of the fantastic until the protagonist chooses to "reach for the stake" (115). The intrusion framework can be broken down into two successive portals. The first instance begins with the introduction of the fantastic: the portal of intrusion; and the second, when the character "reach(es) for the stake" to gain power or agency: the portal of agency/transformation.

The portal of intrusion marks the arrival of the fantastic within the character's world unannounced or without warning. While it symbolizes a direct move from the known to the unknown world, it differs significantly from the portal of exploration due to an important distinction: the character is not aware that movement is going to take place. This is not to say that in a portal of exploration, a character realizes that they are crossing into the fantastic world, but that at the time of crossing they realize that the portal goes somewhere. The difference with the portal of intrusion is also a difference in agency, as the characters do not know that their world is going to be shifted in any capacity, whether physically, psychologically, emotionally, or fantastically, when a portal of intrusion emerges. The border here, or portal, crosses over them, which is reminiscent of how Anzaldúa (29) describes the border of the United States shifting over Chicanx people living between the U.S. and Mexico. In essence, just like Chicanx people, characters have no say in how borders are constructed, which side of their known world they end up on, or how their identity is suddenly reconstructed due to larger socially constructed worlds. The portal of intrusion does not need to be a tangible or visible thing, unlike portals of exploration. Portals of intrusion can be analyzed through lack of agency, as a sense of losing control or power in larger systems.

The question is what the portal of intrusion entails insofar as it refers to identities. First and foremost, Mendlesohn notes this kind of portal is marked by a "denial" of the fantastic (115), a disbelief that fantastical elements are real. This denial can be linked to Holland's conception of naming oneself or situating one's identity within the real world: due to the lack of knowledge and agency that a character has, they may not be willing to position themselves within this new fantastical world and framework. Such rejection centers the identities the character has already constructed for themselves, or for maintaining the cultural point of view of their known world. Notably, however, if the fantastic is situated in a certain cultural mythology or representative of an identity that the character shares, this ideological rejection can also be seen as a "fear of going home" or a fear of the "mother/culture" (Anzaldúa 42) that the fantastic represents. This rejection can be further read as a willingness to sacrifice aspects of one's culture to pass or be accepted within a dominant, hostile, or antithetic culture.

Historically and politically, the portal of intrusion can be read as a fear of the Other, particularly immigrants to colonized spaces, portrayed as fantastic creatures (see for example Christi Cook's article "Bite Me" in the collection *Nerds, Goths and Freaks: Outsiders in Chicanx and Latinx Young Adult Literature*, 64; or Linda Heidenreich "Colonial pasts..." in the *Altermundos* collection, 216-220), positioning any Othered identity associated with the fantastic as a potential "Dark Other" to be destroyed (E. Thomas 23). Yet, notably, the argument made here is that while the intrusion portal can be seen as the fantastic crossing through the portal into the character's world, the arrival of the fantastic in any regard represents an internal shift within the character themselves, thereby signaling a potential warring of understandings, beliefs, and identities. Jeffery Cohen in *Monster Theory* (7-16) puts forth the idea that the monster, or in this case the fantastic, can act as a guard for this portal or as an obstacle for the character to overcome at this "edge of difference" between the protagonist's identity and that which the monster/fantastic represents. Even though rhetorically and structurally the fantastic does cross over, the shift of the borderlands needs to be understood internally as well as externally.

A portal of intrusion can be viewed positively by the character if the fantastic disrupts the known world in a way that empowers, or helps the character formulate their own identity, indicating a societal unease with identities that are centered at large within the known world (Jackson 6-7), creating what José Medina would argue is a type of epistemic friction in not only the character's understanding of the world but also the reader's. A place to look for such a portal is the arrival of "the guide" (J. Campbell 51), a character who arrives from the fantastic world and teaches the protagonist to explore aspects of themselves they never experienced or knew. The portal of intrusion can also be found at any point when a monster appears and disrupts the world, empowering the character in ways that were not previously possible. Characters can view the arrival of the fantastic with a degree of ambivalence: it shifts their world and how they view it, but is seen as neither a negative nor a positive.

An example of a portal of intrusion would be in Córdova's (2016) *Labyrinth Lost*, when a shadow demon attacks the Mortiz family. As per the portal of intrusion, the characters are not aware of the shadow demon, and their lack of knowledge makes the characters question reality: "'Why is it so dark out?' Lula asks. 'It's not even five.' Then Lula shouts as a dark shape slams into her side of the car" (Córdova 53). This lack knowledge about what is going on hampers the character's agency: "'What the hell was that?' I shout. 'I don't know.' Mom white-knuckles the wheel" (53). While the Mom finally puts together that the demon is a "Maloscuro" (54), she lacks specific knowledge about it, requiring the characters to read their *Book of Cantos*, a book detailing all the elements of the fantastic, and thus cross into the fantastic world.

Entering the fantastic world brings into focus Alex's fear of the fantastic and the shifting of her and her sister's agency and identity. As the shadow demon comes from Los Lagos, an island to which brujas banish unfavorable fantastical creatures and people, the shadow demon represents a rejection or fear of Latinx culture otherwise mystified or upheld as perfect by the brujas. The demon represents Alex's fear of the fantastic literally hunting her family, but it also represents her inner warring factions of identity between the known and fantastic worlds. Her fears are fully manifested when her sisters lose their agency and ability to author their identities. Her younger sister, Rose, is possessed by another demon during the fight, thus losing bodily autonomy. Her older sister, Lula, is raked across the face, thus losing her beautiful identity. The converging loss of these identities forces Alex to act:

> I jump in front of my sister, my crazy, rude, wonderful, beautiful sister [...] I take everything I'm afraid of and shove it aside. It's like my body isn't even mine, a bright burning light surrounds me, flows through me and hits the Maloscuro. (57)

While Alex manages to freeze the Maloscuro, allowing her mom to hit it with a mace, it is important to consider what the emergence of the Maloscuro does for Alex and the Mortiz family as a whole. Alex, with the appearance of the shadow demon, must contend with conflicting identities and fears within herself: firstly that her fear of magic and the unknown is well-founded, thus validating her rejection of her magical Latinx identity; secondly, that only by operating within this Latinx magical identity can she save her family. The conflict that Alex faces within this scene indicates the contradiction present in navigating these borderlands between normalcy and hyper-reality, to the point where Alex has to sacrifice what she wants (her identity staying in the known world) and her bodily autonomy to save her family. Alex hence loses the ability not only to author her identity, but to construct the world in ways that she wants to, indicating the sacrifice/loss of her normalized identity.

The appearance of the shadow demon reconfigures Lula's perception of herself and robs her of her romanticized idea of what it means to be "beautiful" (Holland 166). Lula thus continually asks for illusions to cover up her scars as a form of gender performance related to her identity (Butler 177-179), as in Córdova's sequel, *Bruja Born*. This performativity not only reveals a loss of agency for Lula, but also a form of stigma as she fears that she will be Othered by classmates or rejected by her boyfriend. Lula's performance of ideal beauty puts into question other aspects of her identity, such as her femininity, as her body no longer conforms to societal expectations of being "unmarked" (Thomson 18). While this is countered in part when Rose transforms into Lula after being asked to think about the most beautiful person she knows (Córdova *Bruja Born* 285), Lula is effectively scarred emotionally in terms of her identity through the emergence of this portal.

Portal of Agency and Transformation

As has been stated above, the portal of agency and transformation in Mendlesohn's original framework is defined as when a character "reaches for the stake" to kill the fantastic (115). The movement can be described as a shifting of authorship in the role the character plays within the figured world, where an object such as a stake is able to give them the power and ability to act within that world. This portal could be split into two distinctive categories; however, I am combining them into one due to overlapping similarities. If one was to signify the difference between the two, a portal of agency would signify power granted to the character through a porter—meaning an object, person or place that gives magical abilities to a character, according to Lori Campbell (3)—that does not permanently change who they are in terms of identity; whereas, a portal of transformation changes a character fundamentally and/or permanently.

To begin, the emergence of the portal of agency and transformation has to deal with the lack of agency the character has in the fantastical or known world. While the portal of agency and transformation may be opened or initiated by an external porter that acts as a catalyst (L. Campbell 3), when the character crosses through the portal, they are able to gain power, knowledge and agency, indicating an internal shift.

The movement through the portal of agency and transformation turns the character from a human into a denizen of the fantastic, which puts into question what is deemed human (see, for example, Ramírez's arguments in "Afrofuturism/Chicanofuturism"; Cook's arguments in "Bite me"). The movement through this portal usually bequeaths a role within the realm of the fantastic. Stereotypically, in Western European fantasy as defined by Joseph Campbell, the role of hero is bestowed upon the protagonist as they become physically able to repel monsters of the fantastic. A character's willingness to cross through the portal, as well as their agency upon crossing, frame the transformation. The fantastic, or the monstrous, can be seen as salvific, a way to throw off oppression, as a safe haven where certain identities may reside (Clark and Castro 12; Cook 66), or as possibly redemptive (Heidereich 221), thus prompting characters to seek out portals of transformation. For example, as Ella Diaz (94-100) and Domino Pérez (80-84) in the collection *Nerds, Goths and Freaks: Outsiders in Chicanx and Latinx Young Adult Literature* argue, Sierra in Older's *Shadowshaper* seeks to become a shadowshaper in part to get past the outsider-versus-insider elements of her culture, to subvert the issues of male dominant power, and to mark spaces for herself and her ancestors.

However, characters who do not want to move through the portal of agency and transformation tend to value the elements of familiarity or normalcy that the predominant culture or known world has to offer. As Anzaldúa notes, "Humans fear the supernatural" (38), or anything that makes them appear abnormal, and thus "To avoid rejection, some of us conform to the values of the culture, push the unacceptable parts into the shadow" (42). In similar fashion, the rejection of the portal of agency and transformation marks in part a fear of rejection by the predominant, hostile culture or a fear of being, as Goffman in *Stigma* argues, "stigmatized" (3-7). Characters can also be forced through a portal to remove or "cure" identities seen as aberrant: people with disabled bodies often find magical cures, or objects that cure impairment, to achieve the identity of a romanticized hero (Stemp).

This creates the question: which is more problematic, that a character has the agency and desire to remove an aspect of their identity and does so; or if a character has an aspect of their identity sacrificed by someone/something else? On the one hand, if a character has the agency to remove their identity, then by doing so they are sacrificing parts of their identity to appease the predominant culture or to pass as normal (Anzaldúa 42; Thomson 13), which is problematic as it portrays not only a society that does not accept the character but also a character who feels unable to live in their own truth. On the other hand, if a character is forcibly pushed through the portal and finds a marginalized aspect of their identity sacrificed, this is a slaying of the "Dark Other" (E. Thomas 26-27) in which the character is also robbed of voice and agency and forced into a circle of violence. Even when a character appears to have agency and choice to cross through the portal, this agency is at times taken from them due to attendant circumstances.

In Córdova's *Labyrinth Lost,* during Alex's refusal of her magical bruja's power as an emergence of a portal of agency and transformation, Alex has little control over authoring herself and containing her magic. Lula, Alex's older sister, attempts to awaken Alex's power through an ambrosia ritual, an offering to the gods. Thus, the narrative about magic is controlled by Lula, who argues that magic will be good for Alex and by extension for the family: "Magic transforms you. You'll see" (Córdova 13), while also noting, "Waking your magic could really bring us together" (12). The indications are that Alex's non-magical existence is either not necessary or an impediment for their family. Since coming into one's magic is seen as stepping into adulthood, Alex's non-magical self can be read as a form of childhood. Lula's insistence that Alex needs to awaken her magic can then be read as Alex's childhood becoming a necessary sacrifice (Chowdhury 107) to save the sanctity of the Mortiz family: Alex, as Alex currently is, is somehow not enough.

Socially and physically, Alex does not have a choice but to enter this portal of agency and transformation. However, it is clear that she does not want to enter the portal. Alex notes, "It's easy for Lula to talk about power. She sees magic as something to be reserved. All I can think of is the blood and rot and smoke and whispers of my dreams" (Córdova 13). Throughout the text, Alex views magic as a force that has killed members of her family, believing her own magical powers made her father disappear. Alex is cast as a denizen of the fantastic, but one who, understandably, attempts to keep her powers at bay: "Lula thinks my powers are sleeping. She's wrong. I can feel the secrets pushing against my veins, and in turn, I push right back - hiding them deep inside, where I hope one day even I won't be able to find them" (16). The refusal of magic here is a refusal of what Alex views magic to be, "blood and rot and smoke." Magic threatens not only to destroy Alex's identity but also her world and family.

The moment that Alex lets her magic loose is telling. Alex's magic first appears on the page when her best friend and eventual girlfriend, Rishi, is injured by a bully: "I feel my head spin at the sight of Rishi's blood [...] my magic slips" (Córdova 28). Not being able to defend her family in the known world, Alex subconsciously moves across the borderlands to that of the fantastic, giving her the agency to protect those close to her in the non-fantastic world. It is the first step into the portal of agency and transformation. However, the movement also reveals a clear warring of identities and contradictions. The concept of slipping invokes the idea that Alex's movement is unintentional. Yet, Alex is no longer able to author her own world in the known world, thus requiring a catalyst for her to gain power (L. Campbell 3). The irony is striking: in order to save her identities and her friend in the non-fantastical world, Alex must move partly into the world of the fantastic and thus out of the known world. This moment paints Alex clearly as "being and becoming" (Uprichard 1-2) a bruja who can enact magical change, but one who is not fully part of the larger figured world.

Portal of Destruction

The portal of destruction, as I like to call it, can be theorized as a major part of immersion fantasy. In immersion fantasy, Mendlesohn explains, the fantastical elements are centered as natural, and the reader essentially sits upon the character's shoulder with little to no explanation of the fantastical world around them. The fantastic world is centered, and the identities associated with it are also centered. While reconfiguring this framework as a series of portals may seem difficult, the crux of the narrative is concerned primarily with the "entropy of the world" or the destruction of the fantastic (Mendlesohn 61). The portal appears on the horizon, such as a black hole or sinkhole into which the fantastic world, the identities, and the characters will be sucked, destroying their known world: hence a portal of destruction. A definitive feature of this portal is that it is external to the character. While the character may be affected internally by the portal, it affects all characters and the world at large.

The agency of the characters usually revolves around preventing the portal from opening; otherwise they are forced across. In some cases, such as *Labyrinth Lost*, the character creates a portal of destruction; in others, such as *The Sunbearer Trials*, to be discussed shortly, the characters attempt but fail to prevent the portal from opening. Whether the characters can prevent the portal from opening or not, the existence of the portal provides leakage from this newly unexplored world into the known world (Mackley 1). Therefore, the mere knowledge of the portal causes a shifting in the character's identities, as they need to remake their comprehension of the world.

The centering of identity here is clear and prominent. The identities deemed worth saving are those already formatted within the fantastic world, the ones that are considered normal, and this centers the readers' experiences with the primary identities within the world. It then becomes a question of how the characters are going to stop the portal from opening. For example, if characters need to slay monsters on the edge of the portal, or "Dark Others" (Cohen 7-16; Thomas 26), the indication is clear that certain identities need to be slain in order to prevent more broadscale destruction. Similarly, if characters need to sacrifice their childhood (Chowdhury 107) or another aspect of their identity, then the value presented is that a specific identity is worth sacrificing for a greater good.

In some cases, characters want to bring about the entropy of the known world. In this type of case, the emergence of a portal of destruction acts as a commentary on the social world at large, such that only the emergence of a new fantastical force can bring about change. Characters can choose not to close the portal of destruction—as will be described below—which then highlights the identities needing to be sacrificed as being more important than the endangered world. In many ways, a refusal to prevent the portal of destruction from opening reveals the larger social unrest that a given society, for one reason or another, has failed to address.

An example of a portal of destruction appears in Aiden Thomas's *The Sunbearer Trials*. This portal of destruction, which threatens the world with the arrival the Obsidian gods, is complex to analyze in terms of centering identity. The Obsidian gods seem to be referred to as "Dark Others" or monsters that need to be kept out of the idyllic fantasy world. While the novel includes characters of varying colors, genders, sexual orientations, and bodies, all of whom are centered as normal, the theme of the story centers a problematic fantasy binary trope of white versus black, indicating an imagination gap (E. Thomas 6). Characters in *The Sunbearer Trials* are notably not stigmatized and introduced matter-of-factly when their intersectional identities are revealed. One example is Dezi, a deaf character who "was tall and had deep, warm black skin and a high fade with sponge curls. He was objectively beautiful" (A. Thomas 66). It cannot be argued then that Aiden Thomas is not presenting diverse characters, bodies, and identities. The arrival of the Obsidian gods as the portal of destruction is hinted at repeatedly as bringing about an era of destruction, oppression, and chaos. Thus, the portal of destruction as presented within *The Sunbearer Trials* is threatening to take away the diversity that Thomas presents throughout the novel. Yet, it is problematic in that it does fall back on traditional fantasy tropes of a Black-White binary.

The emergence of the portal of destruction changes Teo. Teo is forced to enter a ceremony, where he involuntarily passes through a portal of agency and transformation and is bestowed a sunbearer crown, marking him as a competitor, although he protests, "I'm not - this is impossible! I can't compete in the trials [...] I don't want this!" (A. Thomas 59-60). Portals of destruction, however, demand that heroes close them, reframing Teo into the romanticized role of a hero (Holland 102). Teo distinctly identifies himself outside this role: "How am I supposed to compete with the Golds? I'm not a hero. They have been training their whole lives for this and - I'm not even allowed to go to the same school!" (A. Thomas 61). Significantly, there is a social class difference between Jade and Gold demigods. This manifests itself in a difference of social and cultural expectations, leading to an inequity of education, access to gear, and training. This is most clearly seen when Teo's body does not fit the typical role of hero, consequently requiring modifications to the athletic suits the competitors wear. Teo's suit has holes cut in it for his wings despite the fact that he does not want his wings showing, and has to be reconfigured with Jade markings, all of which clearly depict Teo as Othered and stigmatized in the fantasy world. However, the suit also needs to conform to Teo's body, which pushes back against social class restraints, thus queering social class and the idea of hero.

The closing of the portal requires sacrifice, asking once again for the sacrifice of childhood (Chowdhury 107) and the "dark other" (E. Thomas 23), this time in the form of Auristela, for the world to be saved. The ceremony is presented perversely: "Heads turned to watch and they kept *smiling* [italics original]. A sea of flashing teeth and hungry eyes" (A. Thomas 379). Moreover, the sacrifice of Auristela is painted as a spectacle, something to be celebrated, and so intertwined into the figured world that Auristela is depicted as not only willing to be sacrificed, but regal: "Instead, Auristela looked fearless and ethereal, every bit the Gold Hero she was raised to be. Teo felt like dirt beneath her feet" (380). The implication is a perverse idea of what heroes should be to save the world: self-sacrificing, ready to abandon not only their childhoods but also their lives (Chowdhury 107). Notably, the figured world and the romantic role of hero both frame sacrifice as noble, and those unwilling to sacrifice as ignoble, or dirt in this case, creating a level of estrangement, as Teo feels unwilling and unable to fulfill the role his society has thrust upon him. Thus, when Teo refuses to kill Auristela, Thomas resists centering Teo's own story and identity.

While Teo refuses to sacrifice Auristela and his childhood, his choice notably allows the Obsidian gods to enter the world through the portal of destruction. Immediately, the Obsidian gods capture several of Teo's friends and leave the courtyard in ruins. The portal of destruction, as it is depicted, requires destruction and pain, whether of the individual who prevents it from opening or from the world at large when it does open. Yet, one can read through Teo's actions his argument, and therefore Thomas's, that it is immoral to sacrifice vulnerable populations or individuals for the idea of a greater good.

The Portal not Traveled

The last part of the framework is the portal not traveled. This portal is inspired by Mendlesohn's liminal framework, which, as Mendlesohn notes, is perhaps one of the trickiest and hardest to identify in the genres of fantasy. Mendlesohn describes this as fantasy on the periphery of the character's understanding of the world, but one with which they refuse to engage. When faced with elements of the fantastic, a character: "seems to question whether anything truly fantastical has happened at all. We could even see this as an immersive fantasy because the protagonists take it all for granted. Except that they do not" (Mendlesohn 182). The reconfiguration of this framework in terms of fantasy then is simple: there is a portal to the fantastic world that the character and the fantastic do not cross in terms of the reader's or character's understanding. I would call this then the portal not traveled, as neither the character nor fantastic elements, presumably, cross over this portal.

The positioning of identity and agency here is interesting. Agency requires knowledge and the ability to make an impact upon the world, in this case to engage with the portal and the fantastic; but the portal not traveled, for one reason or another, remains true to its name: it is not traveled. In narratives in which the character is acutely aware of the portal but chooses not to cross it, the narrative then centers the identities and worldviews that the character has when they made the decision, a rebuke of transformation that centers a contentedness with who one is at the current moment. Depending on the scenario, this refusal can also be read as a rebuke of the fantastic and the identities it centers, but in every case, it must be read as a refusal to cross into the borderlands. Characters who are not aware of the fantastic then do not make this decision, nor center the identities within themselves. Rather, the portal acts as acknowledgement by the author of the fantastic that exists parallel to the character's existence.

The engagement and analysis of such a portal is limited, as a reader can only engage with the question of why the portal was not crossed or why the portal was mentioned in the first place. The portal not traveled is usually barely mentioned within, or acts as a parallel narrative to, the main narrative, making its impact upon the character likewise limited.

The best example of a liminal portal I have run across appears in Louis Sachar's 2000 text *Holes*. Latinx speculative YA books have magic and fantastic elements ingrained in them: thus, I have not read a Latinx speculative YA book where the characters do not cross through a portal or at least engage with one. Regardless, the portal not traveled is important to address.

In *Holes*, Stanley Yelnats is sent to a correctional camp to dig holes for allegedly attempting to steal a pair of shoes, a circumstance for which he blames his ancestor, Elya Yelnats, for inadvertently cursing his family into misfortune. Stanley offhandedly mentions the curse throughout the book, treating it as a family mythology, but never spells out how the curse came to be or how it could be broken. The curse thus acts as an object for Stanley to blame, but is not something he actually believes in. As the reader learns, the curse supposedly will continue until one of Elya's descendants carries one of the descendants of Madame Zeroni's, a mystical woman who initially cursed the Yelants bloodline, to the top of a mountain to drink from a lake. Stanley unconsciously does this when he carries Zero (Hector), a fellow camper and his best friend at camp, up the mountain, "breaking" the curse. What follows next is that Stanley's father invents a foot odor-eliminating product named "Sploosh," and the Yelnats family is rewarded with wealth and fame. However, none of the characters believe the curse is real.

The character's refusal to interact with the fantastic elements here, regardless of whether or not they are fully present, then centers the issues, identities, and problems the characters already face: injustice, social inequity, racism, and illiteracy. As Mendlesohn points out, the fantasy within the story is laid out "to explain the conditions of the present—a creation-of-the-land story as it is emerging" (215). The portal not traveled here situates a historical context for the characters, one that gives greater meaning and importance to readers. But, since the characters do not fully engage with this portal, while readers can read it as shaping their destiny and identities, the portal is not fully crossed, and the characters remain as if fastened in their own understanding of the world at large.

Portals in Practice

Breaking a narrative down into portals helps readers identify sites of identity and agency, and doing so moves away from trying to restrict a narrative to a single type, as Mendlesohn's frameworks of portal/quest, intrusion, immersion, or liminal may do. Rather, these frameworks must focus on how these portals operate and how the characters navigate the world through these portals. While Mendlesohn's *Rhetorics of Fantasy* is useful and invaluable, focusing on it solely can become complicated as the frameworks portrayed in it potentially overlap. Reframing the text as a series of portals allows a reader or scholar to analyze these different sites as they appear.

This reframing and fresh approach to analysis, in turn, as has been argued, allows for larger implications and examination of what identities are protected, valued, or sacrificed within the context of the agency offered by portals. For example, Tehlor Kay Meija's *Paola Santiago and the River of Tears*, and the Rick Riordan Presents imprint books, notably have several portals within them: the portal of intrusion, the portal of agency, the portal of exploration, and the portal of destruction. Importantly, the Rick Riordan Presents books are all non-European authors drawing on non-European cosmologies, and thus helping to decenter a Eurocentric literary market. Throughout these books appears movement away from childhood and towards adult responsibilities, but also towards an acceptance of these protagonists' unique identities and cultures within a Whitewashing society.

While this framework allows readers to analyze portals that appear as sites of identity and agency, I am under no delusion that the framework offered here is all-encompassing or addresses all the problems that it seeks to resolve. I am sure there are other instances of portals in academia. But this framework works towards a taxonomy of portals that is useful for engaging how and why characters change as they move through the texts. I also want to use this as a note on the significance of LatCrit scholarship to narratives about fantasy, as Anzaldúa and other Latinx scholars impactfully capture what it means to be trapped between worlds. Commercial fantasy has historically been Eurocentric. It is only through the inclusion of non-dominant narratives, cultures, characters, authors, and scholars, that a community breaks free of Eurocentric thought and advances fantasy to be inclusive of all people, thus pushing fantasy to realize its fuller potential.

Works Cited

Anzaldúa, Gloria. *Borderland/La Frontera: The New Mestiza*. 4th ed., 1987. Aunt Lute Books, 2012.

Anzaldúa, Gloria. *Light in the Dark/Luz en el Obscuro: Rewriting Identity, Spirituality, Reality*, edited by Analousie Keating. Duke University Press, 2015.

Antuna, Marcos de R. "What We Talk About When We Talk About Nepantla: Gloria Anzaldúa and the Queer Fruit of Aztec Philosophy." *Journal of Latinos and Education*, vol. 17, no. 2, 2018, pp. 159-163. *Taylor and Francis*, https://doi.org/10.1080/15348431.2017.1295859. Accessed August 6, 2024.

Butler, Judith. *Gender Trouble: Feminism and the Subversion of Identity*. 1999. Routledge, 1990.

Campbell, Joseph. *Hero with a Thousand Faces*. 1949. Princeton University Press, 2004.

Caroll, Lewis. *Alice in Wonderland*. 1895. CreateSpace Independent Publishing Platform, 2020.

Campbell, Lori. *Portals of Power: Magical Agency and Transformation in Literary Fantasy*. McFarland & Company, 2010.

Chowdhury, Radhiah. "A Chosen Sacrifice: The Doomed Destiny of the Child Messiah in Late Twentieth-Century Children's Fantasy."

Papers: Explorations into Children's Literature, vol 16, no. 2, 2006, pp. 107–111.

Clark, Jessica, and Ingrid E. Castro. "Girl zombies and boy wonders: The future of agency is now!" *Child and Youth Agency in Science Fiction: Travel, Technology, Time*, edited by Ingrid E. Castro and Jessica Clark. Lexington Books, 2006, pp. 1-21.

Cohen, Jeffrey Jerome. *Monster Theory: Reading Culture*. University of Minnesota Press, 1996.

Córdova, Zoraida. *Labyrinth Lost*. Sourcebooks Fire, 2016.

Córdova, Zoraida. *Bruja Born*. Sourcebooks Fire, 2020.

Cook, Christi. "Bite me: The Allure of Vampires and Dark Magic in Chicana Young Adult Literature." *Nerds, Goths, Geeks, and Freaks: Outsiders in Chicanx and Latinx Young Adult Literature*, edited by Trevor Boffone and Cristina Herrera, University Press of Michigan, 2020, pp. 63-73.

Diaz, Ella. "The Art of Afro-Latina Consciousness-Raising in Shadowshaper." *Nerds, Goths, Geeks, and Freaks: Outsiders in Chicanx and Latinx Young Adult Literature*, edited by Trevor Boffone and Cristina Herrera, University Press of Michigan, 2020, pp. 88-102.

Flynn, Richard. "What are we talking about when we talk about agency?" *Jennese: Young People, Texts, Cultures* vol. 8, no. 1, 2016, pp. 254-265.

Goffman, Erving. *Stigma: Notes on the Management of a Spoiled Identity*. New York, Simon & Schuster, 1963.

Hintz, Carrie and Eric L. Tribunella. *Reading Children's Literature: A Critical Introduction*. 2nd ed., Broadview Press, 2019.

Heidenreich, Linda. "Colonial Pasts, Utopian Futures: Creative and Critical Reflections on the Monstrous as Salvific." *Altermundos: Latin@ Speculative Literature, Film, and Popular Culture*, Edited by Cathryn Joesefina Merla-Watson and B.V. Olguín, UCLA Chicano Studies Research Center Press, 2016, pp. 213-232.

Holland, Dorthy, et al. *Identity and Agency in Cultured Worlds*. Harvard University Press, 1998.

Hume, Kathryn. *Fantasy and Mimesis: Responses to Reality in Western Culture.* New York, Methuen, 1983.
Inden, Ronald. *Imagining India.* Oxford: Blackwell. 1990.
Jackson, Rosemary. *Fantasy: The Literature of Subversion.* 1981. Routledge, 1998.
Lee, Nick. "Towards an Immature Sociology." *The Sociological Review* vol. 46, no. 3, 1998, pp. 458-482
Lesko, Nancy. *Act Your Age!* 2nd ed., Routledge, 2011.
Lewis, Clive Staples. *The Lion, the Witch, and the Wardrobe.* 1950. Harper Collins, 2009.
Mackley, J. S. "'It's coming through!' Leakage in Portal Quest Fantasies." The Limits of Fantasy, 11 Nov. 2014, Richmond University, London. Conference Presentation.
Medina, José. "Epistemic Injustice and Epistemologies of Ignorance." *The Routledge Companion to the Philosophy of Race*, Edited by Paul Taylor et al., Taylor and Francis, 2018.
Mejia, Tehlor Kay. *Paola Santiago and the River of Tears.* Rick Riordan Imprint, 2020.
Mendlesohn, Farah. *Rhetorics of Fantasy.* 2008. Wesleyan University Press, 2013.
Older, Daniel Jose. *Shadowshaper.* Arthur A. Levine Books, 2015.
Pérez, Domino. "Afuerxs and Cultural Practice in *Shadowshaper* and *Labyrinth Lost.*" *Nerds, Goths, Geeks, and Freaks: Outsiders in Chicanx and Latinx Young Adult Literature,* Edited by Trevor Boffone and Cristina Herrera, University Press of Michigan, 2020, pp. 74-85.
Pérez, Ashley. "Learning Unbounded: Emancipatory Education in Daniel José Older's Shadowshaper Fantasy Series." *Children's Literature*, 48, pp. 124-152. https://doi.org/10.1353/chl.2020.0006. Accessed August 8, 2024.
Polleck, Jody Nicole. "Constructing Dressing Rooms in Urban Schools: Understanding Family through Book Clubs with Latino and African American Female Adolescents." *Journal of Poetry Therapy*, vol. 24, no. 3, 2011, pp. 139-155. https://doi.org/10.1080/08893675.2011.593393

Pond, Julia. "A Story of the Exceptional: Fate and Free Will in the Harry Potter Series." *Children's Literature*, vol. 38, 2010, pp. 181-206.
Sachar, Louis. *Holes*. Scholastic, 1998.
Ramírez, Catherine. (2008). "Afrofuturism/Chicanafuturism:Fictive Kin." *Aztlán: A Journal of Chicano Studies*, vol. 33, no. 1, 2008, pp. 185-186.
Riordan, Rick. *Percy Jackson and the Lightning Thief*. Scholastic, 2006.
Rowling, Joanne K. *Harry Potter and the Sorcerer's Stone*. Scholastic, 1999.
Stemp, Jane. "Devices and Desires: Science Fiction, Fantasy and Disability in Literature for Young People." *Disability Studies Quarterly*, vol. 24, no. 1, 2004, https://dsq-sds.org/article/view/850/1025. Accessed 26 June 2023.
Thomas, Aiden. *The Sunbearer Trials*. Feiwel and Friends, 2022.
Thomas, Ebony Elizabeth. *The Dark Fantastic*. New York University Press, 2009.
Thomson, Rosemarie Garland. *Extraordinary Bodies: Figuring Physical Disability in American Culture and Literature*. New York, Columbia University Press, 1997.
Tolkien, John Ronald Reuel. *The Hobbit*. 1937. William Morrow, 2012.
Uprichard, Emma. "Children as 'being and becomings': Children, childhood and temporality." *Children & Society*, vol. 22, no. 4, 2008, pp. 303-313.

Time Travel as the Displacement of the Fantastic: The Shifting Temporal Paradigms of Genre and Narratology in the *Outlander* Television Drama[1]

Michael Unger

TIME TRAVEL, as an ever-expanding and historically peculiar trope and sub-genre within the larger literary and visual genres of science fiction and fantasy, has experienced a resurgence and possible high-water mark in the form of numerous televisual productions in the United States. Since 2016, three dramas have premiered across three different networks: *Timeless*, which ran on NBC for two seasons from 2016-2018; *Making History*, which lasted for one season on Fox in 2017, and finally *Time After Time* for ABC which began in 2017 but was cancelled after five episodes. Such hype around these productions prompted *The Wall Street Journal* to call these series the "Hot Concepts for Next Season's New TV Shows" (Jurgensen), highlighting this emergent televisual phenomenon, adding to the intrigue about how each series incorporated time travel in scenarios of adventure, comedy, and dramatic plots to infuse each with an air of quantum-leaping fun. They followed on the heels of the second season of *Outlander* (Starz: 2014-present), a series first shot in Scotland with a cast of Scottish and English actors which, during its first year, won the Critics' Choice Television Awards for the Most Exciting Series in 2014 (Johns). This accolade arguably drew critical attention and success to television dramas with an explicit time travel premise (Ty 58).

While a rapidly growing number of television shows feature time travel as a genre,[2] my concern is to elucidate the appeal and success of a single series, *Outlander*.[3] By interpreting its temporal twist vis-a-vis a love triangle across time between two leading men and a leading lady, this essay examines how *Outlander's* temporal structure of time travel changes through its shift from fantasy to science fiction. Ancillary notions of feminist in-narrative derision by the female lead of Jacobean era societal gender roles in the series' epochal shifts in and beyond Scotland will also be considered. In addition, the blending of innovative thematic and visual motifs regarding the supernatural physics of time travel will be examined.

Outlander[4] begins seemingly as a modernist melodrama in which, at the end of World War II, a young British nurse named Claire becomes reacquainted with her estranged husband Frank. Together they visit Inverness in Scotland to rekindle their marriage and research Frank's ancestral lineage. The narrative transforms into a time travel adventure by the end the first episode, when Claire touches the mysterious standing stones of Craigh na Dun, hereinafter "standing stones," and is magically transported back in time to the year 1743. Marooned in the Scottish Enlightenment, Claire must learn to adapt as a woman from the mid-twentieth century, alone and prey to all forms of patriarchal oppression from British and Scottish forces, utilizing her modern sensibilities and nursing skills to survive as a healer. She attempts not only to return to her present time line but later also to alter past events rather than respecting their temporal integrity against the backdrop of the Jacobite uprising in the Scottish Highlands. As a time traveling drama, *Outlander* hinges on a meta-history of this failed rebellion and other historic markers to punctuate its dramatic effect. However, Claire falls in love with and marries a dashing Highland warrior named Jamie, forming a love triangle between her and her two husbands across two different time lines.

Outlander's construction of time travel in its first two seasons offers a significant example of what I characterize as the displacement of the fantastic. The displacement of the fantastic is an ongoing segue, rather than an overlapping of the generic paradigms of time travel from fantasy as a continual state of wonder in Season 1 and science fiction in Season 2, when the standing stones as a time travel device changes into a causal conceit of science fiction reasoning. While different definitions and taxonomies of the fantastic as a mode exist, ranging from duration of "uncertainty" (Todorov 25), to "a sense of wonder" (Mendlesohn xiii), notions of "magic" (Worley 10), to the "perception of impossibility" (Attebery 9), the key distinction that remains constant between these theorizations of what separates science fiction and fantasy is that science fiction articulates a fictional rationalization, logic, or a fixed set of parameters of cause and effect that counters the inexplicable in fantasy. Claire is in a state of uncertainty throughout the first season as to how and why she is teleported to the past by the standing stones. However, in Season 2 she comes to understand how the stones function, and then she can deliberately teleport herself between the present and past, as do other characters. The displacement of the fantastic thus allows for the viewer to experience two time travel pleasures and premises: the fantasy of the paradoxical time loop, where causality is void and the standing stones operate as a temporal glitch in *Outlander*'s first season; and then as a science fiction theorization of the multiverse in Season 2, when the standing stones function as a time travel portal where the timelines between past and present run concurrent throughout the series.

I will examine how *Outlander* accomplishes this by first unpacking the noted theorist Tzvetan Todorov's concept from *The Fantastic: A Structural Approach to a Literary Genre* (1973), particularly his fantastic marvelous as a literary transitory subgenre in which the fantastic functions as a duration of uncertainty for both protagonist and viewer in the narrative, and then shifts towards the marvelous when the supernatural entity or phenomenon is accepted. Although *Outlander* accomplishes this shift through the changing dramatic portrayal of the standing stones as a time travel narrative device, this displacement stipulates a structural change in the temporal narratology of *Outlander's* first two seasons. Integrated as well into my theory work is David Wittenberg's narratological time travel formulations from *Time Travel: The Popular Philosophy of Narrative* (2013). I utilize Wittenberg's closed paradoxical time loop and the multiverse to demonstrate how this change structurally manifests itself within *Outlander's* serial drama format.[5] My textual analysis of *Outlander* focuses on its first two seasons in which this shift occurs, rather than the novels by themselves or a detailed comparison between the two, although one should keep in the mind that the series of novels and short stories are still being written and are not complete.[6] Be that as it may, based on the novels, *Outlander* will remain within the realm of science fiction regarding time travel because of the notion of a multivariable universe of different time lines co-existing.

In a brief history of Anglo-American quantum leaping, time travel has been a fixture in British and U.S. television since as early as the 1960s. Many notable Anglo-American programs emerged in the United Kingdom, beginning with the cult series, *Doctor Who* (BBC: 1963-89, 2005-present), about an alien who disguises a time machine inside a police call box. It remains one of the BBC's longest-running science fiction television series, using multiverse jumping as one of its prominent features to critique, allegorically, the Cold War and arms race gripping the UK in the 1960s, Britain's industrial decline, Russophilia/Russophobia in the 1970s, Thatcherism in the 1980s, and by the 2000s, class and race relations. In the United States, the Star Trek franchise was more utopian than dystopian in its allegorical reference to internationalism, built on a premise of benign space exploration when its original television series aired on NBC from 1966-1969; its more recent television and film reboots and spinoffs have dramatized theoretical frameworks of time travel as a means to address global concerns in the present century, such as denuclearization, global warming and multiculturalism.[7]

Despite its popularity, according to Matthew Jones and Joan Ormrod, definitions of time travel "as it appears in media texts are difficult to pin down. It has been thought of as a genre, a subgenre, a motif and a narrative device [...] It shifts between fantasy and science fiction, magic and technology" (5). Time travel's unusual ontological narrative flexibility allows for and encourages its continued fictional development among several other media platforms, in addition to the serial drama, while remaining resistant to categorizations that might contain its permutations.

Time travel often revitalizes genres and their codified characteristics because time travel interacts with settings and conventions by introducing its own fantastical set of narrative possibilities that directly impact the thematic and narrative content of a serial television drama. Pamela Achenbach maintains that time travel has to be incorporated into the theme and consequently the purpose of the show to be accepted by the viewer as more than just mere narrative conceit (58-59). For example, the detective procedural format of the original British short-run series *Life on Mars* (BBC One: 2006-2007) features, in each episode, a crime to be solved by the protagonist, while the serial arc consists of his trying to solve his predicament after experiencing a car accident in 2006 and mysteriously waking up in the 1970s (Becker

32). The protagonist of *Quantum Leap!* (NBC: 1989-1993), unlike *Life on Mars*, episodically leaps from one human body to another in a different historical era while trying to return home to the show's diegetic original time of the late nineteen eighties. Making use of newer F/X spectacles and head-spinning writing, the epic serial drama *Lost* (ABC: 2004-2010) includes time travel as one of the central components of the island's supernatural dimensions that directly affects its inhabitants and keeps the viewer guessing from season to season. *Outlander* revitalizes the typical romantic trope of the love triangle by staging it across two different time lines.

While the *Outlander* novels, written by Diana Gabaldon over the last twenty years, have been marketed in the romance genre, where they first received popular acclaim, Gabaldon herself considers her epic time travel romance more as an adventure series that belongs in general fiction (McAlister 94-105). The acclaim accorded to them demonstrates that genre hybrids do not necessarily correlate to an equal sharing between, or eclipse of, different genre conventions. Rick Altman's examination of genre beyond its textual properties in *Film/Genre* (1999) accounts for how genre is also shaped by marketing practices, a means of classifying certain works in academia and media industries, and the genre's reception and acceptance from the public as a viable taxonomy. My view of genre in television falls along the lines of Altman's theory, incorporating different genre characteristics into a hybrid form that reinforces the notion of genre as "fuzzy sets" or taxonomies, described by Brian Attebery in *Strategies of Fantasy* as "meaning that they are not defined by boundaries but by a center" (12). Attebery's textual formulation of an overlapping, porous, and shared clustering of tropes and visual/textual motifs fluidly moves across genres or subgenres within a genre, without each genre losing its foundation or identity. I would link Attebery's notion of "science fantasy" as an example of a hybrid form or mixed mode with *Outlander*'s treatment of time travel, in which the linkage's success "depends upon the writer's ability to handle two kinds of structure independently yet simultaneously" (110) while combining the symbolic and the scientific to comment and complement one another without diminishing each other's value. The essentialist endeavor to classify fantasy apart from science fiction is challenged as time travel, emerging from H.G. Wells' novel set in Victorian London, *Doctor Who* and *Outlander*, comprise a trajectory of time travel texts that simultaneously straddle genres.

As a unique displacement of genre, *Outlander* moves from historical earthbound fantasy to science fiction world-building, or in other words a fictive and explicated (and often couched in scientific terms) logos or rationality. Part of what makes *Outlander* an exceptional television serial drama is that it constitutes a successful combination or mash-up of a variety of genres rather than a blending of two distinct ones: the romance genre, with Claire and Jaime's courtship, marriage, and love triangle; and the historical genre in the show's exploration of the events of the failed Jacobite Rising. Added to this is the adventure genre, travelogue, and ancestry pilgrimage, with Claire's and Jaime's exploits and travels in Scotland, Paris, and colonial North America in the third season and onwards. *Outlander* integrates genre elements of fantasy and science fiction beyond time travel and borrows from other genres, as well.[7] The storyteller relies on the viewer's or reader's familiarity with a genre's narrative and thematic characteristics to satisfy but subvert the viewer's expectations by offering variation on these genre boundaries. Mash-ups, like hybrids, take advantage of expanding genre expectations by destabilizing them through a cross-pollination or combination of their different narrative and thematic characteristics. Brian Bethune observes, "the conventions that once nearly delineated the relationships between genres are not the only ones lying shattered—Gabaldon also cheerfully violates the rules within genres" (np). The displacement of the fantastic in *Outlander* blurs genre distinctions between time travel as fantasy and as science fiction as it eventually edges from the former towards the latter while allowing the viewer to experience genre pleasures from each, without diluting their impact. *Vanity Fair* posits that the great strength "of Starz's most assured, inventive series to date [. . .] is that it continues to challenge expectations, shifting genres sometimes scene-to-scene, but always steadfast in its rich, deeply earnest vision" (Lawson). Time travel amplifies what I consider to be the core identity of the series by reinvigorating the romance genre trope of a couple in love separated not only by nationality and geography but also by time.

Fantasy and science fiction genres not only reflect and refract these aspects of the empirical world, but through their mutual estrangement of the known world, challenge the viewer to reexamine it through metaphor or allegory. *Outlander* accomplishes this by using the narrative device of time travel to juxtapose Claire's sensibilities and experiences as a twentieth-century British woman and those of a twenty-first-century viewer with the plight and social roles of women in the eighteenth century in Scotland, Britain and Europe. Likewise, Claire's temporal dislocation encourages the viewer to dislocate.[8] One prominent example transpires in episode eleven when both Claire and Geillis are put on trial for witchcraft because of their inexplicable healing skills and attitudes that threaten the local male hierarchy and their indigenous/Gaelic superstitions. Time travel in *Outlander* thus activates a feminist twist to the historical, adventure, and romance genres through its dramatization of the temporal contrast and similarity between modern and past European gender sensibilities, social roles, and prejudices that Claire, and other female time travel characters such as Geillis, find themselves having to negotiate.

The method of time travel in Season 1 is a fantastical experience to both Claire and the viewer through the seemingly magical device of the standing stones of Craigh na Dun. The stones themselves are fictional but based on the plethora of actual stone circles found in Britain and elsewhere. Stonehenge is another prehistoric site that leads the imagination to ponder the stones' meaning and mythical power. Like Stonehenge, the standing stones in Scotland are still a mystery, though there is speculation about their function, including astronomical observance and events, rites of healing, and landmarks along energy or "ley" lines that traverse the earth (Frankel *Symbolism and Sources* 86-93). Within the diegesis of *Outlander,* Gabaldon enriches her fictional stones with Druid and Scottish folklore, first with a pagan ritual of a circle dance that Claire and Frank secretly observe in episode one, then as an inexplicable portal that Claire touches, causing her to inadvertently time travel. Claire's displacement is dreamlike; this cosmic place is depicted through expressive sound design so that the stones audibly hum in Claire's ears before she is transported. Visually it is a simple, unanimated process. The mechanics of time travel remain elusive.

This accidental and seemingly mysterious occurrence suspends questions of causality, and within the fantasy realm, renders such questions unnecessary (Cristofari 34); Claire and the viewer must accept this phenomenon, however impossible it seems to be. Claire gradually learns that others could have also used the stones to travel through time. Initially, this possibility is presented as folklore in the form of a folk song that Claire hears at the Scottish court of Lallybroch when both Claire and the reader are still in a state of what Todorov describes as a "duration of uncertainty" (25) between the real and the imaginary. The viewer can revel in the supernatural as a suspension of disbelief in which the standing stones are depicted as an inexplicable temporal glitch.

49 • Michael Unger

Todorov's critical study of fantasy offers a structural template or poetics for how various texts embody the fantastic. His central conceit is that the fantastic is the duration of uncertainty on the part of the narrator and reader between what is real and imaginary within the narrative's diegesis. This status and experience will often change during the narrative: "Once we choose one answer for another or the other, we leave the fantastic for a neighboring genre, the uncanny or the marvelous" (25). Todorov's sub-genre of the fantastic marvelous offers a structural template for narratives that first appear to be fantastic but then change or end with an acceptance of the supernatural. Such narratives, Todorov points out, are "closest to the pure fantastic, [...] by the very fact that it remains unexplained, unrationalized, suggests the existence of the supernatural" (52). Alec Worley contends, in his critical survey of fantasy cinema *Empires of the Imagination*, that Todorov's definition of the fantastic marvelous as a sub-genre is limited because "perceptual ambiguities of the fantastic are rarely sustained throughout an entire story and surely describe a narrative technique, not a genre proper" (9). Even so, Todorov's hybrid terminology effectively encapsulates the changing status of the fantastic as a criterion for this sub-genre that I believe also articulates the viewer's experience of the shift of perception of the fantastic in *Outlander's* first two seasons. Episode eleven in Season 1 accounts for the first significant change of perspective on the fantastic: Claire discovers that the character Geillis Duncan, whom she meets in the past, is also from the modern era, because Geillis bears the mark of a smallpox vaccination on her arm. This pivotal event constitutes the moment of acceptance of the fantastic regarding time travel for both Claire and the viewer, because the presence of another time traveler (in addition to later scenes and storylines of Geillis without Claire's inclusion) confirms its actuality. Todorov's hybrid category, although presented as an overlapping between the fantastic and the marvelous, is actually a trajectory from the fantastic to the marvelous in *Outlander* specifically, and in general when applied to likeminded transformative narrative arcs. Claire's sense of uncertainty about her temporal displacement now gives way to acceptance. Yet the aura of wonder continues in the series through other supernatural forces that seemingly exist as aspects of Scottish folklore. Nonetheless, despite these clues, the function and purpose of the stones remain nebulous.

Worley asserts that "Time-slips are glitches on this cosmic calendar, and most frequently occur in fantasy as earthbound stories, where they are usually the only leap of imagination the film and the audience have to make" (139). Worley's term "glitches" is noteworthy because its connotation expresses time travel as a temporary malfunction, a phenomenon that cannot be explained but must be accepted. Worley's assertion applies to time travel stories that slip into the historic past rather than an imagined future, as does *Outlander*. The series commences at the end of World War II, with London as the initial setting and reference point for Claire's story, as her voiceover reflects on her life in London before her first time-travel experience. Claire's voiceover therefore operates as a reflective framing device for her perspective, from an undisclosed future from which she directly relates her entire story and thoughts to the viewer. Claire's temporal disruption creates a paradox by conflating the distinction between the actual and the fantastical of this historical era. In the words of Geoff King and Tanya Krzywinska, the historical setting "is 'realistic' in one sense, making an appeal to the familiar and quotidian, while entirely 'fantastic' in another: the 'ordinary' becomes unrealistic in an extraordinary setting" (24). The historical setting of the Jacobite uprising is made extraordinary by Claire's fantastical presence within it and as perceived through her modern sensibilities. Likewise, an ordinary convention in the romance genre, the love triangle between a woman and two men, is made fantastic by Claire's temporal displacement: Claire's love for her second husband Jamie stems from the time line of the past, while she holds onto her love for her first husband Frank from her present. This love triangle is further complicated by Black Jack, who is Frank's ancestor, played by the same actor, who pursues and repeatedly tries to rape Claire, and who rapes Jamie.

The serial arc of Season 2 expands upon the stones as a teleportation device, but one that now exhibits a seeming logic when properly enacted, not only by Claire who decides to return from the past to the present, but also by Gillian Edgars. Edgars, Geillis Duncan in the past, decides to travel from the present to the past at the end of Season 2 in episode twenty-nine, in her quest to alter Scottish history. Claire steals Gillian's notebooks that contain her theories and calculations about time travel through the standing stones. This discovery is significant because Gillian's and her husband's research clarifies the causes and effects of temporal teleportation by having certain gemstones, the need for the time traveler to possess certain genetics, and the use of various stone circles at specific times during the year for time travel. This is supported by Gillian's successful passage through the stones—although Gillian misinterprets whether a human sacrifice is also needed to make the journey—and soon thereafter with Claire's passage, and the passages of others, in the subsequent seasons of the series. The temporal consistency of the measured time spans between Claire's time travelling to and from the 1740s and the 1940s suggests that chronological time continues in both time lines at the same rate. The other rules of time travel in *Outlander* are then slowly revealed to Claire and the viewer from season three onwards (Frankel *Symbolism and Sources* 83). By the end of Season 2, the stones are no longer experienced as supernatural to the characters who use them, nor to the viewer. They are, rather, teleportation devices that operate in a reliable manner. This changing perception of the standing stones, from a time glitch to a time portal, situates *Outlander* within Todorov's category of the scientific marvelous as one of his four subsets closest to science fiction, whereby "the supernatural is explained in a rational manner, but according to the laws which contemporary science does not acknowledge" (56). While the stones are eventually afforded a scientific explanation for time travel, their supernatural power still resides in the marvelous as logically possible but at the same time empirically impossible.

Other fantastical elements exist within the series: for instance, Master Raymond and Geillis perform magic, a Highlander ghost appears in modern Inverness in episode one, and Claire hears Frank's voice through the stones in episode eight. Valerie Estelle Frankel argues that the stones belong in the realm of fantasy, but she does admit that "Gabaldon's decision to lay out all the rules and theories of time travel, then have Roger and Brianna do it themselves in a journal, emphasizes the strategic thought needed for proper science fiction worldbuilding" ("Lord John Grey" 141). One can argue that in retrospect, time travel in *Outlander* exists only within the realm of science fiction once its fictional rationality is revealed, but the displacement of the fantastic is a transformation of viewer experience rather than its negation: "Virtually all human beings are futuristic; they transcend their past life" (Ernst Bloch qtd. in Butler 175). This affects not only the perception of the standing stones as a narrative device but more importantly changes the temporal structure of the narratology of time travel in Season 2 and for the rest of the series.

This essay has explicated the value of displacement as a trope and visual motif in *Outlander*. To deepen the analysis of displacement, I now analyze how time travel's narratology in *Outlander* demonstrates temporal and narrative contrasts, elucidating the narratology of this television drama in terms of its gradual unfolding of narrative possibilities that ultimately promise narrative coherence. Umberto Eco points out that viewers watch serial television because "the serial consoles us (the consumers) because it rewards our ability to foresee: we are happy because we discover our own ability to guess what will happen" (86). Narrative chronology depends on a causal relationship between past and present events and replicates experience with time as the immediate sensation of a moment that then shifts into the past and into memory. Though narratives may scramble the order of events, there is inherently a discourse of chronology in the relationship between the events of the story and how the plot unfolds in long form television. Time travel blurs through anachrony when characters intersect, and audiences negotiate their past and present timelines; such a thought process then evokes simultaneity and chronology. If David Wittenberg espouses that narratology "is the very *mise-en-scene* of time travel fiction, and time travel the machinery by which narrative is manufactured" (8), then the displacement of the fantastic in *Outlander* manifests itself through its different temporal constructions of time travel.

In Season 1, Claire's temporal displacement and unfamiliarity with customs of the Scottish Highlanders fuel much of the dramatic conflict in the first season and act as a narrative device that accentuates the time travel paradigm. Claire attempts to return to her present time line without revealing her origins or trying to change the course of history. Claire thus attempts to restore time to its rightful chronological order by going back to the present, which reinforces Matthew Kimberley's and Jason Dittmar's observation that, "even a quick survey of the genre shows that despite this radical potential, most time travel narratives culminate in the restoration of 'our' time line in one way or another" (65). Despite these endeavors, Claire falls in with Jaime, and it is not until episode eleven, when her second chance to return to the present presents itself, that she decides to stay with Jamie and embrace her life in the past. This turning point in her struggle to decide between whether to continue to live in the past or return to the present seems resolved, ending in an open, satisfying conclusion to the first season. Season 1 constitutes what Wittenberg describes as the paradox story phase "in which it is impossible to determine whether a cause precedes or follows its effect" (31). There exists within the closed time loop the notion of the grandfather paradox, in which a time-traveler goes back to the past and either purposefully or inadvertently kills their grandfather, thus negating the existence of the time-traveler in the present. *Outlander* directly presents this causal paradox phase with Jaime and Claire's attempt to avoid killing Black Jack Randall until he produces the offspring that will ultimately lead to Frank's existence two hundred years later. If they do disrupt that past by killing Black Jack and thereby negate the existence of Frank, how would Claire have gone to Inverness in the first place to put these events in motion? While the grandfather paradox is raised in *Outlander*, it is never answered or fully explored.

Season 2 expands upon the temporal contrast between the past and the present. The temporal consistency of the measured time spans between Claire's time-traveling to and from the 1700s and 1900s, which is exactly 202 years, suggests that chronological time continues in both timelines at the same rate. Season 2 also implements chronological jumps or ellipses in the unfolding of the plot in each time line. Season 2 abruptly begins with Claire back in the present three years later in 1948. The viewer at first does not know why and when Claire left the past and Jamie. When Claire reunites with Frank and tells him about her relationship with Jamie, Season 2 then depicts that past with her and Jamie in 1744 in a chronological episodic fashion from its first episode to its last, leading up to the Battle of Culloden in 1746. The last episode takes place abruptly during the year 1968, twenty years after Claire's return to Frank, when she lives in Boston with her adult daughter Brianna, Frank now deceased from a car accident. These chronological ellipses in the plot of the present timeline create suspense and curiosity for the viewer. For example, in this last episode, Claire eventually recounts to Brianna what happened at the Battle of Culloden, and why and when she returned from the past, which is then dramatized in that episode, creating further anticipation for the viewer by finally resolving questions raised at the beginning of Season 2. When Claire learns that Jamie may have survived the battle of Culloden, she vows, "I have to go back." Time is depicted no longer as a closed loop of causality, but coexisting lines of past and present, with certain characters under the right conditions able to jump back and forth between them. As James Gleick comments on the impact of Einstein's research on relativity regarding the theoretical possibility of time travel, "there is no *time*, but only *times*" (81, italics original). Time travel stories that embrace multiple and/or alternate timelines, or hold out that possibility, offer the viewer the fantasy that nothing is permanent, which adds to the fantastical atmosphere of the show.

Season 2's structure of parallel storytelling between past and present embodies the "multiverse/filmic" phase of time travel, which Wittenberg characterizes as the "visualization of parallel or multiplied lines or narrative, and with aesthetic or technological depiction of such multiplicities" (82). A notable example of this is the character Brianna, who is the biological daughter of Jamie from 1745, raised as the daughter of Frank and Claire in the twentieth century. Brianna eventually time travels to the past to meet Jamie. *Outlander's* principal characters can exist and jump back and forth between past and present without having to explore such narrative paradoxes to their logical conclusions. Although change occurs in the personal realm of Claire's life because of time travel, the large historical events that *Outlander* portrays do not change, suggesting that the historical past cannot be changed. Despite their best efforts, Claire and Jamie fail to prevent the Battle of Culloden. It is ironic that the secondary characters who antagonize Claire, such as Colum MacKenzie, The Duke of Sandringham, and St. Germain, end up killed by her actions in Season 2. These deaths do not affect the outcome of depicted historical events either in the 1700s or the 1900s. The possibility of altering the past is a consequence that the closed paradox time loop cannot contain without significant repercussions to its circular order of cause and effect, but that the multiverse narrative structure certainly can allow.

This shift in the narrative temporal structure between the two seasons alters the status of the method by which the fantastic enters the narrative, which is the main criterion that Farah Mendlesohn uses to formulate her rhetorical categorizations of fantasy in her book, *Rhetorics of Fantasy*. Time travel as a fish-out-of-water narrative device operates within Mendlesohn's category of the "Portal Fantasy Quest." Season 1 fulfills many of these characteristics: the fantastic exists only on the other side of the portal; the story proceeds in a linear fashion; the story provides the viewer with a guided tour of the landscape like a travel guide; and the story relies upon the protagonist and viewer gaining experience (Mendlesohn 1-18). However, the consistent use of time travel through the standing stones in Season 2, with Claire purposefully returning to the present and Gillian returning to the past, transforms the experience of fantasy towards Mendlesohn's category of the "immersive fantasy" which she maintains is "closest to science fiction; as such it makes use of an irony of mimesis, which helps to explain why a sufficiently effective immersive fantasy may be indistinguishable from science fiction: once the fantastic becomes assumed, it acquires a scientific cohesion all its own" (xx). Portal quest fantasies are one-way journeys; the magic or the fantastical elements contained in the other world do not leak through. Time travel in Season 2 permeates the entire spectrum of the story; the border between the real and the fantastic is no longer clear. Both past and present are affected by the time travel of respective time-travelling characters, creating a metanarrative for the viewer that belies its materiality. Once explicated, the stones are no longer experienced as magical. Mendlesohn ascertains that as "science moves in, magic fades away, and scrutiny makes it leave faster" (108) which accounts for the lessening, or in Mendlesohn's words, the "thinning" of the immersive fantasy to the point at which, in season three, the standing stones are not featured when Claire travels back to the past for the second time.

Time travel establishes flexible narrative structures that can be adapted in different ways within the genres of fantasy and science fiction but provide a framework by which the viewer can navigate its specific machinations within each story. The displacement of the fantastic from Season 1 to Season 2 in *Outlander* uses the trope of time travel to transition the viewer from one set of genre and temporal possibilities into another. The formation of chronology of the closed causal time loop in Season 1 transforms into multiple timelines that contain different narrative paradoxes. Temporal displacements in *Outlander* revitalize the genres of romance and adventure in the series by making the narrative of Claire's relationships across time—through portals of connectiveness in terms of ideology, customs and even love—whereby other characters and history itself become more complex. As Claire tries to correct the wrongs of her past and history writ large, the narrative of time travel appeals to the viewer's own fantasy to go back in time and perhaps do the same. The time travel narrative offers the viewer pleasures by addressing thematic issues of time and memory and historical revisionism and engages the viewer by raising questions about the viewer's own experiences with time. How does the past influence the present? Can one correct the wrongs of the past?

Cinematic fantasy has the burden to make visible the fantastic, and as Jean Mitry says, "in the cinema 'everything is actual'" (52).

This is a burden that fantasy inhabits and fulfills; the definition of the fantastic in Greek is "to make visible or manifest" (Jackson 13). The displacement of the fantastic in *Outlander* is made visible by the shift in the different narratological structures of time travel that constitute its first two seasons and challenge preconceived essentialist boundaries between the genres of fantasy and science fiction. In an innovative fashion, *Outlander* as a hybrid takes advantage of the trope of time travel to create first a fantastical and then a science fictional experience for the viewer as it changes from the former to the latter in its first two seasons. This transformation is a segue, as a fictional logic eventually supersedes magic through the narrative device of the standing stones, while retaining other fantastical elements in the story that may remain unexplained. Further investigation of genre displacements and how they are implemented by their narrative structures with other television serial dramas, beyond reboots and sequels in which such practices of displacing one genre for another and one set of narrative possibilities for another are commonly implemented, can yield worthwhile answers about time-travel's inventive machinations.

Acknowledgements

This research was supported by the MSIT (Ministry of Science and ICT), Korea, under the Graduate School of Metaverse Convergence support program (IITP- 2024-RS-2022-00156318) supervised by the IITP (Institute for Information & Communications Technology Planning & Evaluation). The author would like to particularly thank Chrissie Mains, Alexis Brooks de Vita, Cat Ashton, and the peer reviewers and editors of the *Journal of the Fantastic in the Arts* for their valuable and detailed feedback.

Notes

1. A previous and abbreviated version of this article as a conference paper was delivered by the author to the University Film and Video Conference of 2018. It was subsequently accepted and presented as a conference paper at the *Outlander* Conference at the University of Glasgow in 2023.
2. A recent example of time travel's resurgence in broadcast television is the critically acclaimed *Russian Doll* (Netflix, 2019- present) with its depiction of an artist in the East Village who finds herself trapped in a time loop. It received four Emmy Award nominations, including one for Outstanding Comedy Series, and was renewed for a second season in 2020, but production was delayed due to the Covid-19 virus until March of 2021.
3. For clarification, *Outlander* in this writing refers to the television serial drama and not the novels, unless otherwise noted.
4. Season 1 of *Outlander* is divided into two volumes that together consist of sixteen episodes. Season 2 comprises thirteen episodes. To avoid confusion, I will use the overall number of episodes in the entire ongoing series for identification. Episodes seventeen through twenty-nine are thus Season 2.
5. As of this writing, the *Outlander* book series encompasses, in addition to several novellas and short stories, eight novels: *Outlander* (1991), *Dragonfly in Amber* (1992), *Voyager* (1993), *Drums in Autumn* (1996), *The Fiery Cross* (2001), *A Breath of Snow and Ashes* (2005), *An Echo in the Bone* (2009), and *Written in My Own Heart's Blood* (2014). The ninth novel, titled *Go Tell the Bees That I Am Gone,* is forthcoming.
6. One of Star Trek's recent incarnations consists of a reboot film series directed by J. J. Abrams, set in an alternative time line known as the "Kelvin Timeline" wherein characters featured in the original television series now lead different lives and are played by different actors, to revitalize the franchise.
7. Brian Bethune cites *Outlander* as a combination of "romance, historical fiction, mystery and the supernatural to wildly popular effect" (2014). Also, Valerie Estelle Frankel mentions paranormal-gothic and military as other subgenres that *Outlander* embraces (126).

8. For a detailed analysis of Claire as a modern feminist see Fernando Gabriel Pagnoni Berns's and Leonard G. A. Lando's article, "Reviewing Linear Time: History Repeating All Over Again (Now, Against You)."

Works Cited

Achenbach, Pamela. "A Tempting Narrative or Temporal Gimmick: A Look at the Use of Time Travel in Unconventional Series." *Time-Travel Television: The Past from the Present, The Future From The Past*, edited by Sherry Ginn and Gillian I. Leitch, Rowman & Littlefield, 2015, pp. 57-70.

Altman, Rick. *Film/Genre*. British Film Institute, 1999.

Attebery, Brian. *Strategies of Fantasy*. Indiana University Press, 1992.

Becker, Christine. "*Life on Mars*: Transnational Adaption." *How to Watch Television*, edited by Ethan Thompson and James Mittell, New York University Press, 2013, pp. 30-37.

Bethune, Brian. "*Outlander* Gives *Games of Thrones* a Run for Its Money." *Maclean's*, 12 June 2014, http://www.macleans.ca/culture/books/outlander-gives-game-of-thrones-a-run-for-its-money. Accessed 12 August 2016.

Berns, Fernando Gabriel and Leonard G. A. Lando. "Reviewing Linear Time: History Repeating All Over Again (Now, Against You)." *Outlander's Sassenachs*, edited by Valerie Estelle Frankel, McFarland, 2016, pp. 105-116.

Bloch, Ernst. *The Utopian Function of Art and Literature: Selected Essays*. Translated by J. Zipes and F. Mecklenburg, The MIT Press, 1988.

Booth, Paul. "Memories, Temporalities, Fictions: Temporal Displacement in Contemporary Television." *Television New Media* vol. 12, no. 4, 2010, pp. 372-88.

Butler, David. *Fantasy Cinema: Impossible Worlds on Screen*. Wallflower Press, 2009.

Cristofari, Cécile. "Time Travel as Trope in Television Series." *Time-Travel Television: The Past from the Present, The Future From The Past*, edited by Sherry Ginn and Gillian I. Leitch, Rowman & Littlefield, 2015, pp. 27-36.

Eco, Umberto. *The Limits of Interpretation*. Indiana University Press, 1990.

Frankel, Valerie Estelle. "The Short Stories on the Science Fiction Shelf, or Lord John Grey Complicates Matters as Usual." *Adoring Outlander: Essays on Fandom, Genre and the Female Audience*, edited by Valerie Estelle Frankel, McFarland, 2016, pp. 125-143.

---. *The Symbolism and Sources of Outlander*. McFarland, 2015.

Gleick, James. *Time Travel*. Pantheon Books, 2016.

Jackson, Rosemary. *Fantasy: the Literature of Subversion*. Routledge, 2003.

Johns, Nikara. "Critics' Choice Television Awards to Honor Ryan Murphy." *Variety*, 9 June 2015, http://variety.com/2014/tv/news/critics-choice-television-awards-honor-ryan-murphy-exciting-new-series-1201216678/. Accessed 10 September 2016.

Jones, Matthew and Joan Ormrod. "Introduction: Contexts and Concept of Time in the Mass Media." *Time Travel in Popular Media: Essays on Film, Television, Literature and Video Games*, edited by Matthew Jones and Joan Ormrod, McFarland, 2015, pp. 5-19.

Jurgensen, John. "Hot Concepts for Next Season's New TV Shows: Time-Travel and Old Franchises." *The Wall Street Journal*, 17 May 2016, http://www.wsj.com/articles/BL-SEB-95357. Accessed 2 August 2016.

Kimberley, Matthew and Jason N. Dittmer. "To Boldly Go Where No Man Has Gone Before: Complexity Science and the *Star Trek* Reboot." *Time Travel in Popular Media: Essays on Film, Television, Literature and Video Games*, edited by Matthew Jones and Joan Ormrod, McFarland, 2015, pp. 63-76.

King, Geoff and Tanya Krzywinska. *Science Fiction Cinema: From Outerspace to Cyberspace*. Wallflower Press, 2000.

Larsen, Kristine. "The Impossible Girl and the New World: Televisual Representations of the Scientific Possibilities and Paradoxes of Time Travel." *Time-Travel Television: The Past from the Present, the Future from the Past*, edited by Sherryl Ginn and Gillian I. Leitch, Rowman and Littlefield, 2015, pp. 213-222.

Lawson, Richard. "*Outlander* is as Odd and Enveloping as Ever in Season 2" *Vanity Fair*, 8 April 2016, http://www.vanityfair.com/hollywood/2016/04/outlander-season-2-review. Accessed 24 February 2018.

McAlister, Jodi. "Travelling Through Time and Genre: Are the *Outlander* Books Romance Novels?" *Adoring* Outlander*: Essays on Fandom, Genre and the Female Audience*, edited by Valerie Estelle Frankel, McFarland, 2016, pp. 94-105.

Mendlesohn, Farah. *Rhetorics of Fantasy*. Wesleyan University Press, 2008.

Mitry, Jean. *Aesthetics and Psychology in the Cinema*. 1963. Translated by Christoph King, Indiana University Press, 2000.

Rabey, Melissa. "Historical Fiction Mash-Ups: Broadening Appeal by Mixing Genres." *Young Adult Library Services* vol 9, no. 1, 2010, pp. 38-41.

Todorov, Tzvetan. *The Fantastic: A Structural Approach to a Literary Genre*, translated by Richard Howard, The Press of Case Western Reserve University, 1973.

Ty, Eleanor. "Melodrama, Gender and Nostalgia: The Appeal of *Outlander*." *Adoring* Outlander*: Essays on Fandom, Genre and the Female Audience*, edited by Valerie Estelle Frankel, McFarland, 2016, pp. 58-68.

Wittenberg, David. *Time Travel: The Popular Philosophy of Narrative*. New York: Fordham University Press, 2013.

Worley, Alec. *Empires of the Imagination: A Critical Survey of Fantasy Cinema fromGeorges Méliès to The Lord of the Rings*. McFarland, 2005.

The Ekphrastic Narrative of the Silmarils: The Prevalence of Ekphrasis in J. R. R. Tolkien's *The Silmarillion*

Patrícia Sá

MARVELLOUS ARTIFACTS ARE AT THE CORE of Tolkien's legendarium, according to Tom Shippey (Shippey 180). Artifacts guide each narrative and the characters' destinies, as in Thorin's obsession with the Arkenstone, the corrosive lure of the One Ring, or the enchanting light within the Silmarils. However, the descriptions of these artifacts are fairly limited, as the main focus seems to be on how they affect each character and how they influence the narrative. In the case of the Silmarils, the way Fëanor builds them and how they affect the world and its inhabitants seems to be far more important than how they look. The initial description of the Silmarils is less ornamental and more narrative, attaching meaning to their making in the way that they both reflect the history of Arda, embodying the light that gave shape to Ilúvatar's creation, and future events, directing the fate of the world. The depiction of the Silmarils surpasses mere description, as it is intertwined with narration. However, the depiction of the Silmarils is not an account of a sequence of actions; this depiction seems to be placed in between description and narration.

Even though contemporary ekphrasis is commonly associated with poems that recreate a visual representation through language, authors such as Michelle St. George and Juliana Carvalho Tavares delve into J. R. R. Tolkien's *The Lord of the Rings* and find instances of ekphrasis in the depictions of the One Ring and the battle at Khazad-dûm, respectively. In this paper, I investigate the uses of ekphrasis in Tolkien's fantasy world in *The Silmarillion* and, specifically, how the depiction of the jewels that seal the tragic fate of the Noldor Elves and aid in the tarnishing of Eru Ilúvatar's vision are an example of ekphrastic writing.

Firstly, it is important to briefly define ekphrasis. James A. W. Heffernan proposes the following definition: "ekphrasis is the verbal representation of visual representation" (3), the same definition suggested by W. J. T. Mitchell in his *Picture Theory* (152). Similarly, Mário Avelar defines ekphrasis as description in his study regarding confessionalism and ekphrasis (40). Thus, a verbal reproduction of a visual object seems to be at the core of ekphrasis.

However, present-day ekphrasis is quite different from ekphrasis as it was understood in Classical Antiquity. One of the earliest examples of ekphrasis can be traced back to Homer's *Iliad*, specifically the description of the Shield of Achilles. Mário Avelar points out a distinctive trait of this technique: the ability of a given discourse to reveal to the reader a painting or an artifact in a vivid way (41). This vividness is important, as a key element of ekphrasis is the reader's ability to recreate the described image in one's mind. Ruth Webb also makes mention of this vividness upon referring to the earliest uses of ekphrasis. Besides the Shield of Achilles, the author points to the *Progymnasmata*, rhetoric lessons from around the first to fourth centuries, which contain myriad different examples of ekphrasis. Its authors, Theon, Hermogenes, Aphthonios, and Nikolaos, define ekphrasis as: "a speech which leads one around [...], bringing the subject matter vividly [...] before the eyes" (Webb, "*Ekphrasis* Ancient and Modern" 11). Besides Theon's suggestion of people, places, time periods, and events as subjects for ekphrasis, Aphthonios proposes plants and animals, and Nikolaos brings up festivals (Webb, "*Ekphrasis* Ancient and Modern" 11). Truly, ekphrasis is a much more complex technique than its prevailing understanding would lead one to believe, which explains Webb's scepticism regarding the modern understanding of ekphrasis as purely an association between word and image. In fact, in Webb's view, "[t]he lure of the modern meaning had too often obscured the ancient meaning, which is worthy of study in its own right" ("*Ekphrasis* Ancient and Modern" 9).

Besides the difference in the range of subject matter, there is one more important aspect to point out about these earlier examples of ekphrasis compared to the way it is often employed now. As previously stated, ekphrasis evokes a physical, visual object, which can be found in the physical world. The Shield of Achilles, on the other hand, is a visual sign that can only be accessed by the reader's imagination; there is no real-world equivalent that Homer's text is referencing. As Avelar points out, the shield only comes to life in the poem, and so the ekphrasis is imaginary (43). John Hollander has referred to this process as "notional ekphrasis":

> [Works of notional ekphrasis] conjure up an image, describing some things about it and ignoring a multitude of others which, [...] we might assume were supplied by any reader who knew what images [...] looked like [...]. The realm of notional ekphrasis is partially extended to include what are virtually notional—ekphrastic poems or passages in literary works which may or may not describe some actual, but totally lost, work of art. (209)

Indeed, James Heffernan contends that classical examples of ekphrasis and present-day ekphrastic sketches are very different. In the introduction to his *Museum of Words*, Heffernan states that the difference between the description of the Shield of Achilles and poems such as W. H. Auden's "Musée des Beaux Arts" hinges on the availability of the image:

> In one sense, the availability of a painting represented by a poem should make no difference to our experience of the poem, which—like any specimen of notional ekphrasis—is made wholly of words. But the availability of the painting allows us to see how the poem reconstructs it, how the poet's word seeks to gain its mastery over the painter's image. (7)

Thus, an ekphrastic poem could be described as a reproduction of a visual object that the reader can compare to its real-world counterpart. However, both contemporary and ancient ekphrasis share a characteristic: "An *ekphrasis* appeals to the mind's eye of the listener, making him or her 'see' the subject-matter, whatever it may be" (Webb, "*Ekphrasis* Ancient and Modern" 11–12).

In addition, ekphrasis is not restricted to descriptions; it is also a narrative form. Doru Pop, for instance, argues that ekphrasis is neither

> a sheer linguistic principle, intervening on the art object, nor can it be a limited approach to visual representations. Ekphrasis includes all forms of narrativities of the visual [...], and it is not only descriptive, but also a form of storytelling of everything that is 'made visible'. Ekphrasis means, not only literary, but practically, to fully express, that is to go beyond all that is visible and everything that is explicit. (6–7)

According to Pop, ekphrasis tells the story of the object it is representing as going beyond the merely visual or recreation of the visual. As Ruth Webb states, "a description deals with objects, while narration deals with actions. *Ekphrasis* in contrast was defined in terms of its impact on an audience" (*"Ekphrasis* Ancient and Modern" 12). The effect ekphrasis has on the reader or listener is key: it is not a mere description of objects, inconsequential to the narrative, nor is it a succession of actions that move the story forward. Webb argues that, according to Nikolaos the Sophist, "[n]arration is a simple account of what happened, while an *ekphrasis* includes the details that tell one *how* it happened, how it looked (one might add also how it sounded and felt). The difference [...] is *energeia*, vividness; an *ekphrasis* in sum is a vivid form of narration" ("Ekphrasis Ancient and Modern" 13).

So, in the epics of Antiquity, the use of ekphrasis can be associated with narration. Heffernan claims that "the making of the [Shield of Achilles] completes a turning point in the poem" as "it is the creation and delivery of this armor that actually sends Achilles into battle" (10). Referring to Kenneth Atchity's argument, Heffernan also states that "the shield microcosmically reflects the whole 'thematic expanse' of the *Iliad* [...], and some of its scenes do mirror the world of the poem" (10). In addition, it is noteworthy that Heffernan uses the term "narrate" to designate the way Homer writes the scene of the making of the shield:

> The fact that Homer narrates the making of the shield of Achilles is one of several things that distinguish it from the shields of Ajax and Agamemnon [...]. To see the passage on the shield simply as description is to miss the narrative force of its principal verbs. Consistently past in tense [...], they satisfy the elementary requirements of narrative by telling the story of how Hephaestus forged, fashioned, and placed the figures on the shield. Yet narrative [...] penetrates that frame, animating the figures within it, and thus

subverting any effort to visualize just where in space the figures are deployed, just what sort of pattern or configuration they assume. (12)

Thus, ancient ekphrasis is description animated by narrative to make a certain subject stand out. As Michelle St. George contends, following Page duBois's theory, ekphrasis operates as a significant turning point in the epic, the mark of a change in the narrative (15).

In contemporary ekphrastic poems, vividness is still an important characteristic. In fact, these often go beyond a simple description of a visual object. For instance, Keats's "Ode on a Grecian Urn" is, according to Mário Avelar, a simulacrum of a meeting with a visual sign which prompts the poetic subject to question it and uncover its mystery (154). So, in this case, the ekphrasis happens as the poet poses questions regarding the subject matter and attempts to devise interpretations (Avelar 156). In the case of Sylvia Plath's "Two Views of a Cadaver Room," the poet connects a detail of Breughel's painting—the depiction of two lovers at the bottom of the painting—to an autobiographical moment; this way, the ekphrasis develops in a mirroring exercise, with two different representations that reflect one another (Avelar 325–27). So, ekphrasis may encase interpretations and elements that are extra to the visual object alluded to.

With such complexity at play, it is unsurprising that ekphrasis, despite its niche standing in the literary sphere, is still used in the present day, and it is not reserved to poetry. In fact, examples of ekphrasis exist in narrative prose. According to Sylvia Karastathi, the association of ekphrasis and poetry has overshadowed its presence in prose texts (107), but it exists nonetheless. From Karastathi's vantage point, "[e]kphrasis in the novel can be approached more as a textual fragment; a detachable unit that can be isolated and studied independently" (107). Karastathi goes on to state: "Far from being a mere ornament, ekphrasis, as a descriptive device, enriches narrative fiction by inviting an already extant image, which has its own historical and theoretical associations, into the fictional discourse" (107). One may be reminded of the classical trait of vividness, which enriches one's reading experience as the object takes shape in one's mind. In fact, Karastathi argues, echoing Louvel's study, *Poetics of the Iconotext*, that while ekphrasis functions as a pause in the text, an insertion into the space of the narrative, a moment in a longer story, it also aids in the construction of an observing subject, a point of view: focalization (108).

Therefore, referring ekphrasis to the realm of description, which in narratology is considered secondary to narration (Yacobi 619), is limitative when all possibilities are taken into account. As Ruth Webb points out, evoking narratology expert Gerard Genette, "the distinction between description and narration is relatively recent and the two are more difficult to separate in practice than in theory. For the ancient rhetoricians, ekphrasis could be applied not only to the background to action [...] but to the action itself" (*Ekphrasis, Imagination and Persuasion* 67). Thus, ekphrasis does not merely reside in the descriptive sphere, but it is still not equivalent to narration. Webb contends that ekphrasis may be distinguished from narration by the fact that narration gives an account of a succession of actions, while an ekphrasis answers the question of how those actions are carried out (*Ekphrasis, Imagination and Persuasion* 71). Therefore, the author claims, "Ekphrasis is [...] not *by definition* separable from narration, nor does it by definition constitute a digression" (Webb, *Ekphrasis, Imagination and Persuasion* 68). Despite this malleability, the modern uses of ekphrasis often render it as a more descriptive process, less associated with narration than in Classical Antiquity. Even though the poet or narrator may add their interpretations or manipulate the images they portray, the modern meaning of ekphrasis deviates from its source, so much so that authors such as Stephen Cheeke and Karastathi consider that "although the term is useful in designating a specific poetic genre, it is also in need of urgent renewal, in order to account for the many and newly-conceived ways in which verbal representations address visual representations" (Karastathi 105).

Accordingly, as Michelle St. George and Juliana Tavares point out, it is possible to find examples of ekphrasis in Tolkien's narrative prose. However, before focusing on those examples, it is important to briefly recall Tolkien's ideas regarding fantasy writing, which he lays out in his seminal lecture "On Fairy-Stories" (1939). To Tolkien, fairy stories are endowed with a special quality he calls "Faërie," a sort of enchantment that aims to satisfy fundamental human desires ("Fairy-Stories" 116) by producing "a Secondary World into which both designer and spectator can enter, to the satisfaction of their senses while they are inside" (143). When successful, this imaginary world retains "the inner consistency of reality" (138) and allows for "the realization, independent of the conceiving mind, of imagined wonder" (116).

According to Dr. Simon J. Cook, *The Lord of the Rings* exemplifies this process in a literal way. Much as fantasy "takes metaphorical constructions literally," as Rosemary Jackson claims (24), and inverts "the literal and metaphoric," as Greer Gilman contends (136), Arda's Elves literalize what human sub-creators can only achieve through language; fantasy takes physical shape in the world (Cook 1). What is more, the narration of Ilúvatar's creation of Arda hinges on the transformation of thought and sound into the Flame Imperishable from which the world emerges. As Cook states, this step "has its analogy in human fantasy (or sub-creation), which, by embodying thought in spoken words, generates in the minds of its audience a vision of a secondary world" (5).

The formation of a vision of the world in the reader's eyes is described by Fanfan Chen as an example of hypotyposis, according to Aristotle's definition of a technique that enables words to "set the scene before our eyes" (Aristotle *apud* Chen 68), and Pierre Fontanier's consideration that "hypotyposis paints things in so lively and energetic a manner that it presents them right before one's eyes, and turns a narrative or a description into an image, a painting or even a live scene" (Fontanier *apud* Chen 68). Likewise, Chen claims, "Tolkien draws on hypotyposis for the fantasy configuration of Sub-creation, which brings before the eyes a Secondary World that entails a Secondary Belief" (68). Similarly, Jeffrey J. MacLeod and Anna Smol argue that Tolkien's writing style is characteristically "painterly," with descriptions that do not denote static images, but moving ones (118–19). The authors argue that this painterly aspect echoes what Steve Walker has termed "invitational prose," that is, "audience-centered. Involving the reader in the very process of creation, Tolkien deliberately stimulates response which is as individual as it is intense" (Walker 6). How is this achieved? Walker considers that it is the lack of many detailed descriptions that enable readers to "fill in the blank," to make use of their own imagination and previous knowledge to picture what is being described. As Walker argues,

> Involving the reader in the very process of creation, Tolkien deliberately stimulates response which is as individual as it is intense. He designs fiction that provokes readers to react personally, even idiosyncratically. [...] [H]is technique is at base a simple matter of alloying vividness with sketchiness. [...] Tolkien's carefully wrought incompleteness lures the reader into personal involvement in the creation. (6)

John D. Rateliff corroborates this point, suggesting that although Tolkien does not supply many endlessly detailed descriptions, he "does tell us everything we need to know, in general terms with just enough specific detail to bring scene home, to guide the reader's imagination, [...] since this participation draws the reader into the work" (6).

MacLeod and Smol are mostly concerned with Tolkien's depictions of the natural world of Middle-earth, and, as they point out, his "painterly" style is not ekphrastic, denoting instead "the sensitivity and awareness of a visual artist" (126). I concur with this assessment, but that does not mean that there are no examples of ekphrastic depictions in Tolkien's fiction, especially those reminiscent of its classical use. Such is the case of the One Ring, as St. George has demonstrated. The Ring is not a mere ornamental object that Tolkien inserts into the space of the narrative; it plays a pivotal role in the main character's destiny, as it is from the moment the Ring is introduced that the story goes from a pleasant account of daily life in Hobbiton to a dark, perilous journey to destroy the one weapon that can doom Middle-earth (St. George 17). Similarly, Tavares highlights how the traditional sense of ekphrasis is crucial to understanding how an event, like a battle, can vividly be conjured by the reader's imagination and generate powerful emotions (15).

St. George expands on the way what she calls the notionality of the Ring allows for a multitude of interpretations. To illustrate her point, the author references Heffernan's considerations regarding notional ekphrasis, which he regards as "much more malleable, much more dynamic than a *one-moment, one-picture* interpretation" and, though these ekphrases "can motivate an endless number of visual translations, ultimately, [...] [their] notionality precludes any singular representation of [them] or the images thereon" (St. George 24). Likewise, St. George argues that Tolkien's notional ekphrasis of the One Ring "prevents static visual translation," yet "does not stop readers from giving sight to the artifact" (26). The author also mentions W. J. T. Mitchell's theory of "ekphrastic hope," according to which, "This is the phase when the impossibility of ekphrasis is overcome in imagination or metaphor, when we discover a 'sense' in which language can do what so many writers have wanted it to do: 'to make us see'" (Mitchell 152). St. George suggests that Tolkien's ekphrastic sketch of the Ring allows readers access to it through their imagination, thereby becoming "active participants in the creative process, capable of drawing on their own artistic abilities, knowledge, and experiences to craft a myriad of unique visual representations of the notional Ring" (28). St. George further points out that, although Tolkien does not use the word ekphrasis, his theories regarding fantasy and story are not so distant from this idea of ekphrastic hope. Recalling "On Fairy-Stories," St. George states:

> Tolkien emphasizes how literature allows readers to create "more poignantly particular" pictures of the described objects and images in their imaginations. Like Heffernan, Tolkien recognizes how the verbal representation of visual representation invites readers to participate in a unique experience, one in which they translate text into dynamic, unique, visual existence. (33)

Having reached this stage in establishing the ekphrastic analysis of the One Ring, I would now like to focus on *The Silmarillion*. Compiled and edited by Christopher Tolkien, *The Silmarillion* tells of the creation of Ëa and Arda by the thought of a primordial being, Eru, the One, also known as Ilúvatar. The story concerns the fall of Melkor, once the most powerful of Ilúvatar's Ainur before his rebellion, as well as the rebellion of the Elves. The falls of the main characters occur, in part, by virtue of their desire to possess what is meant to be shared by all living creatures, the Light of Ilúvatar. This holy light first appears as the Flame Imperishable, the visible manifestation of the Ainur's music, and shines at the centre of the world as the life-force of creation. The Valar bring lights derived from the Flame Imperishable into the world, but these lights are progressively tarnished by Melkor. The first lights shine ceaselessly; then, the Two Trees of Valinor shed an intermittent light, which means that, in Tolkien's world, what is built cannot be rebuilt as it once was. Finally, after Melkor and his ally Ungoliant poison the Trees, Valinor darkens, and the Sun and the Moon are made from the Trees' tainted light. However, that original light is not lost forever, as it was encased in three jewels called the Silmarils, made by the Noldor Elf Fëanor. These jewels do not function as mere ornamental objects in the overall story; their making and disappearance lead to pivotal turning points, and the feelings they inspire in the main characters are crucial to the construction of these characters' portrayals as either greedy and covetous, or heroic and noble. While greed leads to disastrous outcomes, heroism allows for a hopeful turn in the manner of the eucatastrophe, the "good catastrophe" that Tolkien considers key to any fantasy narrative (Tolkien, "On Fairy-Stories" 153).

As Verlyn Flieger states, the Silmarils, like the Arkenstone and the One Ring, represent "the danger of uncontrolled desire, covetousness grown to obsession" ("Jewels" 71). The Silmarils "are a metaphor for the desire of humankind for beauty and for the negative of this desire—possessiveness, covetousness, selfishness, and lust" (Flieger, *Splintered Light* 107–108). However, according to Marie H. Loughlin, these treasures and the places that hold them function, within the narrative, as "the sites where communities and nations are forged and remembered, and where the relationships between peoples and individuals are made the matter of memory, history, and in some cases, oblivion" (21). Indeed, these artifacts are often related to stories and songs that are constantly evoked by different characters as a way to establish "links between present events and a remote past" (Kullmann 200). Therefore, the Silmarils give readers insight into the past of Middle-earth in a way that recalls Page duBois's consideration that classical ekphrastic depictions function as a way to transmit the hero's history to the audience (duBois *apud* St. George 3).

How ekphrastic is Tolkien's sketch of the Silmarils? How do the Silmarils operate throughout the narrative or, more aptly, narratives? Looking at how the Silmarils first come to be, the reader may notice that the description of the jewels is not particularly detailed. How they are built and what effects they will have in the future are far more relevant. Fëanor, their maker, is described as the most gifted of the Noldor Elves, the first to learn how to make gemstones that could not be originally found in Nature (Tolkien, *Silmarillion* 64). This inventiveness kindles Melkor's envy and hatred towards the Eldar, the Elves, who remind him of all that he lost with his revolt (66–67). Melkor hungers for the light he has been deprived of, but he also grows to covet the Elves' inventions—"he looked upon the wealth of bright gems, and he lusted for them" (66)—a desire that will be exacerbated once he learns of the Silmarils.

Fëanor himself is guilty of lust for his jewels. As it is described in the seventh chapter of the *Quenta Silmarillion*,

> In that time were made those things that afterwards were most renowned of all the works of the Elves. For Fëanor, being come to his full might, was filled with a new thought, or it may be that some shadow of foreknowledge came to him of the doom that drew near; and he pondered how the light of the Trees, the glory of the Blessed Realm, might be preserved imperishable. Then he began a long and secret labour, and he summoned all his lore, and his power, and his subtle skill; and at the end of all he made the Silmarils. (Tolkien, *The Silmarillion* 68)

In making the Silmarils, Fëanor sought to permanently preserve the light of the Trees, at first aiming to ensure that their glow remained imperishable, and then by virtue of his desire to be the sole keeper of the holiest light. Flieger equates Fëanor to Prometheus, arguing that "we can see in the stories of both [...] the time-honored mythic theme of the overreacher, the figure whose excess is punished yet whose accomplishments succeed in bringing a spark to humanity that can elevate it above its original condition and carry it forward" (*Splintered Light* 103). Indeed, Fëanor's wish to encase the Light of the Trees of Valinor in his jewels is arguably a Promethean and even a hubristic wish, as he seeks to surpass all that his condition allows. The Silmarils are, thus, symbols, and the narration of their making ascertains that their fate is intertwined with that of world, which echoes Heffernan's previously mentioned theory regarding the Shield of Achilles (Heffernan 10): the Silmarils reflect the scope of motives of *The Silmarillion*, as they hold within them a fire that shines and burns, working as both a blessing and a curse, able to inspire hope and generate misery.

The Silmarils are depicted as three great jewels, but their substance is to remain unknown:

> [N]ot until the End, when Fëanor shall return who perished ere the Sun was made, and sits now in the Halls of Awaiting and comes no more among his kin; not until the Sun passes and the Moon falls, shall it be known of what substance they were made. (Tolkien, *Silmarillion* 68)

With this initial sketch, the reader is introduced to the mysterious properties of the Silmarils and learns that Fëanor will die sometime in the future. The Silmarils are then described as indestructible, built to withstand any hardship despite their beautiful and delicate shell: "Like the crystal of diamonds it appeared, and yet was more strong than adamant, so that no violence could mar it or break it within the Kingdom of Arda" (68). The Silmarils's crystalline exterior is equated to the Elves' earthly forms, establishing that the jewels function as mirrors to them: "Yet that crystal was to the Silmarils but as is the body to the

Children of Ilúvatar: the house of its inner fire, that is within it and yet in all parts of it, and is its life" (68). Subsequently, in describing how Fëanor infused the jewels with the light of the Trees, Tolkien reveals that they will wither and lose their glow forever: "And the inner fire of the Silmarils Fëanor made of the blended light of the Trees of Valinor, which lives in them yet, though the Trees have long withered and shine no more" (68). As the last remnants of Ilúvatar's light live on inside the Silmarils, their inner fire is capable of resisting the densest darkness as they shine with an unending radiance: "Therefore even in the darkness of the deepest treasury the Silmarils of their own radiance shone like the stars of Varda" (68). The jewels have a similar effect on the inhabitants of Arda to the original sources of light, as "[a]ll who dwelt in Aman were filled with wonder and delight at the work of Fëanor" (68).

The Silmarils are not portrayed as mere holders of light; they are likened to living things in the way they reflect the light that glows within them, further cementing their connection to the Elves, who are also often described as shining creatures[1]: "and yet, as were they indeed living things, they rejoiced in light and received it and gave it back in hues more marvellous than before" (Tolkien, *The Silmarillion* 68). This depiction of the jewels as living things creates that vividness Webb views as elemental to ekphrasis ("*Ekphrasis* Ancient and Modern" 13). The Silmarils thus become animated things, not merely passive ornaments, and they take shape in the reader's imagination.

The narration of the Silmarils' making echoes Heffernan's point concerning the storytelling aspect of the ekphrasis of the Shield of Achilles (12), since, likewise, to view the passage of the crafting of the Silmarils as a descriptive example is to completely ignore its narrative facet, which recalls Doru Pop's argument regarding a narration of the visual (6–7). Thus, the verbs employed in the past tense are vital to the creation of the ekphrastic narrative of the Silmarils, as the past tense relays to the reader how Fëanor forged them, infused them with light, and how they themselves shine as living things. The future events woven between the ekphrastic sketch add to this storytelling aspect, as they announce forthcoming sequences directly influenced by the jewels.

The description of the Silmarils is not overly detailed, confirming Tolkien's "invitational prose" style proposed by Walker, and thus allowing the reader to be actively involved in the creative process. This way, there are not merely three jewels, but an infinite number of them, according to each reader's interpretation of them. Similarly, the "ekphrastic hope" suggested by W. J. T. Mitchell (152) is made possible, as the reader conjures an image of the Silmarils based on Tolkien's verbal depiction of them. Could this be considered a description anchored on hypotyposis, according to Chen's proposal, or another instance of Tolkien's "painterly" style, as MacLeod and Smol have suggested? Considering that the Silmarils are, essentially, works of art transformed into words, it seems more apt to consider these ekphrastic sketches, given that, taking MacLeod and Smol's own definition of ekphrasis, "the text aims to describe a piece of art, giving it life and movement that goes beyond the artifact itself" (123). Likewise, the Silmarils could very well be considered another example of Tolkien's use of hypotyposis, which "makes readers 'perceive' the description, fictive and imaginary though it is, as being real or present" (Chen 73). However, the prevalent aspects of the depiction of the Silmarils are not how real or present they appear to the reader, but what they signify in the context of the overall narrative. Therefore, I consider them examples of ekphrastic writing.

Further in the narration, the jewels gain the characteristics that will render them crucial to the story: the Vala Varda blesses them "so that thereafter no mortal flesh, nor hands unclean, nor anything of evil might touch them, but it was scorched and withered" (Tolkien, *The Silmarillion* 68–69); Mandos, the Vala of justice, "foretold that the fates of Arda, earth, sea, and air, lay locked within them" (69), a prediction that will haunt each narrative in *The Silmarillion*. This haunting begins with Melkor's lust for the Silmarils, which have an everlasting effect on him as "the very memory of their radiance was a gnawing fire in his heart" (69), suggesting a rageful covetousness while also evoking the fire burning within the jewels. It is this feeling that leads Melkor to find ways to put an end to the relationship between the Elves and the Valar: "From that time forth, inflamed by this desire, he sought ever more eagerly how he should destroy Fëanor and end the friendship of the Valar and the Elves" (69). In turn, Fëanor's growing possessiveness towards the Silmarils—"The heart of Fëanor was fast bound to these things that he himself had made" (69)—triggers the narrative of the fall of his house, as he turns against the Valar and leaves Valinor with a vow to seek out and keep the Silmarils in his grasp, at all costs. It is noteworthy that Verlyn Flieger relates Fëanor to the fire contained within the jewels, as his own "fire is of such fierceness and intensity that when not properly contained and used, it scorches and destroys what it touches" (*Splintered Light* 109).

When the Valar ask Fëanor to return the light he infused the Silmarils with so that the Trees can be reborn, Fëanor refuses, for he believes he would be unable to remake the jewels as they once were, and equates the Valar to Melkor, convinced that they, too, covet his treasure: "This thing I will not do of free will. But if the Valar will constrain me, then shall I know indeed that Melkor is of their kindred" (Tolkien, *The Silmarillion* 83). Despite Fëanor's insurgence, which somewhat mirrors Melkor's, there is an important difference between these two characters, as Fëanor is not merely fuelled by his greed; it is the death of his father that spurs him further into revolt against the Valar. Indeed, when

Fëanor learns of King Finwë's murder at the hands of Melkor, now called Morgoth, the Black Foe of the World, Fëanor flees, "for his father was dearer to him than the Light of Valinor or the peerless works of his hands" (Tolkien, *The Silmarillion* 84), and Melkor takes the Silmarils for himself. So, Fëanor gathers the Elves of his house and prompts them to rebel with him and return to Middle-earth. With this decision, Fëanor swears an oath to reclaim the Silmarils and "to pursue with vengeance and hatred to the ends of the World Vala, Demon, Elf or Man as yet unborn, or any creature, great or small, good or evil, that time should bring forth unto the end of days, whoso should hold or take or keep a Silmaril from their possession" (Tolkien, *The Silmarillion* 89). This oath binds all Fëanor's descendants in a fate of misfortune and disaster that affects both Fëanor's house and Middle-earth at large, thus fulfilling Mandos's prediction.

Therefore, as St. George contends in regards to the One Ring, while the Silmarils may function as ornaments to a larger epic tale, they also signal important milestones (13), and their ekphrastic sketches provide insight into the history of the world (51). Invoking again Heffernan's views (10), just as with the making of the Shield of Achilles, the making of the Silmarils establishes a turning point in the narrative. Once the jewels are built, the fate of the world is forever changed. With the Noldor Elves's departure from The Blessed Realm, the sons of Fëanor establish their domains in Middle-earth, but they are unable to escape the oath they swore to their father, which will doom them to terrible deaths and leave a trail of destruction, recalling Mandos's prophecy. As an example, in the tale of King Thingol's fall, he orders the mortal man Beren to reclaim a Silmaril from Morgoth's Iron Crown so that Beren may take Thingol's daughter, Lúthien, as his wife. Queen Melian, a Maia, warns her husband of the terrible destiny that will befall him for his treachery: "you have sought cunning counsel. But if my eyes have not lost their sight, it is ill for you, whether Beren fail in his errand, or achieve it. For you have doomed either your daughter, or yourself" (Tolkien, *The Silmarillion* 197), which, indeed, comes to pass, as Thingol dies in part due to the influence of Fëanor's oath and his own desire for the Silmarils. The account of his death begins as the Necklace of the Dwarves, Nauglamír, is brought to Doriath. The necklace is described as "a carcanet of gold, and set therein were gems uncounted from Valinor; but it had a power within it so that it rested lightly on its wearer as a strand of flax, and whatsoever neck it clasped it sat always with grace and loveliness" (130). When Thingol sees the necklace, he decides that the Silmaril Beren retrieved for him ought to be set into it:

> it came into his mind that it [the necklace] should be remade, and in it should be set the Silmaril. For as the years passed Thingol's thought turned unceasingly to the jewel of Fëanor, and became bound to it, and he liked not to let it rest even behind the doors of his inmost treasury; and he was minded now to bear it with him always, waking and sleeping. (278)

So, Thingol instructs Dwarves who had come to Doriath to remake the necklace, but they, too, begin to hunger for the jewel. Thus, they kill the Elven King, who dies "with his last sight upon the Silmaril" (280), at once fulfilling Melian's and Mandos's predictions.

Truly, the Silmarils are at the core of the main narratives of Arda. More than ornaments, they mark significant milestones in the destinies of the characters that shape the fates of Valinor and Middle-earth. As Finrod Felagund tells Beren,

> the Silmarils are cursed with an oath of hatred, and he that even names them in desire moves a great power from slumber; and the sons of Fëanor would lay all the Elf-kingdoms in ruin rather than

suffer any other than themselves to win or possess a Silmaril, for the Oath drives them [...] (Tolkien, *The Silmarillion* 198)

On the other hand, Fëanor's jewels are also central to narratives of heroism and salvation. Beren and Lúthien's tale, for instance, as Tolkien claims in his letter to Milton Waldman,

> is (I think a beautiful and powerful) heroic-fairy-romance, receivable in itself with only a very general vague knowledge of the background. But it is also a fundamental link in the cycle, deprived of its full significance out of its place therein. For the capture of the Silmaril, a supreme victory, leads to disaster. The oath of the sons of Fëanor becomes operative, and lust for the Silmaril brings all the kingdoms of the Elves to ruin. (Tolkien, *The Silmarillion* xviii–xix)

This story, although a sort of palimpsest of medieval tales of chivalry, is an important link between the tale of the making and loss of the Silmarils to Morgoth, and the story of ultimate victory at the end of *The Silmarillion*, which stars Eärendil and his wife Elwing. Beren and Eärendil are contrasting characters to Fëanor, his descendants, and Morgoth, as they feel no covetousness towards the Silmarils when in possession of them. Moreover, Beren seems to be aware of the effect of the Silmarils on holders with malicious intentions, as he thrusts the Silmaril previously set in Morgoth's Iron Crown towards Carcharoth and claims: "Get you gone, and fly! [...] for here is a fire that shall consume you, and all evil things" (214). Indeed, once Carcharoth swallows the Silmaril, "swiftly all his inwards were filled with a flame of anguish, and the Silmaril seared his accursed flesh" (214). Carcharoth grows mad with pain, attacking every creature that stands in his way, and soon "[o]f all the terrors that came ever into Beleriand ere Angband's fall the madness of Carcharoth was the most dreadful; for the power of the Silmaril was hidden within him" (214). Again,

Tolkien does not merely describe; he narrates, vividly, the way the Silmaril impacts the characters: how Carcharoth burns, how it looks, even how it sounds and feels, bringing back Webb's summary of what Nikolaos considers to be the vivid representation of ekphrasis (*"Ekphrasis* Ancient and Modern" 13).

Like Beren, who only sought the Silmaril for Thingol in exchange for his daughter's hand, Eärendil does not keep the Silmaril his wife gave him for himself. Eärendil instead uses it to reach Valinor to ask the Valar to forgive the Elves and Men of Middle-earth and to help them in their impending battle against Morgoth's armies. As Tolkien tells Waldman, Eärendil's

> function, as a representative of both Kindreds, Elves and Men, is to find a sea-passage back to the Land of the Gods, and as ambassador persuade them to take thought again for the Exiles, to pity them, and rescue them from the Enemy. [...] The gods then move again, and great power comes out of the West, and the Stronghold of the Enemy is destroyed; and he himself [is] thrust out of the World into the Void, never to reappear there in incarnate form again. The remaining two Silmarils are regained from the Iron Crown—only to be lost. The last two sons of Fëanor, compelled by their oath, steal them, and are destroyed by them, casting themselves into the sea, and the pits of the earth. The ship of Eärendil adorned with the last Silmaril is set in heaven as the brightest star. So ends The Silmarillion and the tales of the First Age. (Tolkien, *The Silmarillion* xix–xx)

While Eärendil is out at sea, Maedhros and Maglor attempt to force Elwing to give them the Silmaril she inherited as Beren and Lúthien's descendant, hoping to fulfil their father's oath, at last. Neither Elwing nor her people concede to giving up the jewel, as they believe "that in the Silmaril lay the healing and the blessing that had come upon their houses and their ships" (296). However, this decision brings forth a new battle, "the last and cruellest of the slaying of Elf by Elf; and that was the third of the great wrongs achieved by the accursed oath" (296). In the face of such destruction, Eärendil and Elwing set out to sea once more in search of Valinor, bringing the Silmaril with them. Eärendil has the Silmaril "bound upon his brow" and the jewel's light "grew greater as they drew into the West" (297), once more hinging its depiction on narration through a verb such as 'to grow', which conveys a process of change, thereby ensuring the Silmaril is represented in a dynamic way. They do, at last, reach Valinor, a feat none have achieved since the Valar concealed the Blessed Realm from Middle-earth's view, and so "it was by reason of that holy jewel that they [Eärendil and Elwing] came in time to waters that no vessels save those of the Teleri had known; [...] and at the last they cast anchor in the Bay of Eldamar, and the Teleri saw the coming of that ship out of the East and they were amazed, gazing from afar upon the light of the Silmaril [...]" (297).

Eärendil and Elwing's entrance upon the Blessed Realm comes at the cost of not being allowed to return to Middle-earth. As Eärendil sets off eastward on his boat Vingilot, blessed by the Valar to be "filled with a wavering flame, pure and bright" (Tolkien, *The Silmarillion* 300), he ascends into the sky, where he will sail for a long time, "glistening with dust of elven-gems, and the Silmaril was bound upon his brow" (300). He grows to resemble a star, regarded in Middle-earth as a sign of hope, and, according to Tom Shippey, a victory emblem (Shippey 146), as the disappearance of the Silmaril from Middle-earth means that it cannot be possessed by anyone and can now fulfil its intended purpose: to be admired by all. Indeed, as Verlyn Flieger suggests, the Silmarils embody the idea that "[l]ight is not to be held or flaunted as personal adornment or locked away from the sight of all" (*Splintered Light* 107), at the cost of its growing dim for everyone. Thus, Eärendil's tale restores light to its ideal site, not in the possession of a single person, but shared by all. It is noteworthy that Maedhros and Maglor are relieved when they see the new star, "for its [the Silmaril's] glory is seen now by many, and is yet secure from all evil" (Tolkien, *The Silmarillion* 301).

Eärendil succeeds in his quest, and, with Morgoth's defeat, the last two Silmarils fall from his crown, and his evil realm comes to an end. Still, the power of Fëanor's oath is unrelenting, and Maedhros and Maglor are unable to relinquish the two jewels. Accordingly, they suffer the effects of Varda's blessing: Maedhros's hand is burned "in pain unbearable [...]. And being in anguish and despair he cast himself into a gaping chasm filled with fire, and so ended; and the Silmaril that he bore was taken into the bosom of the Earth" (Tolkien, *Silmarillion* 305). Maglor, in turn, "could not endure the pain with which the Silmaril tormented him; and he cast it at last into the Sea, and thereafter he wandered ever upon the shores, singing in pain and regret beside the waves" (305). So, the sons of Fëanor meet their agonizing ends, and the Silmarils are lost forever, "one in the airs of heaven, and one in the fires of the heart of the world, and one in the deep waters" (305).

Ultimately, the tale of the Silmarils suggests that light cannot be contained or kept selfishly for oneself. Light is meant to shine for all, and the catastrophic destinies suffered by those who attempt to possess the Silmarils are testaments to that fact. As illustrated above, the Silmarils are an encapsulation of the ultimate power, which leads to feelings of greed and possessiveness that lead to the characters' unfortunate demises and the destruction of Arda. Nevertheless, *The Silmarillion* does not forgo the eucatastrophe, the hope that, ultimately, good will prevail. This hope manifests in men such as Beren and Eärendil, as well as their elven partners Lúthien and Elwing, who did not covet the Silmarils and were, themselves, shining lights in their stories, heroes that contrast with Morgoth and Fëanor, who, although great in power, were weakened by their greed and hatred. Beren and Eärendil's stories are, thus, examples of a theme that will become central in *The Lord of the Rings*: "the great policies of world history, 'the wheels of the world', are often turned not by the Lords and Governors, even gods, but by the seemingly unknown and weak [...]" (Tolkien, *The Silmarillion* xviii).

This paper has aimed to contribute to the study of ekphrasis in Tolkien's narrative world, and thereby to the studies of ekphrasis in fantasy and narrative fiction, at large. Tolkien's mythological world is rich in ekphrastic sketches, and their prevalence in both *The Lord of the Rings* and *The Silmarillion* suggests that these ekphrases are not incidental; they are at the core of the most important twists and turns in the overall texts. They represent notional objects, meaning imaginary objects that can only be accessed through the text and the reader's imagination, thereby generating more complex images as the reader becomes part of the creative process.

The narration of the making of the Silmarils is intertwined with mentions of future events. The substance they are made of points to the very origin of creation: a pure, holy light that attracts every living creature but burns those who misuse it. Due to these extraordinary qualities, the Silmarils can be viewed as omens, since the future of Arda and its inhabitants is locked within them. Readers may be moved by the characters who lust for the Silmarils, especially those unable to forsake Fëanor's oath, because they know that an inevitable, tragic destiny shadows them. On the other hand, characters who handle the Silmarils with noble purpose revive the reader's hope in the triumph of good over evil, Tolkien's eucatastrophe. This evokes Webb's assertion that ekphrasis, in its ancient understanding, hinges on its impact on an audience (Webb, "*Ekphrasis* Ancient and Modern" 12).

In truth, ekphrasis plays a pivotal role in rousing these feelings, as it is not simply description of a decorative object, a fragment of the text; ekphrasis speaks of how the object looks, how it comes to be, and what sort of feelings it inspires, thereby creating a vivid representation in the reader's imagination.

Tolkien, indeed, creates vivid images of the Silmarils, such that they feel like living things (*The Silmarillion* 68). They surpass mere description, and their imaginary quality allows for an infinite number of representations, as each reader invents their own Silmarils. Thus, readers become a part of the literary process. With the exploration of these ideas, I add to the conversation regarding the ancient use of ekphrasis in Tolkien's fiction and lend weight to the argument that despite its distance in time, ekphrasis in its primordial understanding still has a place in contemporary texts, not only in poetry, but narrative fiction as well, and would therefore benefit from further discussion.

Notes

1. See the description of Lúthien Tinúviel: "and in her face was a shining light" (Tolkien, *The Silmarillion* 193).

Works Cited

Avelar, Mário. *Poesia e Artes Visuais: Confessionalismo e Écfrase*. Imprensa Nacional-Casa da Moeda, 2018.

Chen, Fanfan. "Tolkien's Style of Fantasy: Hypotyposis, Metalepsis, Harmonism." *Caietele Echinox*, no. 26, 2014, pp. 63–82.

Cook, Simon J. Dr. "How to Do Things with Words: Tolkien's Theory of Fantasy in Practice." *Journal of Tolkien Research*, vol. 3, no. 1, 2016, pp. 1–11.

Flieger, Verlyn. *Splintered Light: Logos and Language in Tolkien's World*. Revised Edition, The Kent University Press, 2002.

---. "The Jewels, the Stone, the Ring, and the Making of Meaning." *Tolkien in the New Century: Essays in Honor of Tom Shippey*, edited by John Wm. Houghton et al., McFarland & Company, Inc., Publishers, 2014, pp. 70–84.

Gilman, Greer. "The Languages of the Fantastic." *The Cambridge Companion to Fantasy Literature*, edited by Edward James and Farah Mendlesohn, Cambridge University Press, 2012, pp. 134–146.

Heffernan, James A. W. *Museum of Words: The Poetics of Ekphrasis from Homer to Ashbery*. The University of Chicago Press, 1993.

Hollander, John. "The Poetics of *Ekphrasis*." *Word & Image*, vol. 4, no. 1, Jan. 1988, pp. 209–219. https://doi.org/10.1080/02666286.1988.10436238. Accessed 10 August 2024.

Jackson, Rosemary. *Fantasy: The Literature of Subversion*. Routledge, 2009.

Karastathi, Sylvia. "Ekphrasis and the Novel/Narrative Fiction." *Handbook of Intermediality: Literature – Image – Sound – Music*, edited by Gabriele Rippl, vol. 1, De Gruyter, 2015, pp. 104–125.

Kullmann, Thomas. "Storytelling." *Tolkien as a Literary Artist: Exploring Rhetoric, Language and Style in The Lord of the Rings*, edited by Thomas Kullmann and Dirk Siepmann, Springer International Publishing, 2021, pp. 193–226.

Loughlin, Marie H. "Tolkien's Treasures: Marvellous Objects in The Hobbit and The Lord of the Rings." *Tolkien Studies*, vol. 16, no. 1, 2019, pp. 21–58. https://doi.org/10.1353/tks.2019.0005. Accessed 10 August 2024.

MacLeod, Jeffrey J., and Anna Smol. "Visualizing the Word: Tolkien as Artist and Writer." *Tolkien Studies*, vol. 14, no. 1, 2017, pp. 115–131. https://doi.org/10.1353/tks.2017.0009. Accessed 10 August 2024.

Mitchell, W. J. T. *Picture Theory: Essays on Verbal and Visual Representation*. The University of Chicago Press, 1994.

Pop, Doru. "For An Ekphrastic Poetics Of Visual Arts And Representations." *Ekphrasis*, vol. 1, 2008, pp. 5–12. https://www.ceeol.com/search/article-detail?id=102787. Accessed 25 November 2024.

Rateliff, John D. "'A Kind of Elvish Craft': Tolkien as Literary Craftsman." *Tolkien Studies*, vol. 6, no. 1, 2009, pp. 1–21. https://doi.org/10.1353/tks.0.0048. Accessed 10 August 2024.

Shippey, Tom. *The Road to Middle-Earth: How J. R. R. Tolkien Created a New Mythology*. Revised and Expanded edition, HarperCollinsPublishers, 2012.

St. George, Michelle. *The Lord of the Rings and the Ekphrastic Tradition*. 2012. California State University San Marcos, https://scholarworks.calstate.edu/downloads/0r9674344. Accessed 10 August 2024.

Tavares, Juliana Carvalho. *A Ekphrasis Em Khazad-Dûm de J. R. R. Tolkien*. 2022. Universidade de Brasília, https://bdm.unb.br/handle/10483/36230. Accessed 10 August 2024.

Tolkien, J. R. R. "On Fairy-Stories." *The Monsters and the Critics and Other Essays*, HarperCollinsPublishers, 1997, pp. 109–161.

---. *The Silmarillion*. Edited by Christopher Tolkien, HarperCollins Publishers, 2013.

Walker, Steven C. "The Making of a Hobbit: Tolkien's Tantalizing Narrative Technique." *Mythlore: A Journal of J.R.R. Tolkien, C.S. Lewis, Charles Williams, and Mythopoeic Literature*, vol. 7, no. 3, 1980, pp. 6–7. https://dc.swosu.edu/mythlore/vol7/iss3/3/. Accessed 10 August 2024.

Webb, Ruth. "*Ekphrasis* Ancient and Modern: The Invention of a Genre." *Word & Image*, vol. 15, no. 1, Jan. 1999, pp. 7–18. https://doi.org/10.1080/02666286.1999.10443970. Accessed 10 August 2024.

---. *Ekphrasis, Imagination and Persuasion in Ancient Rhetorical Theory and Practice*. Ashgate, 2009.

Yacobi, Tamar. "Pictorial Models and Narrative Ekphrasis." *Poetics Today*, vol. 16, no. 4, 1995, p. 599. https://doi.org/10.2307/1773367. Accessed 10 August 2024.

Creative Think Piece: A Gift From Pegasus

Jean Lorrah

THE ARTWORK ON THE COVER of this volume, *A Tourist on Mt. Helicon,* was inspired by a trip I took to Greece in the early 1990s. While there, I got some wonderful inspiration for my teaching, but I took home with me something else I did not understand at the time, a gift which manifested years later.

Throughout my life I have followed two paths: teacher and storyteller. I began the second path first, as a child discovering the magic of reading. But as soon as I began to write words and sentences, I began to write stories. It felt like real magic: I could make marks on paper, send it anywhere in the world, and people would know what I was saying.

I was born in 1940, when the written word was the only long-distance two-way communication most people knew. Except for ham operators, something not found in my working-class neighborhood, radio was one-way, while the telephone was limited to important calls only. Long-distance—paid for by the minute—was strictly for emergencies.

People communicated with letters, and discovered the world by listening to the radio, going to movies, reading newspapers and magazines, and—my favorite—reading books. For my sixth birthday, I received my own library card, and that opened whole new worlds to me. I was too young at first to distinguish the worlds I read about in travel books from the worlds in fairy tales, and to this day both still evoke the same excitement.

I was protected from World War II going on oceans away from my home in Ohio. Although my family was touched by shortages, Pathe newsreels, and voices on the radio telling us what was happening, my father, uncle, and grandfather were all over thirty and worked in industries vital to the war effort; thus, we did not share the anxiety of so many families with loved ones on the front lines. But the major reason I did not feel threatened was that it was all over in a victory for our side before I finished first grade.

The Cold War, though—that was the war of my generation, threatening us with spies and atom bombs and creatures born of radiation. Little wonder, as we practiced duck and cover and watched the films of Hiroshima and Nagasaki, that some of us came to prefer science fiction to science! Outer space sounded like a pretty good place to be, and by the time I entered high school I had determined to become a science fiction writer.

Meanwhile, though, America was on the move. With new cars and new roads, we set out to explore our own country. The summer I was seven years old, Aunt Jewel, Uncle Bob, my mother, and I drove all over New England. The next summer we explored the South, including New Orleans, where Uncle Bob bought a single raffle ticket at a church bazaar. I, who read only stories with happy endings, was the only person in the family not astonished when he won a 1949 Pontiac! This event was so significant that he was allowed to take time off from his job as an electrician on the railroad to go back to New Orleans and drive home his brand-new car.

The next summer our trip was to far more exotic locales. I still remember the changing landscape of the American West as we squeezed Pike's Peak and Mt. Rushmore, the Grand Canyon, Yellowstone, and the Painted Desert—each a whole new world—into our three-week vacation span. These childhood trips were where my love of travel was born, and where I saw first-hand how differently people live, and even think, under a variety of conditions. Without realizing it, I was packing away experiences that would one day go into my worldbuilding.

But long before my dream of writing came true, I followed the practicality drilled into my generation by parents who survived the Great Depression: I became an English teacher. In the career so many writers chose because of long summers free to write, I fell in love with teaching. My storytelling skills, not yet good enough for publication, were sufficient to brighten up potentially boring lessons.

Eventually I returned to graduate school for my doctorate and landed my first college teaching job at Murray State University, from which I retired forty years later. But that's not the story I'm telling here. Rather, this is a story about magic, science, travel, and inspiration, and particularly my trip to Greece in the early 1990s, the inspiration for my cover art.

As soon as I could afford it, I began traveling abroad. Each trip provided further understanding of literature set in the places I visited. In 1976 my mother and I walked the remaining sections of the Pilgrim's Way. Years later, some friends and I visited Bayeux, France, to see the famous tapestry. We were professors in our fifties, the last generation of Americans required to study Latin in preparation for college. We started translating, mostly to see if we remembered enough to do so, and soon drew a crowd of English-speaking tourists, demanding that we read it all. When I got home, I added the Tapestry to my curriculum, as I had forgotten what a charming piece of history-as-comic-strip it is.

The more I traveled, the more I felt the significance of place. One of my most dramatic experiences took place in Greece. By the early 1990s I had joined forces with Lois and Eric Wickstrom, who loved traveling as much as I did. Three people made renting a car feasible and gave us much greater freedom to explore. An unexpected delight of that trip was the lack of pollution: the air was clear, the roads were unlittered, and it was safe to drink the water from the numerous public springs.

Tours visit Athens and Delphi and the beautiful islands, but not Plato's Academy. Today that famous spot is still preserved but hidden away in an industrial suburb of Athens. With a car and a map (no GPS yet), we located it, and walked out of hot, gritty city into the literal Groves of Academe. Of course, we had all read that lessons there took place out of doors, but it's very different to experience being among shaded ruins thousands of years old, preserved but not docented—signs marked only the periphery of the site. The remains of so few building foundations, but many little gathering places with what once were benches, allowed us to experience what it must have felt like to be at one end of a bench—or, famously, a log—with Plato, or his most famous student Aristotle, at the other.

The Academy was amazing, but a trip to High Corinth the next day revolutionized my understanding of *Oedipus Rex*. Corinth is also not on most historical tours of Greece, as it is a smallish port city making almost no attempt to attract tourists. Today's city is on the water, but we were there to find the old Corinth, the one where Oedipus was raised as crown prince. There is good reason for that to be called *High* Corinth: it is up on the mountainside, with many buildings still standing along narrow, incredibly steep streets. We three had hiked around such places all over the world, but this was hard work, especially because it was a rainy morning, so what were left of the paving stones were slippery.

94 • Jean Lorrah

As I struggled to negotiate the main street, I suddenly pictured young Oedipus, his damaged feet forcing him to use a walking stick far less well designed than the ones we modern tourists wielded. Many of us know the story. Oedipus was born in Thebes, to a father under a curse that his own son would kill him and take his queen to wife. Laertes, king of Thebes, did what all villains do: instead of killing the cursed child himself, he gave the task to someone else. Furthermore, because he was already out of favor with the gods, he decided to use a traditional means of getting rid of unwanted children: taking them out into the wilderness and leaving them to the will of nature—or the gods.

But Laertes must have known how often in story the child does not die, so he did do one thing himself: he pierced the baby boy's ankles and tied them together with a thong. Bleeding to attract predators and unable even to crawl to safety, the child was certain to perish. Typical of a tyrant, while making sure this baby would not be raised by wolves, he gave no thought to the feelings of the man he sent to do the deed. Wounding the child had been too much for him. Instead of abandoning the nameless baby, he found some shepherds departing for the city of Corinth, gave the boy to them, then ran away himself.

At this point, the Will of the Gods comes into play. We never find out *how* that poor little injured baby ended up being adopted by the childless king and queen of Corinth. But when we realize how radical their decision is, it makes perfect sense for a king and queen determined to have this child they love as their own become the next king that they never tell him he is adopted. So much for a common student objection.

Sophocles's play focuses on Oedipus's tragic end—everything before his dramatic detective work to determine what is causing the series of misfortunes befalling Thebes is mere evidence provided by witnesses who put together the web of coincidences leading to a tragedy it is years too late to prevent. Like most teachers, I had discussed the character of the grown Oedipus, and the tangle of fate he cannot escape. But that rainy day in High Corinth made me think of the hobbling boy negotiating these hills in all weather for his entire young life and gave me a fresh angle: focus on *why* he made those fatal errors that we tend to blame the adult Oedipus for so severely. Normally, the audience entirely forgets how very young Oedipus was when he made those bad decisions, or how deeply traumatized.

In order to qualify for the role of tragic hero, Oedipus must be the best man in either Thebes or Corinth, and his own actions must bring about his downfall. But at the time he begins making decisions that move the plot, Oedipus is just a teenage boy. He has been raised as Crown Prince of Thebes, with no reason to question anything other than why the gods should have placed a person with a physical handicap in that position. He has done everything his parents and society have asked of him in preparation for ascending the throne, except for one thing: he is physically incapable of being a soldier. However, in the *Odyssey,* Homer frequently shows Odysseus outclassed physically by giant cyclops, sorceresses with magical powers, and even pure forces of nature like Scylla and Charybdis. When a capital-h Hero is outclassed physically, he is allowed to use his wits to defeat his enemies. It appears that young Oedipus understands this rule, for he has studied hard to become the smartest and cleverest he can possibly be, with no inkling that it will become his tragic flaw. But it hasn't yet. When he first questions his origins, he is morally superior.

Oedipus is very young—thirteen was the age of manhood in many places in ancient times, old enough to marry and take on other responsibilities. A crown prince with a living father, Oedipus would not be under immediate pressure to take on those responsibilities, so he could be fourteen or fifteen or even a bit older, but still definitely a teen, when one of his father's soldiers accuses him of being a bastard. That starts him on his quest to solve his own mystery—especially when his parents refuse to discuss how anyone in Corinth would get such an idea. But Oedipus knows he has no siblings. It wouldn't take long for him to wonder, "Am I adopted?"

That is the last thing his parents want to hear from their son. We don't know how much they know of who he is, but probably at least that he is of noble blood as they dare raise him to become a king. But they won't tell him anything, which suggests that whether they were told the curse on him when they took him in or have found it out later, they know enough to want to protect him from it. But they have raised him to think like a king. Oedipus decides to find out for himself: he goes to consult the Oracle at Delphi.

The Oracle doesn't accept everyone's question, so when she takes his, Oedipus must know he is going to learn something important. But instead of answering his question, which would have been about his parentage, she straight-out tells him, "You are going to kill your father and marry your mother!"

Before I visited Greece, I used to try to engage my students with the question of what they would do in Oedipus's situation. The image I had of him before I struggled around High Corinth was of a healthy young man with a limp and a chip on his shoulder. We would usually conclude that the first example of his acting on hubris comes when he gets the message from the Oracle: he thinks he can outsmart the gods by never going near his father or mother again. But in doing so, he completely ignores the fact that he has come to Delphi to find out if maybe they aren't really his parents. Anyone who had just been given the message he received would be traumatized, but, apparently, he never again thinks about who his biological parents are until his adult life begins to unravel in the present day of the play.

I never had a satisfactory explanation of how Oedipus could casually kill a man, continue and confront the Sphynx, answer a riddle that was only obvious to someone who walked with a stick, and then accept the kingship of Thebes and take the newly widowed queen as his wife: all this after just being told by a divine source that he was going to kill his father and marry his mother. It made no sense until I started thinking of Oedipus as a teenage boy.

Teenagers may be technically adults with adult responsibilities, but they still live in the moment much of the time. They are also hormonal and volatile. When Oedipus meets Laertes on the causeway, he forgets he is not in Corinth. At home he is the crown prince, and any citizen would stand aside to let him pass. He is also suicidal, on his way to die by Sphynx and thus end all his problems, such a potentially common way of teenage thinking under pressure that it is referred to as "a permanent solution to a temporary problem." We can imagine Oedipus upon hearing the riddle, "What creature walks upon four legs at dawn, two at noon, and three at sunset?" He has "walked on three legs" ever since he got up from four. But his situation is extraordinary. Ordinarily, a man would walk on two legs until he is old. Could the answer possibly be a man?

And it is! Suddenly Oedipus is a hero. He has saved a kingdom from a monster. They want to make him king. What mixed emotions he must have—little wonder he just goes with the flow. From the depths of despair, he is welcomed into a new family and position to replace the ones he sacrificed. Was the sacrifice of leaving his parents so he wouldn't harm them what the gods wanted? If he marries the Queen of Thebes, then he won't be available to marry his mother. It appears that he has no idea that the man he hit with his stick died. He has undoubtedly hit people before without killing anyone and doesn't know that, that day, the gods were directing the upper body strength he built up negotiating High Corinth. And he doesn't know until the day many years later, when he finally gathers the facts of that fateful day, that the king's guards lied, saying that they were set upon by a whole band of attackers because they could not admit to not being able to protect the king from a disabled teen with a stick. Oedipus has fulfilled the first part of the prophecy, and the gods make certain that he not only completes the second but is persuaded he has outwitted them. *They* know what he has been through in the past few days, and simply expect him to act like a teenager—which he does. Thus, he is allowed to make the tragedy worse, incestuously bringing four innocent children into the world to suffer their own tragedies.

The pivotal events of *Oedipus Rex* make much more sense when the young Oedipus who committed them is read as a confused and traumatized teenage boy, and I find that my students are more interested in the play when read that way. But this insight into Oedipus was not the only thing I brought home from that trip to Greece. Only in recent years have I realized that something else happened to me on that journey.

As I mentioned, we spent our whole trip drinking the clear, cold water from the many springs we encountered. Only much later did I learn that some of those springs—in and around Mt. Helicon—were brought to flow when the flying horse Pegasus struck the earth with his hoofs. These springs were associated with inspiration and creativity and dedicated to the Muses.

It seems that I absorbed some unexpected creativity on that journey. I was already a writer of fiction, but something that had frustrated me all my life was that I could not draw or paint. Over the years I made numerous attempts to learn, all failures. Eventually I stopped trying.

After my trip to Greece I continued my writing and teaching, eventually retired from teaching but continued writing, and then, at a time when I was caught up on obligations, I stumbled on a book that challenged me to *Learn to Draw in Thirty Days!* It was not the first time I had tried. But perhaps because I was otherwise in a lull creatively, I started each day for a month with an exercise from the book. And at the end, for the first time ever, I could draw a house that looked like a house, a flag that looked like a flag, a flower that looked like a flower. I still have the sketchbook I used—yes, they were very childish houses, flags, and flowers, but when you've always before had people guessing that your attempt at a bluebird is an elephant, recognizability is success!

Now, most of us know that it takes a million words of practice to become a writer. I learned that it takes ten thousand drawings to become an artist. In each case, of course, we usually mean adequacy, not mastery. But at that particular time, I was retired from teaching and between other projects, so I decided I would see how far I could get—because I could see progress, something that had never happened in my earlier attempts. Fortunately, I did not show my work at that time to a real artist. Anyone would have told me, "Go back to writing stories."

So, I didn't tell anyone, but continued to start every day with a sketch of some kind. I took an online course in—of all things—portraiture and failed abysmally at its promise (lifelike portraits). But I learned how to use value, how to measure, and above all practice-practice-practice. Once again, there was clear progress, which gave me the hutzpah to enroll in Art 101 at Murray State, to get some formal training. I was definitely one of the bottom three students in the class, but I was there to learn—and learn I did. I continued into Life Drawing, in which course I finally produced a graphite drawing that came out looking exactly as I intended. Of course, I couldn't do that with the next one, but as I continued, just often enough to keep me going, something would turn out right.

As I look back on those four years, including the two we all lost to COVID, something kept me going—and I'm convinced it was the inspiration I gained by drinking from Pegasus's spring. My progress was so slow at first that in any other time of my life I would have quit again and spent my spare time reading. But just as the restrictions lifted, I discovered pastels, and suddenly everything I had learned in my classes came together. An artist friend looked at my work, and took me to a local gallery, where for the past two years my work has sold steadily. I began entering contests, and winning recognition. I have had four works accepted into juried museum shows.

How could someone who could not draw at all her whole life suddenly blossom into a respectable artist in her 80s? The only answer I can see is magic—the magic of reading, the magic of writing, the magic of travel, all available to everyone—but in this case, I think there was some special extra magic from Pegasus, one day in Greece.

David G. Hartwell Award Winner

"The Beauty of the House is Immeasurable": Susanna Clarke's *Piranesi* on the Uses of Speculative Fiction for Escape During the Covid Pandemic

Liz Busby

WHEN SUSANNA CLARKE WROTE her novel *Piranesi*, she could not have predicted that it would be published during a global pandemic. Yet this coincidence in timing has overwhelmingly affected the reception of the book. One review notes, "Like many of us during quarantine, the protagonist Piranesi can barely remember life before the House" (Schroeder n.p.). The book's narrative of being trapped alone in an infinite interior space resonates with the enforced social isolation during the Covid-19 pandemic (Walton; Vinson; Holub). Many people coped with quarantine by reading books or watching media, particularly varieties with an escapist reputation including speculative fiction, which made up seven out of the top twenty most-watched shows during the early pandemic (Gentile n.p.). Similarly, Piranesi copes with his isolation through his study of the symbolic statues that line the halls of the House: their stories become a lifeline, enabling his survival in otherwise insufferable circumstances. The House itself becomes a constructive Escape from an unjust world, as described by Tolkien in his classic essay "On Fairy-Stories." Indeed, Clarke's novel illustrates both in its content and in the context of its release how stories provide a way for humanity to cope with injustices and why fiction—particularly speculative fiction such as *Piranesi*—is not merely entertainment, which might be considered frivolity.

The attitude that art should be of practical use is represented by Piranesi's one-time research companion and, the reader eventually discovers, his jailer, Valentine Ketterley. "The Other," as Piranesi names Ketterley, values the House only as a means to an end, the container of a "Great and Secret Knowledge" (Clarke 7). The novel draws the metaphor between this utilitarian attitude towards the House and the consumption of literature: Ketterley sees the House as "a text to be interpreted, and that if ever we discover the Knowledge, then it will be as if the Value has been wrested from the House and all that remains will be mere scenery" (Clarke 60). This sentiment reduces story to two purposes: information-dissemination and decoration. Literature from this perspective is propaganda, a clever way to conceal and deliver a message to the human mind, but otherwise a frivolous ornament not worthy of serious consideration. It's easy to see why, from this perspective, narrative media—whether television shows or novels—might be considered a waste of time, with the possible exception of historical fiction as a metaphorical spoonful of sugar to deliver unappetizing but important facts. Certainly, from this perspective, there would be no purpose for speculative fiction.

Piranesi's reaction to the House is a counterpoint to this perspective, one that feels familiar to those who love speculative fiction. When Raphael, Piranesi's rescuer, explains to him that the statues in the house are "only" a representation of the real world, Piranesi argues against this reduction of his world to a mere copy: "You make it sound as if the Statue was somehow inferior to the thing itself. [...] I would argue that the Statue is superior to the thing itself, the Statue being perfect, eternal and not subject to decay" (Clarke 221). Dugger notes that Piranesi inverts Plato's theory of forms, claiming art not as an imitation of the imitation, but as a true form in its own right (Dugger 77-78). A thorough examination of Piranesi's view of the symbolic world he inhabits reveals three different uses of the non-mimetic story, which I will tie to Arthur Frank's theory regarding cognitive capacities of story.

Firstly, though the statues in the House are not direct representations of any particular thing, they reflect a distilled essence of the outside world that has been transformed into something new that can stand on its own. Laurence Arne-Sayles, the scientist and mystic who initially discovered the alternate dimension that makes up the House, describes it to Piranesi as "a Distributary World [. . .] created by ideas flowing out of another world" (Clarke 88). Although this statement implies that the story-world is inferior, Arne-Sayles then clarifies that the world now exists in its own right through the metaphor of a cave: "Imagine water flowing underground. [...] Millennia later you have a cave system. But what you don't have is the water that originally created it. That's long gone" (Clarke 90). The ideas flowing out of the real world may have created the symbolic world of the House, but those ideas have been transformed into something that now stands on its own, a story capacity that Frank calls "symbiosis" (37).

Because of this independence, Piranesi, who no longer remembers the outside world, can nonetheless derive meaning from the statues. The clearest example is Piranesi's interpretation of the statue that readers may recognize as Mr. Tumnus from *The Lion, The Witch, and the Wardrobe*, but that the narrator has no context for understanding. Still, when Piranesi sees this statue, he intuits the symbolism of the finger across Mr. Tumnus's lips: "I have always felt that he meant to tell me something or perhaps to warn me of something: Quiet! He seems to say. Be careful!" (Clarke 15). That statue conveys the meaning of caution and secrecy because of the story it is connected to, even when that direct connection is severed. Piranesi gives other statues a list of virtues that show how the story presented even by just a single static image affects him: the statue of the gorilla "represents many things, among them Peace, Tranquility, Strength and Endurance" and "The Horned Giants [...] represent Endeavour and the Struggle against a Wretched Fate" (Clarke 15–16). These statues symbolize the interior human world, even without direct referents, much the same way that speculative fiction conveys information about humanity without being directly mimetic.

The second way that the statues function for Piranesi is by giving him a means to interpret his own experiences. As Piranesi realizes halfway through the book, by combining the meanings of the statues together, he is able to understand concepts that don't exist in his world, such as gardens or universities, when he reads about them in the journal of his former life (Clarke 120). This makes the statues similar to speculative fiction: they can't tell Piranesi anything directly about how to survive in the world he lives in by instructing him in fishing or informing him about what he has forgotten; yet, lacking an informative function, the statues are nevertheless far from simply decorative. In fact, Piranesi believes that "the World still speaks to me every day" through the statues (154).

Piranesi's experience of the statues changes over time. Piranesi encounters the Tumnus statue again just after he has realized that he has lost a significant portion of his memories. Where he had previously seen the Tumnus statue as a symbol of caution, "today it seemed to mean something quite different: Hush! Be comforted!" (Clarke 108). Piranesi also strings the statues' meanings together transformatively into messages by watching which ones a flock of birds land on (39–42). The statues become part of Piranesi's personal vocabulary of meaning, allowing him to understand them in new ways at different times.

This sort of divination from stories may seem odd on the face of it, but drawing wisdom from stories is, in fact, a common practice. Frank writes that stories have a capacity for "inherent morality" in that they depict "the necessity, the difficulty, and the inherent danger in choosing how to live" and that people are able to "respond [to life] because stories taught them how" (36–37). It is not surprising that Piranesi's belief in the power of these statues becomes religious, as many religions use stories to understand correct behavior. Much of the Christian practice of reading the Bible relies on this notion: while parts of scripture contain treatises on correct behavior, most are stories that must be internalized and interpreted and reinterpreted, as needed. Similarly, scholars have recognized that "fairy tales send powerful, practically irresistible messages about what life is about that resonate with both children and adults," even though their specific lessons about the nature of fairies or dwarves may not be applicable (Rudy 173). Although the stories represented by the statues don't tell Piranesi about his world, they inform his ability to act and live within it.

Finally, within these more practical views of story as a means of understanding and interpreting the world, *Piranesi* also asserts the intrinsic value of story. While the Other sees the labyrinthine House as a means to obtain power, and the Prophet (Piranesi's name for Laurence Arnes-Sayles, the original discoverer of the House) uses the House as a means to assert his influence over others, Piranesi exists in a state of constant appreciation of the House as itself. While contemplating the beauty of "the sight of the One-Hundred-and-Ninety-Second Western Hall in the Moonlight," Piranesi realizes that "The House is valuable because it is the House. It is enough in and of Itself. It is not the means to an end" (Clarke 60). Indeed, perhaps one of the most unique things about reading *Piranesi* during the pandemic is its reframing of a quiet life confined to an interior space as tranquil and beautiful rather than constricting and claustrophobic. This perspective on abiding in a work of art echoes a formalist appreciation of story: story doesn't need to mean anything or have any practical application in the world to be valuable. Narrative is an innate human need and activity, not something done for practical purposes but because readers and listeners are human with the story capacity Frank calls "imagination," the fact that stories "arouse emotions" and are "compelling" in their own right (Frank 41).

This imaginative capacity of story as an escape from reality was widely used during the pandemic, as people escaped from what was called endless doom-scrolling of the news into novels and Netflix binges. My own unhealthy obsession over unchangeable circumstances during the pandemic is echoed in Piranesi's reaction when he finally learns the truth about his imprisonment: "I did not think to rest. I did not think to eat. I did not think to drink water. Hours passed – I do not how many [....] My thighs ached, my back ached, my head ached. My eyes and throat were sore with weeping and shouting" (Clarke 189). The recovered pages of his journal indicate this obsession has happened to Piranesi once before, when he was first brought to the House, and his inability to change his circumstances nearly led him into madness (190). The only way for Piranesi to cope with the situation was to tear "into pieces the description of his enslavement that he had written in his Journal," casting aside his unchangeable circumstances (190).

In order to recover from this realization, Piranesi seeks Escape through the statues and their stories: "I revisited all my favourite Statues [. . .] Their Beauty soothed me and took me out of Myself" (Clarke 109). This desire to flee from an intolerable world into a different world is defined by Tolkien as one of the three major purposes of fantasy: "Why should a man be scorned if, finding himself in prison, he tries to get out and go home? Or if, when he cannot do so, he thinks and talks about other topics than jailers and prison-walls?" (Tolkien 148). The critics to whom Tolkien is reacting see fantasy as the irresponsible abandonment of reality, "the Flight of the Deserter" (148), whereas Tolkien sees the Escape of speculative fiction as a rational coping strategy in an intolerable world, "the Escape of the Prisoner" (148).

This sense of story as Escape from intolerable reality is exemplified in the characters who continue to return to the labyrinth with Piranesi after he is freed from his imprisonment. The first is a young man named James Ritter who struggles with mental health issues and drug addiction, who is often homeless and sometimes does sex work. He is imprisoned in the House by Laurence Arnes-Sayles years before Piranesi, but justice is eventually served when Ritter is rescued and Arnes-Sayles is incarcerated. But Ritter has been permanently altered by his time in the labyrinth: Arnes-Sayles mentions he could "barely string a sentence together by the end" (Clarke 90). A decade later, Ritter states that "working at Manchester Town Hall was what had saved him; [...] The resemblance to the other house – the one Arne-Sayles had taken him to – calmed him" (119). When the freed Piranesi seeks him out, Ritter is a "thin, ravaged-looking man who smelt strongly of cigarettes," still coping with the damage done to his mind (239). When Piranesi conducts Ritter back to the House, the return provides the solace Ritter has been seeking: "he started to cry, not for fear, but for happiness. He went immediately and sat under the great marble sweep of the staircase; the place where he used to sleep. He closed his eyes and listened to the sounds of the tides" (239). The sensory experience of the House—being immersed in a narrative divorced from his reality—provides solace, helping Ritter to heal in a way the retributive justice of the British legal system cannot.

Even for those not directly victims of injustice, art can be a solace from the world's imperfections. Raphael, the police officer who rescues Piranesi, is the novel's enactor of justice as she doggedly pursues clues to the whereabouts of Matthew Rose Sorensen, Piranesi's lost identity. Raphael is at first amazed by the House, calling it "an astonishing place. A perfect place," but later she comes to realize that even this alternate world contains injustice (Clarke 224). She is disturbed by the fact that Ketterley will "never be punished for what he did to you [. . . .] There's nothing I can do. Nothing he can be charged with" (225). Raphael realizes that the failure of retributive justice has followed her even into what she regards as the imaginary world of the House. Nonetheless, she continues to find solace there: "she returns to the labyrinth often. Sometimes we go together; sometimes she goes alone. The quiet and the solitude attract her strongly. In them she hopes to find what she needs" (242). The House cannot fix the injustice of what has happened to Matthew Rose Sorensen, nor the many other crimes Raphael has no doubt seen, but its nature allows a respite from that pressing reality, a Tolkien-esque Escape from the imperfect justice system.

Both Raphael and Ritter show the value of story as an Escape from an unfair world, but in examining Piranesi's experience the reader finds something more. Piranesi has been in the labyrinth for years, longer than anyone else. When Arne-Sayles visits him, he finds it remarkable that Piranesi has been able to maintain his sanity for so long when the typical effects of lingering in the House are "amnesia, total mental collapse" (Clarke 90). Indeed, Piranesi has suffered from amnesia, but why has he not suffered the total mental collapse that happened to Ritter?

Perhaps it is because Piranesi went beyond simply experiencing the House as an escapist respite from the world, but instead sought to derive meaning from it. There is no indication that either Ritter or Raphael, regardless of their appreciation of the House's aesthetic value, ever saw the statues as full of meaning, full of story, in the way that Piranesi does. Only Piranesi interacts with story in more of its capacities—the imagination of Escape, yes, but also symbiosis and inherent morality. Rather than only pushing the injustice of the world out of his mind, Piranesi allows his experiences in the House to teach him about humanity, to actively shape his character.

While Matthew Rose Sorensen spent days obsessing over getting retributive justice against his captor, the House has made Piranesi into someone who is merciful. Even when he finds that Ketterley intends to kill him, Piranesi cannot countenance doing the same: "To be honest, I do not think that I would ever want to kill him—the idea of it is abhorrent to me" (Clarke 100). Even when contemplating violence in self-defense, Piranesi's morality stands firm: "Even the wicked deserve Life. Or if they do not, then let the House take it from them. Not me" (130). As Matthew Rose Sorensen was not this kind of person, the reader is left to assume that he has acquired this inner moral code as a result of living in the peaceful House.

Using story to grow as a person might sound superficially similar to Ketterley's desire to extract information from the House, but I would argue that Piranesi's use of the House is inherently different. Whereas Ketterley wants a straightforward meaning that can be extracted, Piranesi's method of obtaining meaning reflects Frank's story capacity of "interpretive openness" (Frank 34). Piranesi's interpretations of the House change and grow with him; to him, the statues are "several things at once, and they are good at equipping humans to live in a world that not only is open to multiple interpretive understands but requires understandings in the plural" (Frank 34). When he returns to the real world, Piranesi realizes that his experiences help him understand it:

> I thought that in this new (old) world the statues would be irrelevant. I did not imagine that they would continue to help me. But I was wrong. When faced with a person or situation I do not understand,

my first impulse is still to look for a statue that will enlighten me. (Clarke 240)

Piranesi uses analogies to specific statues to illuminate the character of the various people involved in his experience in the House: Raphael is "a queen in a chariot, the protector of her people," Arnes-Sayles a "heretical pope seated on a throne" (Clarke 241). Characterizing these people via the statues allows Piranesi to interpret his experience—not in a closed way that defines people with a singular meaning, but an open way that casts them as characters in a story that may grow and change.

As he walks down the street at the end of the novel, Piranesi offers this same hopeful vision to those he meets on the street:

> An old man passed me. He looked sad and tired. He had broken veins on his cheeks and a bristly white beard [. . . .] I realised I knew him. He is depicted on the northern wall of the forty-eighth western hall. He is shown as a king with a little model of a walled city in one hand while the other hand he raises in blessing. I wanted to seize hold of him and say to him: In another world you are a king, noble and good! I have seen it! (Clarke 244)

Piranesi's time among the statues has given him a vocabulary for humanity's potential, a positive template through which to interpret life.

Limited studies on the cognitive effects of media-watching during the pandemic indicate that this ability to apply story to real life may indeed be protective from the harmful effects of what is referred to as binge-watching media. In a study of 715 Italian adults during April 2020, researchers found that "both non-problematic and problematic TV series watching behaviors were equally induced by anxiety symptoms and escapism motivation" (Boursier et al. 1). However, Boursier et al. observed that those who stated that they were "watching TV series for exploring new ideas, increasing knowledge, and enriching one's own perspective on contexts and situations" were less likely to display problematic behaviors such as saying their watching was "compulsive and uncontrollable" (7). Though all media provided an Escape from the stress of the pandemic, the real benefit came as people engaged with those stories on a deeply moral level, using them as Piranesi does to enrich his humanity through personal growth.

In my own media consumption during the pandemic, I found that the cooking competitions I watched compulsively left me feeling worse, resulting in an endless cycle of watching what I thought of as "just one more episode." But picking up Susanna Clarke's novel transported me to a world where I found my own world reflected back to me in a more comforting form. The peace of the House reconciled me to the tranquility of this time of more limited options. The careful consciousness and repetition of Clarke's prose calmed me as it does the characters in the House. And the eventual resolution of the novel served as a template for finding serenity even in a world where it seemed none of the options were good, fair, or just. *Piranesi* is the novel I needed to get through the pandemic because it engaged directly with the meaning and beauty of stories in a world where nothing seemed to make sense. The novel provided an Escape, yes, and Escape is necessary at some points of human experience, such as a global pandemic. But *Piranesi* also forced me as a reader to consider the uses of the stories I was consuming. Clarke's novel makes the argument that stories are not just an escapist pastime, but a vital part of one's humanity. In speculative fiction, where stories don't reflect the realities of current or historical experience, they still do real work within the human soul.

Works Cited

Boursier, Valentina, et al. "Is Watching TV Series an Adaptive Coping Strategy During the COVID-19 Pandemic? Insights From an Italian Community Sample." *Frontiers in Psychiatry*, vol. 12, 2021, https://doi.org/10.3389/fpsyt.2021.599859. Accessed 28 May 2022.

Clarke, Susanna. *Piranesi*. Kindle edition, Bloomsbury Publishing, 2020.

Dugger, Julie M. "Lewis and Clarke in the Caves: Art and Platonic Worlds in Piranesi." *Mythlore*, vol. 40, no. 1, 2021, pp. 63–83.

Frank, Arthur W. *Letting Stories Breathe: A Socio-Narratology*. University of Chicago Press, 2012.

Gentile, Dan. "The 20 Most Popular Shows People Started Watching during the Pandemic." *SFGATE*, 5 May 2020, https://www.sfgate.com/tv/slideshow/most-popular-shows-people-started-watching-202049.php. Accessed 5 June 2022.

Holub, Christian. "Quarantine Book Club: How I Got Lost in 'Piranesi' during the Pandemic." *Entertainment Weekly*, 17 Sept. 2020, https://ew.com/books/quarantine-book-club-piranesi/. Accessed 25 May 2022.

Rudy, Jill Terry. "Socializations: Traditional Wonder Tales and Other Guides for Growing Up." *A Cultural History of Fairy Tales in the Modern Age*, edited by Andrew Teverson, vol. 6, Bloomsbury Academic, 2021, pp. 159–180.

Schroeder, Jack M. "'Piranesi' Is a Beautifully Infinite Quarantine." *The Harvard Crimson*, 3 November 2020, https://www.thecrimson.com/article/2020/11/3/piranesi-review/. Accessed 25 May 2022.

Tolkien, J. R. R. "On Fairy-Stories." *The Monsters and the Critics and Other Essays*, edited by Christopher Tolkien, George Allen and Unwin, 1983, pp. 109–61.

Vinson, Jodie Noel. "'Piranesi' Is a Dispatch from the Kingdom of Chronic Illness." *Electric Literature*, 28 January 2021, http://electricliterature.com/piranesi-susanna-Clarke-chronic-illness-long-covid/. Accessed 28 May 2022.

Walton, James. "Infinite Quarantine." *New York Review*, 8 April 2021, https://www.nybooks.com/articles/2021/04/08/susanna-Clarke-piranesi-infinite-quarantine/. Accessed 25 May 2022.

David G. Hartwell Award Winner

Toxic Tales: The Craft of Enchantment in Fiction and Memoir

Sasha Bailyn

ENCHANTMENT IS, BY DEFINITION, SUBJECTIVE: a feeling of great pleasure; something that is thought to have magical power over someone (*Cambridge Dictionary*). All stories arguably cast a spell. Readers enter an implied contract with the author, a magical exchange, and step into a world not their own. Preconceptions slip and give way to what the author weaves in readers' minds. Writing is spellcasting. Occasional readers and avid bibliophiles will likely agree that the act of reading is itself a form of enchantment.

Magic is usually linked to fantasy: stories with otherworldly creatures, worldbuilding that overtly distinguishes itself as other from accepted reality. Enchantment is a cousin of magic, having more to do with myth and fairy tales, but also, ironically, ordinary life. The worldbuilding of an enchanted tale isn't a distant planet, or even a separate reality. It's magic-adjacent, right next door to everyday experience. Many would broadly label enchantment as a speculative genre, or even "magical realism," a "narrative mode that discusses alternative approaches to reality to that of Western philosophy" (Bowers 1). But magical realism has its own complicated, canonical history in the twentieth century, spanning Germany and Latin America (8). Enchantment is not a genre in and of itself, falling somewhere between speculative and magical realism; it's a craft approach that takes the reader out of a linear, logical experience of reality, while highlighting and exploring the complexities of human life. What distinguishes enchanted storytelling is its form, which references or directly imitates classic European fairy tales.

This is not a study of enchantment as genre, but as craft device: what are its uses in prose, and how is it deployed in both fiction and creative nonfiction? How are *Gingerbread*, a novell-length fairy tale retelling by Helen Oyeyemi, and the fairy-tale-like memoir *In the Dream House* by Carmen Maria Machado, alike or different in their enchanted prose? I end not with a conclusion but an opening, an invitation for further exploration. Enchantment—that is, magic and delight—is meant to be tricky to pin down. The important thing is to pursue it, not to quantify and over-define it.

As witches have grimoires, it's helpful to have an implement, guideposts for identifying the elements of enchantment. The grimoire for this study is Kate Bernheimer's craft essay "Fairy Tale is Form, Form is Fairy Tale," in which she outlines four techniques of classical European fairy tale writing: flatness, abstraction, intuitive logic, and normalized magic.

1) Flatness: Characters and settings read as one or two-dimensional, with limited depth.
2) Abstraction: Description lacks detail, is deliberately vague.
3) Intuitive Logic: Events are connected by syntax, narrative proximity, rather than logic.
4) Normalized Magic: Wondrous things occur amid everyday life, and characters aren't surprised. This is perhaps the most exciting, most obviously enchanting aspect of fairy tales.

Carmen Maria Machado's memoir *In the Dream House* and Helen Oyeyemi's *Gingerbread* are enchanted tales of home, belonging, and relationships. Toxicity is their shared spine, the primary villain in these tales of dreams—of hopes for the future, altered states of being and consciousness. *Gingerbread* is a blended rewrite of two trickster fairy tales, "Vasilisa the Fair" and "Hansel and Gretel" (Tatar 236, 263). But unlike Hansel and Gretel's spiced cake, Oyeyemi's gingerbread is not an innocent treat, but a dangerous travel agent, toxic when mixed with the wrong ingredients, or when given to celiac protagonist Perdita, who learns that family doesn't always look out for its members' best interests. Likewise, Machado's Dream House and dream relationship turn out to be laced with malintent and danger: "The Dream House was never just the Dream House. It was, in turn, a convent of promise (herb garden, wine, writing across the table from each other) [...] a haunted house (*none of this can really be happening*), a prison (*need to get out need to get out*), and, finally, a dungeon of memory" (72).

Unlike Helen Oyeyemi's *Gingerbread*, whose magic is baked into its nature as a riff on "Hansel and Gretel," Carmen Maria Machado's memoir *In the Dream House* is not an obvious fairy tale. It takes a more slanted approach to enchantment. Its prominent craft mechanism is point of view, spliced between second and first person:

> You were not always just a You. I was whole—a symbiotic relationship between my best and worst parts—and then, in one sense of the definition, I was cleaved: a neat lop that took first person—that assured, confident woman, the girl detective, the adventurer—away from second, who was always anxious and vibrating like a too-small breed of dog. (Machado 14)

116 • Sasha Bailyn

A splitting of the self; therein lies the fairy tale flatness and abstraction. The self is flattened as "You," and abstracted into two perspectives. Machado's prose alternates between the narrator "I" of the innocent past and the wiser future and the "You" sandwiched in-between, in the years Machado felt like a victim. The second person illustrates the flattening effect of victimhood. Machado's dream relationship, "the woman from the Dream House" (10), is introduced with similar flatness and abstraction. She's not a three-dimensional person, but The Woman from the Dream House, with capital letters. This drips of villainy and fairy tale foreboding. The reader sees her through the flattening, rose-colored glasses the "You" Machado once had, before her lover's abusive side revealed itself. "She loves you. She sees your subtle, ineffable qualities. You are the only one for her in all the world" (29). This narrative style of telling rather than obliquely showing stokes the reader's sense of mistrust for the information presented and heightens suspense for what's to come. In this memoir, flatness and abstraction strengthen the reader's understanding of the "You" narrator as hapless and unreliable.

Like *Dream House*, there are villains and hapless victims in the novel *Gingerbread*. Billionaire Clio Kercheval neglects struggling farmstead families, except for choice malnourished daughters, whom she plucks out of their homes, moves to the city, and turns into actresses—Gingerbread Girls—in what she calls her "authenticity theme park." Perdita's mother was one such Gingerbread Girl, whose story begins with fairy tale flatness: "A girl grew up in a field" (Oyeyemi 49). The Gingerbread Girls sleep in a cinnamon-colored house with a sugar-dusted effect on its roof, but live far from a sweetened life, fending off perverts, earning what turns out to be counterfeit money, and choking down strange regimens of rotten egg-flavored gruel. The public sees them "as the epitome of plump-cheeked country childhood [...] Their eyes and teeth sparkled, their skin was smooth, and their pigtails were extra-bushy" (Oyeyemi 90). Clio Kercheval and the Gingerbread Girls are rendered with exquisite detail and specificity, but their roles in the story, monstrous villain and helpless victims, are flattened fairy-tale tropes.

Oyeyemi also incorporates fairy tale abstraction in her use of symbols, enchanted props that occupy the landscape. In the hidden land of Druhástrana, Perdita's matrilineal country of origin, Oyeyemi flattens recognized elements of fairy tales, omitting their backstories: "It was a wooden clog the size of a caravel, a relic from the days of the giants. The Coopers were convinced the shoe belonged to a giant Cinderella, and they gave the youngest among them the task of keeping it polished in case someone came back for it" (50). There's also a giant Mr. Jack-in-the-Box, and a broken loom. *Gingerbread* is sprinkled with abstracted fairy-tale references that are insignificant to the plot. Who were the giants, and will they ever return? Who broke the loom and why? The reader will never know, nor will they care for very long because the plot moves like quicksand. The abstract props are shallow objects instead of completed metaphors, landmarks without deeper meaning. Like a good fairy tale, *Gingerbread* uses abstraction to leave one wondering, teetering on the edge of *Ah-ha!* and fascination.

In the Dream House has a tighter calibration than *Gingerbread*, exploring all metaphors, leaving little unexplained. Machado establishes authority as a narrator through her intellect, the breadth of her well-researched musings. Chapters evoke the pages of an encyclopedia in their titles ("Dream House as Folktale Taxonomy," "Dream House as Inciting Incident"), but their order seems nonsensical, a piecemeal narrative constructed by Machado's emotional experience. It's an arc that's challenging to anticipate, an enchanting mystery: intuitive logic at play. *Consider this, now imagine the opposite of that, and what about this other idea?* Machado communicates, urging one not to worry about the path, but to follow her breadcrumbs. When Machado describes how she's cleaved in two, "a neat lop that took first person [...] away from second" (14), she announces the mechanism of her memoir in the way that a fairy tale may introduce its unique logic with the opening line, "'There was once'" (Bernheimer 66).

Fairy tale logic, nonsensical sense, also relates to how Machado brings the reader into the experience of abuse:

> Her grip goes hard, begins to hurt. You don't understand; you don't understand so profoundly your brain skitters, skips, backs up. [...] *This is not normal, this is not normal, this is not normal.* Your brain is scrambling for an explanation, and it hurts more and more, and everything is static. (57)

Machado likens this moment to the wife's experience in the fairy tale "Bluebeard," musing: "[the wife] hadn't protested when [Bluebeard] told her her footfalls were too heavy for his liking [...] it made logical sense that she sat there and watched him spinning around the body of wife Number Four, its decaying head flopping backward on a hinge of flesh [...] You are being tested [...] look how good you are; look how loyal, look how loved" (60). In fairy tales, things happen for seemingly no reason other than proximity. *In real life, this is how abuse feels*, Machado conveys.

To temper the heaviness of her story, she infuses unexpected playfulness in the "Choose Your Own Adventure" section (Machado 162), where the reader can choose to flip to different pages. This, too, illustrates the illogical, no-win situation of dealing with an abuser, with dark humor that conveys, *can anyone believe this insanity?* With experimental form, here ostensibly nonsensical narrative progression, Machado stokes a sense of unexpected enchantment—delight—in readers that, if absent, would make readers want to give up on reading her story.

Gingerbread, too, uses intuitive logic as a vehicle for lightness. This is most evident in the made-up country of Druhástrana, whose lottery is nonsensical, using alternative methods to announce its winners. Each Thursday, lottery participants must keep their eyes open for clues, because "any string of nine numbers written on a wall or a pavement could correspond to the ticket you were carrying around that week [...] The majority of players who won that 'rigged' prize never found out that they had" (Oyeyemi 57). The citizens of Druhástrana don't protest or boycott the lottery. Like Oyeyemi's readers, they accept its illogical nature because it fosters an ambience of playful mystery, as fairy tales do with their whimsical plot sequencing. Fairy tale logic enchants even when *Gingerbread*'s plot turns to unpleasant topics, such as Perdita's near-death experience eating gingerbread, which turns her hair grey at a young age. This isn't standard medical logic; it's delightfully poetic: a symbol for Perdita's alignment with her matrilineal line. "From a distance, [they] look like three grannies" (7).

For the most part, *Gingerbread*'s magic isn't to be feared. The everyday billionaires, corporations, impoverishment, emotionally withholding family members—these are the antagonists. Normalized magic carries the wonder, lightness, and humor of the novel. One of the best examples is Perdita's collection of dolls, Bonnie, Sago, Lollipop, and Prim, who chime in like a Greek chorus at various instances of the plot: "But before Harriet can begin, Sago pipes up. She'd rather go to bed without a story tonight, if that's all right with the others" (47). The dolls have thoughts and opinions. No one bats an eye at talking dolls because they're an accepted feature of Perdita's bedroom, a normalized part of her life. They're also a nod to the fairy tale "Vasilisa the Fair," wherein Vasilisa's mother gives her a doll before she dies, and the doll helps guide Vasilisa safely through life.

Magical happenings abound in *Gingerbread*. Handwriting cakewalks across the page, ink flying off like soot, multiplying and settling into a chair as a soot figure (32); a real estate agent tries to sell an enchanted, Baba Yaga-like house (Estés 73) that has been built by fireflies and is constantly on the move: "'I don't think you can count on viewing it any time soon...we've just confirmed it went out to sea last night'" (Oyeyemi 255). There's so much magic in *Gingerbread* that it's easy to forget that the characters live in present-day England. And perhaps this is the point. Mother Harriet and daughter Perdita aren't sure whether they really exist in England. Perdita and her mother have a shifting sense of belonging and homeland.

Oyeyemi doesn't let fairy tales do all the magical work. Normalized magic also appears in the form of unexpected interiority:

> Harriet heard someone saying SHHHHHHHH so loudly and for so long that she felt she should check on the situation, and realized it was water falling down rocks....the waterfall never stopped saying, SHHHHHHHHHHH, *this is no laughing matter, young lady,* so she stayed straight-faced and giggle-free. (133)

The personification of the waterfall is an instance of the everyday turning wondrous, a way of elegantly—enchantingly—revealing Harriet's feelings of unease and displacement.

As in *Gingerbread*, unexpected metaphors crop up in *Dream House*, delighting even as they describe disturbing imagery: "There is something desperate about the house; like a ghost is trying to make itself known but can't, and so it just flops facedown into the carpet, wheezing and smelling like mold [...] the house inhales, exhales, inhales again" (Machado 73-4). Personification is an enchanting technique in and of itself, but especially so in the context of a trauma memoir. Normalized magic is "the day to day collapsed with the wondrous" (Bernheimer 69). The day to day of Machado's relationship collapses with wondrous metaphor.

Readers experience normalized magic in Machado's memoir in her sparing shifts in perspective. For most of the book, she communicates her thoughts and feelings through the ominous, tonal flatness of second person. When she breaks from second person, it's an overwhelming relief:

> [O]ur bodies are ecosystems, and they shed and replace and repair until we die. And when we die, our bodies feed the hungry earth, our cells becoming part of other cells, and in the world of the living, where we used to be, people kiss and hold hands and fall in love and fuck and laugh and cry and hurt others and nurse broken hearts and start wars and pull sleeping children out of car seats and shout at each other. If you could harness that energy–that constant, roving hunger–you could do wonders with it. You could push the earth inch by inch through the cosmos until it collided heart-first with the sun. (13)

This passage is one of the few kernels of inspiration in Machado's memoir that functions as normalized magic does in a fairy tale. Readers aren't surprised to encounter the magical feeling of hope, though they may be glad to cling to what feels sublime, just as young Machado does in the rare instances of first person: "As long as I can remember, I have been obsessed with physical and temporal limits [...] Once, when I was a kid, I stood in that wonderful sand right at the lip of the tide [...] there was a line on the map between the land and the water, and I was *on it*, precisely" (63).

While *Gingerbread* must reassure its readers that the plot has somewhere to go, *Dream House*, as a memoir, must reassure that all will be well in the end. In the final stretch of the book, Machado is left with a special ability:

It goes off at random times—meeting a new classmate or coworker, a friend's new girlfriend, a stranger at a party. A physical revulsion that comes on the heels of nothing at all, something akin to the sour liquid rush of saliva that precedes vomiting. Inconvenient, irritating, but important: my brilliant body's brilliant warning. (238)

To survive the Dream House, Machado develops a sixth sense to predict her partner's shifting moods and impending storms. In other words, abuse can produce magical abilities for protection in the everyday.

These toxic tales caution readers through fairy tale language not to fall for fantasies, while guiding them towards hope and the survival of one's dreams. But toxic tales do so with an undertone of hauntedness. The past haunts the present through fairy tale form, nested stories, disorienting, unexpected plot twists in the case of *Gingerbread* and point of view shifts in *In the Dream House*. Must enchantment always pair with trauma? Indeed, most fairy tales have haunting undertones. "In a fairy tale, inside that lyrical disconnect, resides a story that enters and haunts you deeply" (Bernheimer 68). Folded into the magic are morals, lessons about how to live, as Bruno Bettelheim explains in *The Uses of Enchantment*, when he states that fairy tale lessons "answer the eternal questions: What is the world really like? How am I to live my life in it? How can I truly be myself?" (45). Bettelheim makes the case that "fairy tales leave to the child's fantasizing whether and how to apply to himself what the story reveals about life and human nature" (45). He sees fairy tales as a way for children to metabolize psychological anxieties and Freudian taboos. Perhaps it's not so different for adults, who must metabolize trauma from a mature narrative viewpoint and confront cultural taboos.

Gingerbread has taboo baked into its retelling of "Hansel and Gretel": the taboo of child abandonment. When protagonist

Perdita, hungry for answers about her paternal bloodline, finds herself at the Kercheval mansion, she's met with an attitude of withholding from her grandmother and told she'll get no money, despite the Kercheval's wealth. The true stinginess is that the Kerchevals treat love as if it is a dangerous folly. It's taboo to even ask for love. Machado, too, explores taboos associated with the pursuit of love and one's sense of identity, noting, "*queer* does not equal good or pure or right" (Machado 48). Machado points out that just because queerness and women have a history of being oppressed and abused doesn't make them immune to being agents of oppression; relationships between women can also house abuse. Through her slanted take on fairy tale-like writing, Machado speaks about the unspeakable.

Family, relationships, and falling in love are not straightforward, as original fairy tales and Disney film adaptations might have one believe. Maria Tatar notes, "In real life, every unhappy family may be unhappy in its own way, but in fairy tales unhappy families are all very much alike" (229). There is power in words and in who tells the story. Machado knows this, having structured each chapter as a survey of idioms and terms to push back on the "dislocation" she experienced: "a common feature of domestic abuse [...] the victim [...] has been otherwise uprooted from her support network, her friends or family, her ability to communicate" (Machado 72). In *Gingerbread*, mother Harriet and daughter Perdita also struggle to find a support network. Magical gingerbread doesn't grant them the ideal community, even if it can transport them back to Harriet's homeland of Druhástrana. Whereas fairy tales generalize for a wider audience, enchanted language is a tool to explore more deeply, expressing greater maturity, more realistic complexity. In a word, what Machado and Oyeyemi accomplish with enchantment is nuance.

Enchantment is a perspective, a slanted look at reality. It asks readers to let go of expectations and whisks them out of the ordinary, away from linear, logical lives. But to be convincing, enchantment must occur in the day-to-day, with a sense of depth and purpose—reflection, as opposed to pure escape. Where myths and fairy tales simplify stories about human lives in their polarizing flatness and abstraction, enchanted books make use of these same tools to explore ambiguity and subtlety, challenging cultural norms—even the norms set forth in myth and fairy tales. Like Machado, readers can engage in direct discourse with fairy tales in creative nonfiction, rewriting and challenging the messaging, and using this form to "[put] language to something for which [we] have no language" (134). Like Oyeyemi, who litters the landscape of her prose with fairy tale symbols, readers can keep the tales of yore that still captivate imaginations, treating fairy tales as landmarks to write around and through, rather than fixed talismans one must carry down every path. Most readers have pined for the magic that fairy tale characters encounter, those who "embark on adventures that take them from the drab world of everyday reality—a place of suffering, deficiency, and lack—to a shining new reality" (Tatar 229). Intelligent authors can harness this desire to tell new tales and invent their own magic, so to speak, through the language of enchantment.

Works Cited

Bernheimer, Kate. "Fairy Tale is Form, Form is Fairy Tale." *The Writer's Notebook*. Portland: Tin House Books, 2010, pp. 61-73.

Bettelheim, Bruno. *The Uses of Enchantment*. New York: Vintage Books Edition, 2010.

Bowers, Maggie Ann. *Magic(al) Realism*. New York: Routledge, 2004.

"Enchantment." *Cambridge Dictionary*, https://dictionary.cambridge.org/us/dictionary/english/enchantment. Accessed 14 Aug. 2024.

Estés, Clarissa Pinkola. *Women Who Run With the Wolves*. New York: Ballantine Books, 1992.

Machado, Carmen Maria. *In the Dream House*. Minneapolis: Graywolf

Press, 2019.

Oyeyemi, Helen. *Gingerbread*. New York: Riverhead Books, 2020.

Tatar, Maria. *The Classic Fairy Tales*. 2nd ed. New York: W.W. Norton & Company, 2017.

Walter James Miller Memorial Award Winner

Resurrecting Indigenous Sciences from the Prehistoric Myths of Chinese Ancestral Tribes: The Whimsical Cosmographer in Weiyu's *Great Fable* Tetralogy

Yuheng Ko

WEIYU (尾鱼), A PROLIFIC WRITER featured on Jinjiang Literature City (*jinjiang wenxue cheng*), the major Chinese-language platform for serializing internet literature, has long been celebrated within her fandom and has recently gained critical attention for her adept synthesis of two distinct sub-genres prevalent in Chinese popular literature: "female-channel novels" (*nüpin xiaoshuo*; 女频小说) and "novels of the spiritual and the strange" (*lingyi xiaoshuo*; 灵异小说). Presented from a distinctly female perspective and primarily directed toward a female audience, her stories typically revolve around female protagonists who collaborate with male counterparts, embarking on journeys to unravel mysteries while fostering romantic relationships.[1] Most ambitious among her works is the *Great Fable* tetralogy published between 2013-2019, named after the final book of *The Classic of Mountains and Seas*, an ancient Chinese compilation of mythology and folklore. Drawing inspiration from diverse speculative genres within the

Chinese literary tradition, such as *zhiguai*, *chuanqi*, and Chinese mythology and folklore, the tetralogy stands as an exemplar of Chinese-written Indigenous science fiction long-awaited in the realm of science fiction and fantasy scholarship.[2] Notably, it rejuvenates the supernatural elements entrenched in prehistoric myths by rationalizing them as ancient advanced sciences, and by reimagining the ancestral Chiyou tribe, who harnessed these sciences, as an early human species capable of auto-reproduction, and thereby of enjoying immortality. By translating mythical narratives into rationalized constructs, the tetralogy playfully teases modern scientific discourse, revealing its speculative dimensions and exposing the inherent epistemological uncertainties within.

Central to her discursive enterprise to navigate the ambiguities between rationalization and speculation is the whimsical character who recurrently appears throughout the tetralogy, known as the "godly trickster," or the god's fellow—a term rooted in a Chinese idiom *shen-gun* 神棍, which historically refers to charlatans who offer services such as divine communication, miraculous healing, misfortune deflection, and aversion of evil, while exploiting their clients for financial gain. Superficially, the godly trickster assumes the role of a jester-like figure, whimsically emerging out of nowhere to offer vital clues for unraveling mysteries, then vanishing into the woods for investigations into peculiar occurrences. Yet, this whimsical character serves narrative purposes beyond mere plot advancement and playful amusement. With his consistent self-identification as a scientist, the godly trickster, I contend, can be legitimately regarded as a whimsical cosmographer delving into the anomalies of the universe, echoing Robert Campany's conception of the Chinese *zhiguai* stories as cosmographic accounts laden with investigative intent and observational significance. Through his whimsical rhetoric, the godly trickster blurs the lines between fact and fiction and between cognition and imagination imposed by scientific discourse, inviting readers to suspend their disbelief, and thus setting the stage for a reinterpretation of prehistoric myths and folklore. In essence, by examining the godly trickster as a whimsical cosmographer, this paper explores how the tetralogy offers a whimsical approach to Indigenous Chinese science fiction.

The May-Fourth Movement: Literary Modernity, Chinese SF, and Internet Literature

To fully illustrate the discursive baggage at stake in placing Weiyu's *Great Fable* tetralogy within the context of Indigenous science fiction, I begin by integrating three disparate discourses—namely, Chinese science fiction, internet literature, and mythological studies. On the one hand, Chinese science fiction has been seen as a cultural product stemming from China's modernization around the early 20th century, during which Chinese epistemological traditions clash fiercely with modern science in the wake of Euro/colonialist imperialist conquest, with the most recent case represented by the Eight Nations Alliance Invasion (Britain, the U.S., Australia, India, Germany, France, Austria-Hungary, Italy, Japan, Russia) in 1900 (Isaacson 2; Han Song 15). On the other hand, internet literature, appearing online in the forms of full-length novels and thereby falling into the category of modern Chinese fiction, can be seen to have built upon the vernacular literature movement, which also begins during the early 20th-century Chinese Modernization Movement, more formally known as the May Fourth New Culture Movement.

The core spirit of the May Fourth Movement lies in the promotion of a new culture imported from Europe and its colonies, which particularly refers to science and democracy, while renouncing traditional Chinese values—namely, the Confucian orthodoxy. One of the famous manifestos attesting to the May

Fourth revolutionary spirit is Chen Duxiu's "A Vindication of *New Youth*," published in the *New Youth* journal in 1919, in response to criticism of the journal for destroying Chinese traditional values. Chen Duxiu, the founder of the journal and one of the earliest leaders of the New Culture Movement, asserts that

> To endorse Mr. Democracy, we could do nothing but reject Confucian teachings, traditional rituals, chastity, old ethics, and previous political systems; and to endorse Mr. Science, we could do nothing but reject old arts and old religions; and to embrace both gentlemen, we could do nothing but reject all traditional heritages and old literature. (Chen Duxiu, "Vindication of *New Youth*," my translation)

Alongside the wholehearted embrace of science as a rejection of Confucianism, what is noteworthy here is the declaration to reject old literature, which later evolves into a staunch promotion of the use of vernacular language in literary composition, particularly in the European-influenced form of fiction—namely, prose fiction at various lengths, as opposed to verse poetry and performative drama. In his article "Preliminary Proposals for Literary Reform," Hu Shi, another prominent scholar active during the May Fourth Movement, outlines eight principles for vernacularizing Chinese literary language, all of which advocate for a complete rejection of established components in classical literature. The eight principles caution writers against traditional clichés and set phrases, classical allusions, the rhymes and meters of classical verse, and the long-entrenched tendency for literary parallelism, while encouraging the incorporation of everyday language and popular slang. As shall be seen, Weiyu's whimsical treatment of internet memes and popular slang can be seen as paying tribute to the anti-orthodoxical tenets of the vernacular literature movement. It is indeed in writing in the less patrolled realm of online platforms that Weiyu is able to use whimsical narrative strategies and language disdained by the literary establishment of modern Chinese literature, which holds that there is an opposition between serious literature and popular literature. Weiyu's use of scientific speculation in rationalizing Chinese prehistoric myths aligns with the endorsement of Mr. Science. In hindsight, it is arguable that science fiction is the most appropriate literary form to promote, considering the New Culture movement's call for a literary form using vernacular language and the form of prose fiction while demanding a scientific spirit. In fact, Lu Xun, the prominent writer and scholar often dubbed "the father of modern Chinese literature," ardently translated Euro/colonial science fiction, hoping to enlighten the nation with the scientific concepts introduced in SF novels.

However, the most intriguing question confronting one here is the ambiguously anti-rationalist endorsement of Chinese mythology among May-Fourth intellectuals, which reveals a tension between the anti-Confucian sentiment and the enlightening drive to promote modern science. Three major pioneers in Chinese mythological studies form a lineage originating from the May Fourth period: Lu Xun, Mao Dun, and Yuan Ke. Surprisingly, all of them defend the cultural values of Chinese mythology, despite the prevalence of supernatural accounts within these myths, a stance which clearly contradicts the scientific spirit of the May Fourth movement. Such a resolute affirmation of traditional myths appears particularly unconventional amid the prevailing May Fourth cultural trend to disparage and abandon traditional Chinese cultural heritage. Instead of viewing Indigenous myths as superstitions, these pioneering May Fourth mythologists eagerly establish Chinese mythology as emblematic of national identity and revolutionary spirit. These two factors then combine to elevate Chinese mythology as a valuable cultural heritage for serving their nationalist agenda in reviving the nation both spiritually and politically. The main strategy taken by the May Fourth mythologists is to reject the historization and rationalization of mythical accounts in order to retain Chinese mythology within the realm of imagination. An important question immediately arises here: how to account for Weiyu's approach to prehistoric myths in her tetralogy, which is exactly one of historicization? If one situates Weiyu's tetralogy within the May Fourth discourse in connection to Indigenous science fiction, it is necessary to examine why the mythologists reject historicization, despite their rationalist emphasis on scientific thinking.

Debating Mythology: Between Historicization and the Reconstruction of National Identity

In his seminal work *A Brief History of Chinese Fiction*, Lu Xun, a scholar-writer often celebrated "the father of modern Chinese literature" (Cheng), identifies Chinese mythology as the birth of writing in general and by extension, the earliest root of Chinese prose fiction. He presents two reasons explaining why existing Chinese mythology lacks the systematic organization found in its Euro/colonial counterpart (Lu 23-24). While the first reason glorifies early farming ancestors' prioritization of practical affairs over myth-making as a result of their industrious endeavor to cope with a challenging geographical environment, the second reason singles out Confucianism for blame. Lu argues that Confucian thought's privileging of ideological utility and practical teachings results in a dismissal of mythology as primordial absurdity unworthy of serious consideration or transmission—reflecting the famous rationalistic decree from the *Analects*: "Master Confucius never speaks of the strange, the violent, the disorderly, and the spirits." Expanding upon Lu's insights, Mao Dun, another prominent May Fourth scholar-writer, who now has the highest literary award in mainland China named after him, elaborates that it is not just Confucian disapproval that prevents the compilation and transmission of mythology, but that mythical accounts have been distorted in a long process of historicization. Mao argues that many accounts labeled as historical, about the prehistoric era, were originally myths. As demanded by the Confucian decree to "preserve orthodoxy" (守正), earlier official historians integrated these mythical fragments into ancient texts through a strategy of historicization (29-33). To recover mythology from the distorted records of prehistory, Mao advocates for mythologists to reconstruct it from existing textual remnants about that period. Exemplary of this de-historicization approach is his reconstruction of the prehistoric rivalry between Huangdi or the Yellow Emperor and Chiyou as a mythical clash between the race of gods led by Huangdi and the race of titans led by Chiyou, in rejection of the official account that it is a historical war fought by two tribal leaders. Mao's choice to focus on this epic rivalry is significant because the triumph of the civilized Huangdi force over the barbarian Chiyou tribe has been regarded as marking the birth of Chinese civilization in official history. As it turns out, it is no surprise that Weiyu's tetralogy is also centered on reinventing this epic rivalry between Huangdi and Chiyou through scientific speculation.

Following in the footsteps of Lu and Mao, Yuan Ke also highlights how Confucianist historicization has distorted many ancient myths in his *Ancient Mythology in China* (5-6). Notably, he cites some brief yet powerful examples representative of Confucianist historicization and rationalization. In traditional legend, Huangdi, the military sage-hero whose conquest of the barbarian tribes allegedly gives birth to Chinese civilization, is described as having four faces. However, Confucius shrewdly reinterprets this as a tale about Huangdi dispatching four representatives to govern four pieces of land in the four cardinal directions (Yuan 6).³ In another example, Kui, described as a mythical creature having only one leg in *The Classic of Mountains and Seas*, is "historicized" as a court musician to Emperor Shun, one of the saint-kings canonized by Confucius for their exemplary governance by virtue and wisdom in an idealized yet lamentably irrecoverable past—with the historical existence of Shun remaining debatable.⁴ Based on the semantic ambiguity of the character 足, which means both "leg" and "sufficient," the original text "夔一足" (literally, "Kui one leg") is reinterpreted by Confucius as "For such a person as Kui, one is sufficient" (Yuan 6).⁵ What can be observed from these two examples is that Confucianist historicization is nothing but a method of reducing imaginative elements rich with interpretative potential into mundane trivialities—reminiscent of their Euro/colonial counterparts found in Euhemeristic historization and Palaephatusian rationalization of Greek mythology.⁶ Citing Zhou Yang, an influential Marxist intellectual during the May-Fourth period, Yuan highlights a distinction between myths and superstitions, despite their similarities in "a naive understanding of the world and a belief in supernatural forces" (14). Superstitions often promote a passive acceptance of one's inability to challenge authority, legitimizing submission to a fate determined by gods and thus the need to obey the ruling class. Unlike superstitions, myths encourage individuals to liberate themselves from preordained subjugation, celebrating human disobedience to the mighty gods. Given that the May Fourth movement also advocates for a revolutionary spirit for challenging the Confucian orthodoxy and conducting political and cultural reforms, it is no wonder why the May Fourth mythologists deeply admire the cultural values of Chinese mythology and reject any attempt to historicize and rationalize mythical accounts, despite the May Fourth emphases on rationalism and scientific thinking.

Closely intertwined with the revolutionary ethos of the May-Fourth movement is a nationalist agenda focused on revitalizing the nation through scientific enlightenment and Euro/colonial modernization. Lu Xun's earlier endeavors between 1898 to 1906 in learning Euro/colonial scientific subjects and translating European/American science fiction undoubtedly laid the groundwork for the development of a scientific spirit that would later thrive during the peak of the New Culture Movement in the 1910s and 1920s (Sun 32). However, beginning in 1907, Lu published several long essays that reflect upon the Chinese intellectuals' unthinking commitment to European/American science and learning. In the essay "On Condemnation against Superstitions" (破恶声论), Lu Xun provocatively proposes the thesis, "pseudo-scholars should be banished; superstitions could be preserved" (伪士当去，迷信可存), challenging the prevailing scientific ethos dominating the intellectual landscape of that era. This thesis notably brings the problem of interpreting ancient Chinese myths to the forefront. Lu Xun, designating adherents of scientism as "pseudo-scholars," criticizes their wrongful misconception of Chinese myths as superstitions in the name of Euro/colonial scientific thought.[7] Lu argues that dismissing belief in the mythical Chinese dragon (龙) as superstitious amounts to eradicating the very essence embedded within Chinese civilization (Tan Jia, Chapter 3). This, in his view, indicates a misapplication of scientific standards to the domain of mythology and underscores an unjust treatment of mythology due to an excessive preoccupation with scientific thinking and an unquestioning acceptance of European cultural superiority in devaluing Chinese Indigenous cultures. To sum up, within modern literature, Chinese mythology holds a unique cultural status, representing distinctive Chinese identity and a revolutionary spirit against authority and orthodoxy. As shall be seen, the nationalist and revolutionary sentiments of May Fourth mythological scholarship have strong resonance with the recent discussion of Indigenous science fiction, which celebrates Indigenous mythical and fantastical elements in terms of Indigenous sciences as an effort to challenge the dominance of modern scientific discourse.

Zhiguai as Cosmography: The Whimsical Cosmographer and Scientific Speculation

The previous section delved into the effort to firmly establish a stance favoring de-historicization within earlier mythological scholarship amidst the conflicting sentiments of anti-Confucianism and scientific rationalism prevalent during the May Fourth era. Until now, this essay's exploration of Chinese mythology has remained confined to scholarly discourse. What about the use of ancient myths in literary works? Weiyu's tetralogy provides an invaluable opportunity to scrutinize the issue of myth historicization within literary appropriation. Indeed, the extensive utilization of ancient myths and scientific elements qualifies Weiyu's tetralogy as Indigenous science fiction. Yet, this tetralogy displays a significant departure from the generic conventions of SF: the whole narrative is set in the contemporary era of its composition—namely, to adopt Darko Suvin's terms, the "empirical reality" of the author and her implied readers, rather than an alternative reality set in the future. One crucial question arises in regard to such a contemporary setting: how does Weiyu convince 21st-century readers, who are deeply entrenched in modern scientific thought, about a story set in contemporary time that retells ancient myths filled with supernatural elements? The answer lies in her brilliant appropriation of the Chinese literary tradition of *zhiguai* 志怪 or "recording the strange," a generic liminality that straddles the epistemological boundary between creative fabrication and historical cosmography. At the core of this approach is precisely the whimsical characterization of the charlatan-scientist shen-gun, or the godly trickster, as a cosmographer echoing the *zhiguai* tradition.[8]

Challenging the received notion that *zhiguai* marks the birth of Chinese fiction as propagated by DeWoskin, Robert Campany, in his book *Strange Writing: Anomaly Accounts in Early Medieval China*, makes a compelling argument that anomaly accounts in *zhiguai* should be viewed as rooted in historical events to which the authors or their reporters bear witness—what he calls "cosmographic collecting"—rather than something born out of literary imagination; that is, a product of "fiction."[9] Central to the tradition of cosmographic collecting is the distinction between center and periphery: "the peripheral is, from a centrist perspective, the anomalous, the external other" (9). Cosmographic collecting is defined as "the variety of ways in which anomalies are domesticated and represented in the interest of, and from the point of view of, the center" (9). Campany convincingly shows how the early Chinese tribute system (贡 gong) and the tour inspection (巡守 Xunshou), among others, serve as precedents of "cosmographic collecting" that *zhiguai* writers have drawn on. In these two examples, Campany highlights how cosmographic collecting is in fact a "creation of order out of disorder" and how the geographical mappings of anomalies entail a centrist ideology in terms of ethical, epistemological, and ontological domestication (103-07). Similarly, in Weiyu's tetralogy, the anomaly accounts investigated by the protagonists, along with the trickster, predominantly cover untrodden or forbidden terrains in rural areas that remain relatively unaffected by urbanization. For instance, events in books 1 and 2 occur in various places such as Ganai of LanZhou, Lijiang of Yunnan, Yadan of Dunhuang, Xiahe, Qinghai, and Gannan. Book 3 delves into stories about the three lineages of "water spirits" (水鬼 shui-gui) reigning over the drainage areas of the Three Rivers: the Yellow River, the Yangtze, and the Lancang-Mekong River. Book 4 focuses on stories about the "mountain spirits" (山鬼 shan-gui), set in the mountainous regions traditionally associated with the mythical prehistory of China, including the Xiangxi 湘西 area, or Western Hunan, and the Kunlun 昆仑 mountains, as depicted, respectively, in the two earliest sources of mythical accounts, *Chuci* 楚辞 and *Shanhaijing* 山海经.[10]

These anomaly tales from the periphery constitute curious objects of "cosmographic collecting" for the pleasure of online readers, who now occupy a position at the center. Their access to internet not only attests to their urbanized residency, removed from the wilderness where anomalies abound, but also reflects the modern scientific worldview represented by the very technology facilitating such a display of cosmographic collection. The center-periphery power dynamic takes on a whimsical twist as the center shifts to the internet reading platform, where an array of collected anomalies flows in for display. Works published online are often deemed vulgar and lacking literary value by mainstream writers and critics entrenched in the literary establishment, which is the old center. In the tetralogy, characters speak an everyday language incorporating internet slangs and memes, a playful deviation from orthodox vernacular (baihua 白话).[11] Vividly representing the dynamic evolution of language at the diegetic level, Weiyu's literary treatment of such an "online vernacular" based on a whimsical aesthetics signals a rebellion against orthodox vernacular, aligning with the revolutionary ethos of the May Fourth movement. The transition from physical publications to online releases marks a paradigm shift in reading mediums, inevitably leading to the widespread infiltration of online vernacular into everyday life.[12] Although often derided as "the

Martian tongue" or deemed inferior or corrupted, online vernacular has now become the true vernacular that reflects the most updated vibrancy of contemporary spoken Mandarin.[13]

In addition to her rebellion against the orthodox vernacular of serious literature, Weiyu's use of whimsical language that massively draws on internet memes and popular slang also plays a significant role in another discursive feat: she evokes Suvinian cognition among readers in appreciating incorporated scientific elements, while simultaneously demanding that they estrange themselves from their modernized epistemological criteria and engage in speculating about the historical authenticity of fantastical phenomena in ancient myths. Due to the limited scope of this paper and the extensive length of the tetralogy, which spans thousands of pages, my discussion here will concentrate on Book 1, *The Vengeful Tolls of the Windchimes*, where the godly trickster makes his debut, and Book 4, *Dragon Bones and the Burning Chest*, where the ultimate worldview of the *Great Fable* universe is revealed.[14] Just like zhiguai cosmographers, the godly trickster believes that folklore about the anomalies he collects in his notebooks is historical and scientific in terms of cosmographical collection. After opening with the folk belief that ringing bells on the streets at night might attract ghosts, a notion that Yue Feng, the male protagonist, dismisses as mere "superstition" (*Tolls* 272), the trickster goes on to discuss the popular account that when windchimes ring for no apparent reason, it indicates a ghost passing by. Rather than outright refuting this thesis, he tries to make sense of it in quasi-scientific terms by speculating about the nature of a ghost: "it is a kind of *qi*, a flow of air, a sort of energy. The windchime is a highly sensitive object. So when this kind of energy appears, it disturbs the surrounding field of *qi*, causing the windchimes to make sounds" (*Tolls* 273; my translation).

The trickster's whimsical rhetoric that coopts scientific speculation is perhaps most exemplified in the following passage, where he references Newton's law of conservation of energy to elucidate how the lingering vengeance of wrongfully murdered victims manifests as an intangible energy, causing a windchime to ring in a manner imperceptible to observers[15]:

> Although many ghost stories depict ghosts as fierce and harmful, I personally believe that ghosts are quite pitiable. Think about it, ghosts are just a form of *qi*. What can this *qi* do? It doesn't even have a smell; it can't even produce a fragrance to fumigate people. But we can't just let this *qi* linger, can we? *After contemplating it, I've developed my personal theory. I believe the human body is positive, and the soul, which is this qi, is negative. Either both the positive and the negative exist; or both of them don't exist—only in this way can the world's energy be conserved.* But when the body kicks the bucket and this *qi* still sticks around, the energy isn't conserved anymore. If it's not conserved, even Newton wouldn't agree. So, this vengeful *qi* must be dissolved, it must be eliminated. How to eliminate it? It can't do it by itself, right? It needs external force, doesn't it? But how does it access external force? Qi can't speak, so what to do? The vengeful *qi* energy collides with bells. The sound of bells is the only thing that can pass from the human world to the ghost world, and vice versa [. . .] (Weiyu, *Tolls* 274; my translation and emphasis)

When the female protagonist Ji Tangtang, though finding his reasoning deductively solid, chuckles at his bizarre appropriation of European studies and scientific theories, the trickster responds to her doubt by stating that it is just a hypothesis, which he calls the "Trickster's Hypothesis." He then goes on to claim scientific authority for his whimsical speculation:

> "Currently, there isn't substantial theoretical support for it. But, Little Tanggie, you must know, many scientific theories start as hypotheses. We first propose a hypothesis, then we go on to prove it. Additionally, academic knowledge knows no boundaries; we can

apply valid scientific theories to any field, even to the study of the supernatural. You agree, right?" (Weiyu, *Tolls* 275; my translation)

By comparing his whimsical reasoning to the production of scientific knowledge, the trickster playfully teases modern scientific discourse, shaking its epistemological foundation and thus setting the stage for a reinterpretation of prehistoric myths with recourse to scientific rationalization in later books.

Severing through the Biological Lens: The Sense of Wonder Bridging Science and Myth

Book 4 introduces the most important setting that governs the worldbuilding of the whole *Great Fable* universe: "Severing the Passage between Heaven and Earth" (绝地天通 jue ditiantong), hereinafter "the Severing." In the history of Chinese religion, the Severing is regarded as a monumental event signifying the shift from decentralized forms of primitive shamanism to the state's monopoly on religious power. Sacrifices, rituals, or any forms of divine communication became centralized under the state's control, resulting in people on Earth being completely severed from Heaven. In supplement to the conventional historicization of the Severing as a religious reform, Weiyu presents a biological interpretation that still retains a modicum of mythical elements, in which the Severing is reconstrued as a "Generational Traverse from Gods to Humans" (神人跨代, hereinafter, the Traverse), occurring after Huangdi's triumph over Chiyou. Traditionally historicized as two leaders of ancestral tribes, Huangdi and Chiyou here are reimagined as representing two fractions of the ancient humanoid species capable of auto-reproduction while wielding advanced technologies. The illusion of immortality generated by their auto-reproduction, combined with the seemingly supernatural effects of their advanced technologies, bestows upon them a divine aura in the eyes of the early ancestors of the modern human race, who worshipped them as gods—hence their half-god-half-human status in ancient texts.

The epic rivalry between Huangdi and Chiyou stems from their differing approaches to the impending extinction of the god race due to the slow yet irrevocable dilution of their auto-reproductive ability across generations. While the Huangdi tribe proposed assimilation into the human race by altering their genes for sexual reproduction and destroying advanced technologies to prevent misuse, the Chiyou tribe resisted assimilation. They believed that their technological advancements would eventually resolve the dilution problem of auto-reproduction, thereby averting their extinction. Following their victory, the Huangdi tribe led the entire god race to assimilate into the human race, becoming the early founders of Chinese civilization. On the other hand, retreating underground after their defeat, the Chiyou tribe devised a clandestine resurgence plan by preserving their consciousness in the form of "mind-files" and hiding away an assortment of advanced technologies from Huangdi's eradication campaign. These cached technologies could be used in future conflicts against the human race, into which the Huangdi tribe has now assimilated, when the Chiyou tribe revives at a propitious time. While awaiting the grand revival, some Chiyou descendants remain active underground guarding the plan. The effects of the technologies wielded by Chiyou descendants are then recorded as anomalies in Chinese myths and folklore, and the mysteries of resurfacing anomalies are investigated and unveiled by protagonists in the tetralogy.[16] Prominent examples of these rationalized technologies are the Road Bell 路铃 and the Ghost Bell 鬼铃 for harnessing the power of vengeful spirits in the first book, the seven Bamboo Strips of Evil 凶简 for manipulating human minds in the second, and the Ancestral Tablet 祖牌 and the magical

Xirang soil 息壤 for preserving human consciousness and reconstructing human bodies in the third.[17]

Recruiting modern bio-science as a tool for rationalization in service of her speculative aesthetics, Weiyu undertakes an ambitious reinterpretation of the Severing not only as a historical event but also as a biological transition from gods to humans. Mythical divinity is thus brilliantly historicized as the capacity for auto-reproduction, which is taken as a form of quasi-immortality by borrowing from the concept of digital immortality of consciousness informed by modern bio-informatics. Her appropriation of the concept of auto-reproduction is hinged on a clever play on a key fragment from ancient texts describing the begetting of Emperor Yu 禹, the legendary founder of the quasi-mythical Xia夏 dynasty, who is also credited as a mythical hero for fixing the mythical Great Flood: "Gun the father gave birth to the Emperor Yu from his belly" (gun fu sheng yu 鯀复生禹).[18] This textual oddity has confused mythologists and historians alike for centuries. Weiyu's explanation contends that the statement is every bit true: the Emperor Yu does come from his father's belly—but in the form of auto-reproduction. Here lies the most notable departure of Weiyu's scientific speculation on myths from the examples of Confucian historicization cited before and from its European counterparts found in Euhemerus and Palaephatus. Unlike mythological historicization, which relies much on common-sensical reasoning that undermines the imaginative capacity of ancient myths, Weiyu's approach actually supplies to them a sense of wonder derived from the plausibility of techno-scientific feats, a narrative strategy evidently inspired by typical tropes in science fiction.

Weiyu's whimsical speculation, driven by the trickster's impulse for cosmographical collecting, adeptly co-opts modern scientific discourse into her creative reinvention of ancient

Chinese myths.[19] Her use of ancient myths, marked by meticulous attention to and close engagement with textual details, transcends sheer rehashing and superficial touting of traditional elements as mere labels. Instead, mythical tales are revitalized with scientific elements, becoming captivating and relevant for the contemporary audience—all the while without compromising the cultural value of these myths for asserting national identity, as a pure historicization-rationalization approach would do. Overall, Weiyu's whimsical approach to sci-fi is genuinely indigenous in the sense that it intimately engages with Indigenous discourses. Her incorporation of modern science not only echoes the May Fourth revivalist embrace of science, but her whimsical language, heavily borrowing from the internet vernacular, also pays homage to the May Fourth anti-orthodox spirit. Remarkably, she accomplishes all this in a manner that defuses tension surrounding the problematic historicization of myths and resists the tendency toward canceling Chinese cultural identity at the risk of self-orientalization.

Notes

1. In considering the significance of female readership and authorship, Ni Zhange has explored the feminist implications in the tetralogy through the concept of "materialist feminism," which reconfigures sex and reproduction in the digital era. In her *Romancing the Internet*, Jin Feng has also pioneered the study of internet literature from feminist perspectives, focusing on "web romance" that is predominantly produced and consumed by women.

2. See Lisa Raphals, who has envisioned a form of "Chinese indigenous science fiction" that draws on the rich literary tradition of zhiguai, or tales of the anomaly, and does not simply feed into the model of European/colonial science fiction. Although Weiyu's work does not directly incorporate or appropriate the theories and practices of Chinese indigenous sciences, her engagement with premodern zhiguai narratives through rationalization and speculation notably introduces non-

European elements into the sci-fi discourse, while also departing from the concerns of imperialism and epistemological crisis typically associated with the orthodox lineage of Chinese sci-fi. For a more general discussion of the relationship of non-European sciences and science fiction, see Amanda Rees and Iwan R. Morus.

3. The earliest fragment that features the persona of Confucius rationalizing the quadruple-faced Huangdi appears in the *Taiping Yulan* 太平御览 of the Song dynasty, in which an even earlier text *Shizi* 《尸子》, whose full text is lost, is cited for that fragment.

4. In fact, the historical existence of Yu is central to the debate ignited by Gu Jiegang's influential thesis, which asserts that all textual records and accounts of Chinese prehistory, including the Xia dynasty and earlier, are mythological and ahistorical (Wang 25). For a review of Gu's thesis and its ongoing repercussions in mythological and historical scholarship, see Wang Hui.

5. Relevant fragments on Confucius rationalizing 夔一足 appear originally in earlier texts such as the *Hanfeizi* 《韩非子·外储说左下》 and the *Lüshi Chunqiu* 《吕氏春秋·慎行论之六·察传》.

6. See Stern, "Heraclitus" for a distinction between Euhemeristic historization and Palaephatusian rationalization. This classic example from Palaephatus's *On Unbelievable Tales* should suffice to demonstrate how commonsensical reasoning spoils the imaginative capacity of the original tale with trite explanation: "The story about Callisto is that while she was out hunting she turned into a bear. What I maintain is that she too during a hunt found her way into a grove of trees where a bear happened to be and was devoured. Her hunting companions saw her going into the grove, but not coming out; they said that the girl turned into a bear" (Stern, *Palaephatus*). For a comprehensive treatment of rationalization as a widespread phenomenon in classical mythology in terms of intellectual history, see Hawes.

7. Lu Xun also wrote several whimsical stories in the collection *Old Stories Told Anew* 故事新编, pioneering in rewriting ancient myths. In the preface, he mocks himself as being "*you hua*" 油滑 (literally "oily-slippery," which means "elusive," "frivolous," or "whimsical," which is a good translation in this context) in writing these stories. Though often represented as a May-Fourth leader devoted to literary orthodoxy of

realism for its socio-political functions in enlightening the people, Lu Xun's affinity for the Chinese underground tradition of the strange and the abnormal has been uncovered by revisionist commentators. For example, see Leo Lee for a reading of Lu Xun's "heart of darkness" in being a secret patron of the alienated tradition of non-realisms in his earlier scholarly practice. Also see Wang Hui for a very instructive comparison of approaches to mythology and anomaly tales in Lu Xun's *Stories* and Gu Jiegang's historical skepticism 疑古.

8. There is a substantial body of scholarship exploring the trickster as a mythological and cultural figure that disrupts established social orders and challenges orthodox epistemological frameworks, often through humor and boundary transgression—a characteristic closely aligned with the *shen-gun* in the tetralogy. Notable examples of tricksters discussed by scholars include Coyote from North American Indigenous cultures, Hermes from classical Greece, and Sun Wukong, the Monkey King, from China, all of which are characterized as mischievous, deceptive, comical, and yet didactically creative. While there is ample opportunity to explore further connections between these figures and the *shen-gun* to enrich understanding of the trickster's historical significance, space constraints prevent a more detailed investigation here. For more extensive discussions on the trickster figure, see the works of Radin, Douglas, Hynes, and Hyde.

9. Indeed, it is debatable whether the idea of literary fiction in the Euromodern context of Platonic mimesis can be applied to the Chinese context or whether the Chinese concept of *xiaoshuo* 小说 is fictional. See Plaks for a discussion on the lack of clear distinction between history 史 and fiction 文 in Chinese literary tradition. What distinguishes them, in Plaks's view, is simply a different level of emphasis on the content. "History" is more concerned about the public sphere, while "fiction" about the private sphere.

10. Water spirits and mountain spirits here apparently correspond to the seas and mountains in the title of *Shanhaijing*, or *The Classic of Mountains and Sea*.

11. One prominent case is the "verb + 了都" construction, which is a grammatically unconventional, if not illegitimate, inversion of the standard "都 + verb + 了" construction.

12. The theme of transgressions related to Chinese internet literature has garnered significant scholarly interest. See Michel Hockx, for a discussion of the questions of censorship, free speech, and online publication. While Hockx has examined the interplay between political and moral transgressions in internet literature, Weiyu's internet vernacular here is better characterized as transgressing literary and linguistic conventions upheld by the literary establishment of the May Fourth lineage.

13. Shao Yanjun has made a similar point in discussing the crucial role of media in shaping the distinctive characteristics of internet literature, as compared to oral and print-based literature ("Internet-ness" 143-44). Drawing on Marshall McLuhan's influential insight, "the medium is the message," Shao argues that internet literature shares a stronger affinity with oral literature than with print-based literature, due to its reliance on oral circularity and instantaneous interaction, which in turn reflects the most current and active use of language. See Shao's "Reckoning" and "Chronicle" for more discussion on the problem of canonization in internet literature.

14. *Great Fable* is translated from *da huang* 大荒, which also means Great Bleakness, Great Wilderness, or Great Absurdity. The term *da huang* comes from the name of the mysterious "third space," in addition to water and land, described in *The Classics of Seas and Mountains*.

15. Passages such as this, where the trickster suggests his investigation and speculation are scientific while comparing himself to scientists actually recur throughout Books 1, 2, and 4, where the trickster appears.

16. Weiyu specifically refers to Nuo shamanism (巫傩) in Xiangxi (湘西), the Western part of Hunan. Since Chiyou is allegedly from the south, the geographical locations are preserved, showcasing the cosmographic precision inherited from zhiguai.

17. This motif of fantastical technologies can be compared to the interpretative strategy of the "first-inventor" (*protoi heuretes*) in Palaephatus's rationalization of unbelievable tales. For instance, the Centaurs are explained as the first horse riders, while Medea, who allegedly rejuvenates old men by boiling them in a cauldron with magic herbs, is rationalized as the inventor of hair dye and the sauna (Stern, *Palaephatus* 20). The first witnesses of these technological

innovations, unable to provide a rational explanation for what they observe, mistakenly attribute them to supernatural phenomena.

18. Again, in addition to this fragment, there are more fragments or textual details reinterpreted by Weiyu in her historicization of Chinese myths. In fact, she spends the entire books 3 and 4 on such reinterpretation and speculation. Also, another rationalizing approach is to understand the account of King Gun giving birth to Yu as indicative of what cultural anthropologists call "couvade," which refers to a symbolic or ritualistic labor performed by husbands to reinforce their status and power in a patriarchal family structure (Yuan, *History*, Chapter 2). Typically, during a couvade, the husband pretends to be a postpartum wife, lying in bed and feigning pain and sickness, while the actual wife, who has just undergone labor, is sent to the farm to work.

19. As revealed in the later chapters of Book 4, the trickster is actually descended from Huangdi's bloodline, which explains his inner urge for anomalies as they are traces of his ancestors' historical existence. In addition to the trickster's divine bloodline, another case that demonstrates Weiyu's preservation of mythical elements is the mysterious realm of Great Fable, which the protagonist couple of Book 4 enters through the Heavenly Stairs in Kunlun.

Works Cited

Campany, Robert Ford. *Strange Writing: Anomaly Accounts in Early Medieval China*. Albany: State University of New York Press, 1996.

Chen Duxiu .陈独秀《文学革命论》. February, 1917.

Cheng, Eileen J. "Lu Xun." In *obo* in Chinese Studies. https://www.oxfordbibliographies.com/view/document/obo-9780199920082/obo-9780199920082-0218.xml. 31 Oct. 2024.

DeWoskin, Kenneth Joel." The Six Dynasties *Chih-Kuai* and the Birth of Fiction." *Chinese Narrative: Critical and Theoretical Essays*, edited by Andrew Plaks, Princeton: Princeton University Press, 1977, pp. 21-52.

Dillon, Grace L. *Walking the Clouds: An Anthology of Indigenous Science Fiction*. University of Arizona Press, 2012.

Douglas, Mary. "The Social Control of Cognition: Some Factors in Joke Perception." *Man*, vol. 3, no. 3, 1968, pp. 361–376.

Feng, Jin. *Romancing the Internet: Producing and Consuming Chinese Web Romance*. Brill, 2013.

Han Song. "Chinese Science Fiction: A Response to Modernization." *Science Fiction Studies* vol. 40, no. 1, 2013, pp. 15-21.

Hawes, Greta. *Rationalizing Myth in Antiquity*. Oxford: Oxford University Press, 2013.

Hockx, Michel. *Internet Literature in China*. Columbia University Press, 2015.

Hu Shi. 胡适《文学改良刍议》January, 1917.

Hyde, Lewis. *Trickster Makes This World: Mischief, Myth, and Art*. New York: Farrar, Straus and Giroux, 1998.

Hynes, William J. and William G. Doty. *Mythical Trickster Figures*. University of Alabama Press, 1993.

Isaacson, Nathaniel. *Celestial Empire: The Emergence of Chinese Science Fiction*. Middletown, CT: Wesleyan University Press, 2017.

Kao, Karl S. Y. (Gao, Xinyong). *Classical Chinese Tales of the Supernatural and the Fantastic: Selections from the Third to the Tenth Century*. Bloomington: Indiana University Press, 1985.

Leo Ou-fan. *Voices from the Iron House: A Study of Lu Xun*. Bloomington: Indiana University Press, 1987.

Liu Mingming. "Theory of the Strange: Towards the Establishment of Zhiguai as a Genre." PhD Dissertation. University of California-Riverside, 2015.

Lu Xun. 鲁迅《破恶声论》December, 1908.

Lu Xun. 鲁迅《中国小说史略》Originally published between 1923-1924.

Lu Xun. 鲁迅《故事新编》1936.

Mao Dun. 茅盾《中国神话研究初探》1928.

Ni, Zhange Nicole. 倪湛舸. "Sexuality in the Digital Era: Material Feminism and Weiyu's *Lingyi* Novels" (数字时代的性——物质女性主义与尾鱼灵异小说的共鸣). *Theory and Criticism of Literature and Art* (文艺理论与批评). April 2023.

Plaks, Andrew H. "Toward a Critical Theory of Chinese Narrative." *Chinese Narrative: Critical and Theoretical Essays*, edited by Andrew H. Plaks. Princeton, NJ: Princeton University Press, 1977, pp. 309-352.

Radin, Paul. *The Trickster: A Study in American Indian Mythology*. N.Y.: Schocken Books, 1955.

Raphals, Lisa. "Chinese Science Fiction: Imported and Indigenous." *Osiris* vol. 34, no. 1, 2019, pp. 81-98.

Rees, Amanda, and Iwan R. Morus. "Presenting Futures Past: Science Fiction and the History of Science." *Osiris* vol. 34, no. 1, 2019, pp. 1-15.

Shao, Yanjun. 邵燕君. "On 'Internet-ness' and Classicalness of Internet Literature."(网络文学的"网络性"与"经典性")北京大学学报 vol. 25, no.1, January 2015, pp. 143-52.

Shao, Yanjun. 邵燕君. "Reckoning with Internet Literature: The Academia's Attitude and Method." 〈面对网络文学：学院派的态度和方法〉. *Southern Literary Forum* 《南方文坛》 2011, pp. 12-18

Shao, Yanjun. 邵燕君. "The 'Chronicle' of Web Literature and the Canonization of 'Traditional Web Literature'" 〈网络文学的"断代史"与"传统网文"的经典化〉 *Modern Chinese Literature Studies*《中国现代文学研究丛刊》, vol. 2, 2019, pp. 1-18.

Song Xiaoke. 宋小克 *Ancient Myths and Literature*《上古神话与文学》. Jinan University Press 暨南大学出版社，2013

Spence, Lewis. *An Introduction to Mythology*. George G. Harrap & Co., 1921

Stern, Jacob. "Heraclitus the Paradoxographer: Περὶ Ἀπίστων, 'On Unbelievable Tales.'" *Transactions of the American Philological Association (1974-)*, vol. 133, no. 1, 2003, pp. 51–97.

Stern, Jacob. *Palaephatus: On Unbelievable Tales*. Wauconda, IL: Bolchazy-Carducci, 1996.

Sun Yaotian. 孙尧天. "Scientificism in the Late Qing and Lu Xun's Breakthrough: A Historical Examination of Lu Xun's Early Proposition 'False Scholars Must Go, Superstition May Remain.'" 〈清末科学主义与鲁迅的突破———对鲁迅早年"伪士当去,迷信可存"主张的历史考察〉. *Literature, History, and Philosophy* 《文史哲》 vol. 2, 2023, pp. 31-43.

Suvin, Darko. "Science Fiction and the Novum (1977)." *Defined by a Hollow: Essays on Utopia, Science Fiction and Political Epistemology*. Bern: Peter Lang, 2010.

Suvin, Darko. *Metamorphoses of Science Fiction: On the Poetics and History of a Literary Genre*. New Haven: Yale Univ. Press, 1979.

Tan Jia. 谭佳《神话与古史：中国现代学术的建构与认同》社会科学文献出版社，2016.

Wang Hui. 汪晖〈历史幽灵学与现代中国的上古史———古史／故事新辨(上)〉 *Literature, History, and Philosophy*《文史哲》vol. 1, 2023, pp. 5–41.

---. 汪晖〈历史幽灵学与现代中国的上古史———古史／故事新辨(下)〉*Literature, History, and Philosophy*《文史哲》vol. 2, 2023, pp. 5–30.

Wang, David Der-wei. "Confused Horizons: Science Fantasy." *Fin-de-Siècle Splender: Repressed Modernities of Late Qing Fiction, 1849-1911.* Stanford, CA: Stanford University Press, 1997, pp. 252-312.

Weiyu (尾鱼). *Dragon Bones and the Burning Chest* (龙骨焚箱 longgu fenxiang). Jinjiang Literature City (晋江文学城), 2019.

---. *The Seven Bamboo Strips of Evils* (七根凶简 qigen xiongjian). Jinjiang Literature City (晋江文学城), 2015.

---. *The Three Routes in Loop* (三线轮回 sanxian lunhui). Jinjiang Literature City (晋江文学城), 2018.

---. *The Vengeful Tolls of the Windchimes* (怨气撞铃 yuanqi zhuangling). Jinjiang Literature City (晋江文学城), 2013.

Xu Lingyuan. 徐令缘. "昆仑系"神话传说的类型学思考. 国学, vol. 9, no. 3, 2021, pp. 20-30. https://doi.org/10.12677/CnC.2021.93005

Yang Lihui. 杨利慧《21世纪以来代表性神话学家研究评述》,《长江大学学报》, 2014年第6期.

Yuan Ke. 袁珂 *Ancient Mythology in China*《中国古代神话》, 2006.

Yuan Ke. 袁珂 *A History of Chinese Mythology*《中国神话史》, 2015.

Analyzing Works Of James Baldwin, Toni Morrison, and Octavia E. Butler as Prophetic Literature in American Society

Stevens Orozco

IN LITERATURE, THE IMPULSE FOR SURVIVAL in postcolonial society has been culturally influential on writers and their stories. In some instances, these impulses to proactively imagine survival have in turn affected the society that consumes the literary work. As the result of a growing canon of historically predictive and influential works, critics and philosophers have attempted to find methods for using literature as a measuring tool to achieve an accurate reading of a shifting society and its changing conditions, and to foretell its inevitable direction and fate.

One cannot apply literature as a measuring tool without creating a formulaic approach. It is necessary to identify elements in a literary work that can be applied to other works in that genre, in the search for an analytical equation that can yield the same results consistently. The task of achieving such a formula becomes daunting when attempting to apply it accurately across differing cultures, identities, and nations. In the last century alone, the literary canon has expanded internationally, with contributions from writers of different cultures, languages and philosophies.

This complicates any formula's application and yields results that are not consistent over the long run.

French critic and historian Hippolyte-Adolphe Taine proposed just such a formula when he published *The History of English Literature* one hundred and fifty-eight years ago, in 1863. In its introduction, Taine offers his formula—based on *race, milieu,* and *moment*—with the goal of predicting future trends in society. Taine's contemporaries and fellow philosophers, sociologists, and critics criticized and disregarded his formula because of its limited success in accurately predicting nineteenth-century social trends, and it became a footnote in his otherwise highly accomplished academic career. It would take the dawn of a new century for Taine's formula to encounter the needed conditions in order to produce a legitimate and functioning formula. The elements of Taine's formula, when applied more specifically to the precise social setting and the writer of the literary work being analyzed, begin to work together to produce a new element, arguably the result that Taine attempted to achieve.

Even though Taine's contributions to literary criticism, historical analysis, and sociological theories have earned him the title of founder of the sociological science of literature, the discarding of his race-milieu-moment formula for literary analysis has been largely due to its overbroad scope, making it incapable of reliable predictions. There are plenty of shortcomings in Taine's original theorization of race-milieu-moment. For example, Taine's concept of race was centered on a nationalistic identity defined by his European experience as a French citizen who had observed wars and politics between the French as a race, the German as a race, and the English as a race, rather than the subsuming of all Europeans into one classless, newly invented continental race. Taine's concept of moment is similarly outdated. It is his concept of milieu which critics of Taine found the most useful. In his article "Hippolyte Taine's Literary Theory and Criticism," René Wellek states:

> The term "milieu" is the only one which has preserved its usefulness and has survived intact. It is a catch-all for the external conditions of literature: it includes not only the physical environment (soil, climate), but also political and social conditions. It is a conglomerate of everything which even remotely can be brought into contact with literature. (Wellek, "Hippolyte Taine's Literary Theory and Criticism," 2)

In considering these criticisms of Taine's formula, it becomes clear that it would be improved by using more current concepts of race and moment. The goal of this essay now becomes this: if many factors can determine what is milieu, then by considering multiple factors to analyze race and moment, one can begin to understand with better clarity how to apply Taine's formula with more success.

The determining factor is the prophetic element—the writer—responding to the moment, interacting with the milieu of their society or civilization. During Taine's lifetime, scholars and analysts had not yet discovered the need for an additional element in order for prophetic predictions to function. For this formula to be successful, the importance of the human element, the writer, cannot be overstated. It is the writer who lives the shared experiences of the society they inhabit. The writer's sense of identity depends on the systemic beliefs of their homeland in regard to race, ethnicity, and faith. These beliefs shape the social conditions, the political environment, and the power dynamics that exist between the social classes of people. The tension of the social climate is influenced by how these sub-elements interact with and react to one another. As a civilization develops documentation and record keeping, it constructs historical narratives of a people, race, and nation that shape identity and society. These historical narratives find their supporters, who see themselves in these accounts. Such narratives also expose society's victims and resistors in the margins of its neglected storylines. This has led to moments in which the morality of a nation is confronted, and the threat of a collapse looms larger, as the balance between social classes becomes overburdened by greed, selfishness, and hatred.

Taine did not live long enough to witness the possibilities for massive data collection and historical documentation created by the information age. For future writers who critically analyze their society through works of fiction and non-fiction, the opportunity to absorb near-infinite amounts of historical data and philosophical works has become the most invaluable development for prophetic writing. The success of Taine's formula relies on the passage of time and technological advancement for writers to develop a keener literary lens for predicting future trends and civilizations.

Taine's view of history is most closely aligned with German philosopher Georg Wilhelm Friedrich Hegel's concept "that history recurs in cycles: that civilizations rise, flower, and decline like organisms" (Wellek 12). When coupled with this cyclical framework for analyzing history, the works of prophetic writers become more accurate—and as a result more potent—as the twentieth century has provided large amounts of data and analysis of the historical cycles of past trends and civilizations. When applying Taine's formula to U.S. society, the works of James Baldwin, Toni Morrison, and Octavia E. Butler reflect the fruits of decades of research and investigation of the past and the present works of a race-based colonized and self-liberating history.

In the midst of a global pandemic that forced the world to seek safety through quarantines, masks, and a heightened sense of hygiene, the United States observed its 2020 presidential election cycle. After four days of counting all the votes in the historic turnout, the results declared former Vice-President Joe Biden the winner. With the procedural stages of confirmation still ahead, outgoing President Donald Trump's accusations of a stolen election would fan the flames of an already-growing political division. This fracture between the two dominant political parties had been turning more volatile and dangerous in its rhetoric over the previous twelve years, since the election of the nation's first African American President in 2008. With the power of social media, the oppositional forces that rejected the results of the election would organize a rally to reclaim the country they affirmed as theirs. On January 6th 2021, with the presidential inauguration only two weeks away, former President Trump and other Republican hardliners would speak at a massive rally in the nation's capital. By the early afternoon, the Capitol building was stormed by thousands of the rally's attendees while Congress was in session. Images of Congressional officials seeking shelter and safety—while men and women paraded the anti-U.S. Confederate flag through the halls of Congress—spread across international news networks and social media. This moment in U.S. history had never occurred before. Yet, it was not a surprise to many observing the trajectory of the U.S. since before the election of President Barack Obama. Whether analyzing through the Hegelian historical cycles or the prophetic writings of Baldwin, Morrison, and Butler, this moment had been foreseen and had arrived.

In the wake of the January 6th storming of the Capitol, national intelligence and security institutions have begun directing their efforts towards the rise of social media organizing. This response to the dangerous rhetoric and acts of right-wing extremists is being tailored to fit all ideological opposition to the governing state. Social media companies have begun to de-platform user accounts that express right-wing extremist views, but many leftist and social justice user accounts have been targeted as well. The country's Black Liberation Movement has begun to experience blanket censorship as a result of the government's newfound concern for the threat of domestic terrorism. As with the response to the 9/11 attacks twenty years ago, the proposal of a new and revised Patriot Act—with an increased emphasis on data collection and internet surveillance—has been set forth as a consequence of the storming of the Capitol (Downs et al). The monitoring of speech has made public discourse a dangerously fine line to walk in the face of the most socially and politically tense era in U.S. history since the days of the Civil Rights and Black Power Movements. The path to the alarming endangerment of the right to free speech as laid out in the U.S. Constitution was paved by the technological advancement of social media and its unregulated consumer-based capabilities.

The power of language is multiplied when that language is spread to as many individuals as possible. The invention of the printing press, the advancement of communication through radio and telephone, and the cultural revolution of television broadcasting have all maximized the power of language as readers, listeners, and viewers are transformed into consumers by a capitalist society. Language, as Toni Morrison emphasized throughout her career, can be a vessel to liberate minds or trap them in dangerous ideological trances (Kapitan). The intentions of those who use euphemizing or obfuscating language become clear when observing their efforts at outright censorship and mass manipulation through misinformation. The impact social media has had on the world is immediate. When the ability to instantly broadcast oneself to the world through a cell phone became a reality in 2010, social movements for democracy spread across the Middle East and North Africa in what became known as Arab Spring (Wolfsfeld et al). This would become the infancy of social media organizing for social justice and democracy. Three years later the hashtag #BlackLivesMatter went viral after the not-guilty verdict of George Zimmerman in the case of the murder of

Trayvon Martin, and since then the organizing power of African American and other non-Anglo communities in the U.S. has only increased in influence. During the 2016 presidential election, the social-media-based movement was still coming into its full potential and identity as it began to force a tense confrontation between the failed history of race relations in the U.S. and the electoral aims of both political parties beginning to adapt to the capabilities of social media.

When observing the current moment and milieu—eight years after the start of the Movement for Black Lives and the rise of social media organizing—there is no denying that the social and political landscape has been transformed by the power of social media. The presidential campaigns for both Biden and Trump employed messaging and mobilizing tactics that mimicked the efforts of social justice organizers who had learned to channel the full capabilities of the revolutionary technological advancement of a generation. These tactics have resulted in the co-opting of the movement's liberationist identity and have become a tool for propaganda and misinformation. Social media's infinite reach and capacity for conflicting narratives, and conspiracies alongside facts, has flooded social consciousness and, as a result, accusations of fake news have entrenched political divisions even further (Austin Community College Library Services). The goals of the Black Liberation Movement that had been echoed throughout U.S. history now confront the next challenge of censorship and increased military response to social unrest. The killings of George Floyd and Breonna Taylor by police in 2020 sparked a new wave of mass protests and unrest during the global Covid-19 pandemic. The responses to these protestors were sharply different from the responses to right-wing armed protests including the siege of the Capitol on January 6th (Cachelin). Mirroring the years leading to the Civil War, as well as the years leading to the Civil Rights and Black Power Movements, this current moment has been constructed by the same oppositional forces and narratives that have plagued the nation since its founding. In W. E. B. DuBois's 1920 speculative essay "The Souls of White Folk," in which he speaks as the legendary Sphinx, he sets a precedent for the prophetic African American tradition by stating, "Instead of standing as a great example of the success of democracy and the possibility of human brotherhood America has taken her place as an awful example of its pitfalls and failures, so far as black and brown and yellow peoples are concerned" (Chapter II). These "failures" highlighted and analyzed by DuBois become the same cycle of failures that have plagued the U.S. through the past centuries of political and social turmoil, since its inception. Today's American writers have the opportunity to speak to the moment as James Baldwin dares to do when confronted with the duty and burden to do so. In order to execute this literary task, writers must look to the work of the past to address their present condition and envision the future that has been hoped for, century after century.

U.S. identity has in many ways embodied the plateau of Euro-colonial civilization. Its roots in White supremacy are intertwined with the historical weaponizing of Christianity. The mainstream consciousness of the U.S. has been centered on the morality of Christian theology, but it has consistently resisted the recognition of its diverse population and true history of human rights violations, African enslavement, and Native American genocide. The prophets and prophecies of the Bible have provided a space for advocates for equality to speak to their present time in hopes of connecting Scriptures to reality (Harriss, "The Bible in American Literature," and *Bible, King James Version*).

A prophet is recognized only after the moment to act has passed. The function of prophecy has historically been to warn against impending struggle or catastrophe. It is also a social justice practice that connects to the universal struggle against oppression, as evidenced by Rev. Martin Luther King, Jr. and the early abolitionist efforts of the African Methodist Episcopal (AME) Church. Baldwin himself, once a child pastor, employed language rooted in Christian theology throughout his liberationist nonfiction work. George Shulman explores these relational dynamics between prophets and society, stating:

> Prophecy is a changeable and contested social practice. After all, there was profound conflict between those (call them "house prophets") who worked for the royal house of Israel and voiced god's unconditional support for it and those canonized now as "the" prophets, whose god condemns idolatry and holds both monarchy and nation to account. (Shulman, 712-713)

When considering the self-promoted image of the U.S. as a Christian nation, one can argue that Baldwin's ability to employ language that utilizes Christian doctrine to appeal to the morality of the nation's Anglo citizens increases his effectiveness to make the prophetic argument for both self-evaluation and the urgency to act. In *The Fire Next Time*—a title that itself is taken from an African American Christian spiritual—Baldwin emphasizes the urgency of the moment with the hope of breaking through and helping to steer the nation's conscience towards justice and equality. Through dire and prophetic warning, Baldwin places hope and responsibility in the hands of the reader: "And here we are, at the center of the arc trapped in the gaudiest, most valuable, and most improbable water wheel the world has ever seen. Everything now, we must assume, is in our hands; we have no right to assume otherwise" (105). Shulman contrasts Baldwin's urgency with the biblical echoes of scripture:

> We can feel the aggression in Jeremiah's or Baldwin's voice, tied to indignation—at injustice and denial of it, at idolatry and attachment

to it, at repetition and blindness to it. The aggressive assertion about how it is with us—about how we *must* see our situation and history *if* we are to bring ourselves out of it—sounds like a 'thou shalt,' even though it is a conditional claim in an imperative voice. (Shulman, 726, italics original)

Despite Baldwin's attempts to shake the conscience of the nation through echoing the voice of biblical prophecy, the result of his mission—to not only witness the moment, but to speak directly to it—is a social detachment from the prophetic warning signs as media and politics change the topic of conversation, tuning out the urgency of the historical moment that was the Civil Rights and Black Power Movements. The mainstream narrative is manufactured to lionize Rev. King Jr. as an American hero, demonize the Black Panther Party and Black Power Movement esthetics, and begin the militarization of police departments across the country. During his final years, Baldwin witnessed the nation elect former actor Ronald Reagan as president. As governor of California, Reagan had led efforts to silence the Black Panther Party, which resulted in targeted killings of its leaders and the political imprisonment of those who survived attempts on their lives (Vankin). When visiting the site of Baldwin's home in Paris—after it had been demolished for a new housing development—Eddie S. Glaude reflects on this period of the U.S. as it entered the 1980s, stating, "The ruins were a fitting description for what Baldwin saw in the latter part of his life in the United States. He saw decay and wreckage alongside greed and selfishness" (xvii). Today, Baldwin's words decorate many social media posts, protest signs, and speeches that have emerged during the early twenty-first-century effort for justice and equality for African Americans. This fulfillment of prophecy has elevated Baldwin as one of the U.S.'s greatest thinkers and writers. In considering his hopes and aspirations for a better U.S. future, there are still those who continue in his legacy to prophesy for the realization of a decaying American dream.

Baldwin addresses Taine's element of race by filling in the sub-elements of Person, People, Identity, Spirit, and Nation through the practice of sharing personal stories and inner thoughts, feelings, and fears. This practice follows in the tradition of African American writers and academics such as Frederick Douglass, Richard Wright, W.E.B. DuBois, and Ralph Ellison. Baldwin, by embodying the sub-element of person, is able to reach deeply within himself in order to pull out the human vulnerabilities that have always existed. As a result, *The Fire Next Time* serves as a prophetic warning in which Baldwin begins with his most personal duty to warn his own flesh and blood about the nation he calls home and moves forward to warn the nation he chooses to confront in the hope of a better future. Baldwin explains to his nephew this fear and sense of identity that both threaten and define their American experience:

> To act is to be committed, and to be committed is to be in danger. In this case, the danger, in the minds of most white Americans, is the loss of their identity. Try to imagine how you would feel if you woke up one morning to find the sun shining and all the stars aflame. You would be frightened because it is out of the order of nature. Any upheaval in the universe is terrifying because it so profoundly attacks one's sense of one's own reality. Well, the black man has functioned in the white man's world as a fixed star, as an immovable pillar: and as he moves out of his place, heaven and earth are shaken to their foundations. (*Fire Next Time*, 9)

In an attempt to relate to the fear felt by Anglo-Americans who have not considered or read an African American person's thoughts on race or living in America, Baldwin draws a comparison between the certainty of the universe and the natural disposition of the stars with the role of African American people in the minds of Anglo-Americans. He does this in order to explain the conditioned fear that is triggered by the Anglo-American's white identity when this role is challenged. By allowing all readers--especially Anglo readers--into this intimate and loving expression towards his nephew James, Baldwin opens a space for a vulnerable journey through his thoughts on the increasingly tense social setting of the 1960s.

If Baldwin's work functions as a direct confrontation against the manufactured historical narrative and identity of the U.S., then Morrison and Butler stand alongside Baldwin as a functioning effort to rearrange the U.S.'s historical timeline. If Baldwin writes to his present moment, then Morrison's career is a collection of works that write through the past, and Butler's career in this instance is a clear effort to write towards and into the future. Baldwin's moment and audience exist in a heavily Anglo-male and Christian-dominated United States. During Morrison and Butler's careers, the nation had begun to shift in its identity as media spaces began to provide more opportunities for diverse voices and images. The cases of Morrison and Butler stand as examples of works of literature that carve out spaces for future diverse voices, both in the U.S. literary canon and in the speculative and science fiction genres, respectively. The prophetic capabilities of both Morrison and Butler benefit from the expansion of identities and escape from the theological confines of Christianity. Their radical imaginations allow for them to create narratives that speak to a broader range of human conditions that exist in the realities of Euro-colonial society, making many previously unseen or ignored realities unavoidably visible. M. Cooper Harriss explores this greater reach of freedom for prophetic literature by both Morrison and Butler:

At the same time, Morrison and Butler represent exemplars of a post-Christian (and thus a postbiblical-theological) America that contends with inescapable biblical echoes and legacies (for good and ill) while simultaneously striving to reimagine its certain textual futures that respond to and move beyond these legacies and their innovations. Morrison recasts this biblical mode by looking backwards and renovating the terms of its contribution to American literary expression. Butler looks ahead, innovating not only the meaning of the Bible but its canonical possibilities for the future tense. (100)

The collective works of Morrison reach as far back in scope as the nineteenth century and move through the twentieth century, exploring the nuances and conditions of different decades. Morrison is successful in unearthing untold stories of the African American people who form so much of the U.S.'s foundation, creating a need to reassess U.S. identity and deconstruct the manufactured narrative of U.S. exceptionalism. The power of Morrison's work aligns with her literary and historical criticisms, as she often emphasizes the ties that bind:

> Just as the formation of the nation necessitated coded language and purposeful restriction to deal with the racial disingenuousness and moral frailty at its heart, so too did the literature, whose founding characteristics extend into the twentieth century, reproduce the necessity for codes and restriction. (*Playing in the Dark*, 6)

Morrison's work stands as an example of the practice of conscience in the literary imagination that does not erase, misrepresent, or demonize any other identity, avoiding the marginalization of any racial or social group.

In October of 1993, Morrison was awarded the Nobel Prize for Literature. This prize marks the highest recognition for a writer by an international audience of readers, critics, and scholars. For

Morrison, this was the culmination of a twenty-three-year literary career that expanded the scope of U.S. literature, a career that also helped mold U.S. literary identity. Morrison's literary journey began during the twilight of the Civil Rights and Black Power movements. U.S. social consciousness had been awakened to a dangerously tense social climate. This tension had been stirred by opposing reactions to the African American community's efforts to achieve social equality since the mid-1950s. By 1970, the assassinations of Rev. Martin Luther King Jr., Malcolm X, Medgar Evers, and both President John F. Kennedy and his brother Robert Kennedy had exhausted the nation's morale, and disrupted the momentum of change. The leaders of the Black Panther Party had been targeted through politically motivated killings and imprisonment. The milieu of the nation had shifted from a cautiously optimistic orientation towards unity in its racial conversation into a more politically charged stand-off between communities who did not know one another well, if at all. With this rupture, the moment for writers to predict future trends and civilizations had passed, and the history of the 1960s was set for future revisions, manipulations and re-imaginings. The release of Morrison's first published novel, *The Bluest Eye*, in 1970 would be the beginning of the formation of a new moment in U.S. literature and history, a moment in which Morrison's prophetic abilities would be on full display through her artistic use of language.

As Morrison's work began to open U.S. consciousness to the untold stories of the African American community, the revisiting of purportedly classical U.S. literature became more urgent for the recognition of the nation's true identity. The reach of Morrison's artistic abilities for the purpose of unlearning biased and incomplete U.S. history would be paired with her scholarly work to examine the U.S.'s literary canon for purposes that are just as important to the nation's identity. The expansion of critical race studies—through the literary analysis of Morrison and her observations on whiteness in the literary imagination—has contributed to an increase in White Studies in other academic fields since the 1990s. The examination of how Whiteness functions in history, sociology, politics, psychology, and other academic disciplines has become a post-modern practice that Morrison's published work of literary criticism, *Playing in the Dark,* helped elevate into greater visibility. This academic trend is crucial for the understanding of U.S. identification of race since the definition of race itself has long been separated from its Eurocentric roots of nationhood. In a research study on Whiteness, Tammie M. Kennedy, Irene Middleton, and Krista Ratcliffe clarify the difference of race in the U.S. when compared to European identity:

> Although race initially referred to ethnic groups (as in the Irish race), by the time the US Constitution was signed in 1787, race had shifted to signify color and blood as designators of biological differences. Within the cultural logic of white supremacy, these so-called biological differences were employed to justify social and economic hierarchies: That is, "white people" were presumed to be the superior race. (Kennedy, et al, "The Matter of Whiteness," 365)

This deconstruction of the use of Blackness and Whiteness in the formation of U.S. history through the use of language becomes a priority for the evolution of the nation's future identity. Morrison reflects on this responsibility by stating,

> for both black and white American writers, in a wholly racialized society, there is no escape from racially inflected language, and the work writers do to unhobble the imagination from the demands of that language is complicated, interesting, and definitive. (Morrison, *Playing in the Dark,* 13).

In recognizing the misuse of racialized language, Morrison has identified the battle line for future writers and scholars to unravel the words of the past for a more responsible use of language in the future.

When Morrison accepted the Nobel Prize in Literature and gave a lecture to the guests present for the ceremony in her honor, this historic moment of recognition and praise was the result of over two decades of work totaling six novels that expanded the U.S. canon. She became the tenth U.S. writer to receive the prize, and only the second woman to do so. But Morrison was the first and remains the only African American writer to receive this highest international honor in literature. Her identity as an African American woman had provided her with the insights and language to do more than just speak about racial matters. Her own identity optimized her ability to see language more deeply through the lens of U.S. society and history. With the moment to speak and reflect on the power of her work fully in her possession, Morrison chooses to use her acceptance speech as an opportunity to tell a story. The use of this narrative would function as an allegory for matters far greater than celebrating a successful and decorated literary career. Through her prose and imagery, Morrison speaks her own prophetic warnings to those present and to future generations of writers.

The story that Morrison shares with the audience is simple in its premise: an old blind and wise woman is visited by a group of young people who want to test her power and wisdom by asking her if the bird that one of them is holding in their hand is dead or alive. Morrison primes the allegory by using the bird and the old woman as metaphors for language and a writer, respectively. She proceeds to explore the possible intentions and purposes of the question asked by the group of youths. If language is dead or alive in one's hand, are its proponents responsible for either? The blind woman explores the depth of these intentions as Morrison warns of the misuse of language:

> The systematic looting of language can be recognized by the tendency of its users to forgo its nuanced, complex, midwifery properties, replacing them with menace and subjugation. Oppressive language does more than represent violence; it is violence; does more than represent the limits of knowledge; it limits knowledge. ("Nobel Lecture," 320)

Morrison expresses through the blind woman the wisdom gained through the experience drawn from recorded history, as the warning continues to point to the various platforms in which language has been and continues to be abused and manipulated:

> Whether it is obscuring state language or the faux language of mindless media; whether it is the proud but calcified language of the academy or the commodity-driven language of science; whether it is the malign language of law-without-ethics, or language designed for the estrangement of minorities, hiding its racist plunder in its literary cheek––it must be rejected, altered, and exposed. ("Nobel Lecture," 320).

The story advocates for and defends the responsibility of language and the power behind its use. Echoing Morrison's prophecy, today's current use of social media for the purposes of consumerism, nationalism, and fearmongering has exploded over the last decade. In the U.S., the result of such irresponsible use of language through this high-speed technology has been an increasingly tense political climate since 2012. The culmination of this exploitation of language reached uncontrollable heights during the first presidential election of Donald Trump, which led to the inception of fake news accusations, fact-contradicting claims, and vicious oppositional ideologies competing for consumption. In a research article conducted by The Institute for National Security Studies, the recent addition of the word Post-Truth to the *Oxford Dictionary* is recognized as a significant moment in the evolution of language, and within that recognition lies the danger Morrison warns about:

> Only in 2016, against the backdrop of the United States presidential elections and the United Kingdom referendum about withdrawal from the European Union (Brexit), did the new and rather obscure term (Post-Truth) become prevalent, and its use in the political context skyrocketed by thousands of percentage points. It was for this reason that Oxford Dictionaries selected it as the "Word of the Year" in 2016 and defined it as "a term relating to or denoting circumstances in which objective facts are less influential in shaping public opinion than appeals to emotion and personal belief." (Brahms, *Philosophy of Post-Truth*, 1)

As the world becomes more interconnected through technology and the internet, the ability to spread massive amounts of information at the speed of light creates an extreme vulnerability for the abuse of language. The moral responsibility of the writer—represented by the blind woman, in her age and wisdom—is the rallying cry Morrison has been advocating for through her work and her critical analysis of literature.

Octavia Butler's work absorbs the milieu of her lifetime and combines it with the explosion of the information age that has expanded the capabilities of data collection. This mixture facilitates Butler's imagination to envision a future U.S. and world that, if the warning signs of social unrest, political instability, and climate science go unheeded, will find a dystopian future unavoidable. Her most successful novel series—*Parable of the Sower* and *Parable of the Talents*—demonstrates her sharp ability to use social, historical, and scientific analysis to create a potent vision and a warning. Butler's achievement is a prophetic prediction of where the U.S. and the rest of the world may be headed if conditions do not change. The recent posthumous re-emergence and success of Butler's *Parables* demonstrate that her vision has captured the imagination of readers around the world, with *Sower* reaching the *New York Times* bestseller list twenty-three years after its release. In an interview speaking about the *Parables*, Butler reveals:

> It is to look at where we are now, what we are doing now, and to consider where some of our current behaviors and unattended problems might take us. I considered drugs and the effects of drugs on the children of drug addicts. I looked at the growing rich/poor gap, at throwaway labor, at our willingness to build and fill prisons, our reluctance to build and repair schools and libraries, and at our assault on the environment. In particular, I looked at global warming and the ways in which it's likely to change things for us. (Butler, *Parable of the Sower*, 337)

Butler continues, listing the effects of drugs, extreme economic inequality, labor exploitation, the growing prison industrial complex, failing school systems, and the long-term concerns of environmental pollution and decay on society. Through this collective capturing of many social, political, historical, and environmental elements, Butler stands as an exemplary representation of how prophetic power can manifest in literature. Butler presents and addresses a wider scope of social and political issues that expand further beyond the limitations of gender-specific narratives of writers such as Leni Zumas (*Red Clocks*) and Margaret Atwood (*The Handmaid's Tale*), or the monolithic theme of (Anglo) man versus a high-tech surveillance state (George Orwell's *1984*). Butler's *Parables* breaks away from the early dystopian model and tells the story of an African American teen who is coming of age in a chaotic U.S. where climate change and economic collapse have left the people outside of the wealthiest class vulnerable to instability, ideological extremism, and violence.

Without the contributions by Baldwin and Morrison to the conversation on race relations and racialized language in America, Butler could not have written as freely, without the limitations of identity politics. This freedom facilitates Butler's imagination, contributing to the SF genre and the growth of Afrofuturism, which had begun to coalesce as a genre in the 1990s, as more African American writers published speculative fiction. Butler's visions of the future include diverse identities and, as a result, activists and organizers of all backgrounds today can see themselves through her prophetic imagination. As the works of Baldwin, Morrison, and Butler remain widely read and influential, both their sense of urgency and their prophetic warnings become the responsibility of the U.S. reader and writer to contend with during this moment of U.S. decay and potential collapse. As analysts, pundits, and politicians seek answers in order to respond to this moment, the works of U.S. writers continue to hold many of the imagined possibilities of the future that can save the nation.

The determining factor for the successful application of Taine's formula has been the prophetic element—the writer—responding to the moment, interacting with the milieu of their society or civilization. In revisiting Taine's idea to quantify literary works into a functioning scientific formula for the successful prediction of future trends and civilizations, one must consider the material available for the formula to be executed correctly. The identification of the prophetic element allows readers today the ability to update Taine's formula and visualize it in formulaic language as $(rmm)^w$. It is the writer who determines the functionality of the formula and its success. The present condition and milieu of the U.S. today is confronted by Baldwin's warning against failing to act in the moment and Morrison's plea to protect language and to be fully responsible with its power; in case these warnings go unheard, Butler's dystopian *Parable of the Sower*, which begins on July 20, 2024 in an environment of climate disaster and social collapse, may soon become fully realized.

For some, the signs of these incipient dystopian conditions have begun to form clearly enough to mobilize in the hope of saving the nation from such a dark fate. In the resulting analysis of these three American writers' works, one can see how the social, cultural, and intellectual trends of today's social justice movement are fully rooted in their prophetic words. The power of language remains at the root of civilization. The role of its artists, writers, and creators becomes increasingly socially recognized as the ongoing mission to learn from the past, observe the present, and envision a better future.

Works Cited

Atwood, Margaret. *The Handmaid's Tale*. New York: Vintage Books, 1998.

Austin Community College Library Services. "Fake News and Alternative Facts: Finding Accurate News: Why is Fake News Harmful?" https://researchguides.austincc.edu/c.php?g=612891&p=4258046. Accessed 25 November, 2024.

Baldwin, James. *The Fire Next Time*. 1963. New York: Vintage Books, 1993.

Bible, King James Version, https://quod.lib.umich.edu/cgi/k/kjv/kjv-idx?type=DIV2&byte=4800788. Accessed 25 November 2024.

Brahms, Yael. *Philosophy of Post-Truth*. Institute for National Security Studies, 2020, https://www.jstor.org/stable/resrep23537. Accessed 31 July 2024.

Butler, Octavia E. *Parable of the Sower*. New York: Grand Central Publishing, 2019.

Butler, Octavia E. *Parable of the Talents*. New York: Grand Central Publishing, 2019.

Cachelin, Shala. "The Suppression and Othering of Black Lives Matter Protests Through Tear Gas." *Journal of Black Studies*. 54:6, 1 July 2023, pp. 513–533. https://doi.org/10.1177/00219347231184234. Accessed 25 November 2024.

Downs, Jim, Ed. *January 6 and the Politics of History*. Athens: University of Georgia Press, 2024.

Du Bois, W.E. B. "The Souls of White Folk." *Darkwater: Voices from Within the Veil*. 1920. Project Gutenberg, http://www.gutenberg.org/cache/epub/15210/pg15210-images.html#Chapter_II. Accessed 31 July 2024.

Glaude Jr., Eddie S. *Begin Again: James Baldwin's America And Its Urgent Lessons For Our Own*. New York: CROWN, 2020.

Harriss, M. Cooper. "The Bible in American Literature." *The Bible in the American Experience*, edited by Claudia Setzer and David A. Shefferman, The Society of Biblical Literature, Atlanta, 2020, pp. 93–112. *JSTOR*, https://www.jstor.org/stable/j.ctv16obtr9.8. Accessed 14 Feb. 2024.

Kapitan, Alex. "Toni Morrison and the Power of Language." *The Radical Copyeditor*, 14 August 2019, https://radicalcopyeditor.com/2019/08/14/toni-morrison/#:~:text=There%27s%20no%20way%20to%20overstate%20the%20significance,deepest%20wounds%20and%20try%20to%20comprehend%20them.%E2%80%9D. Accessed 25 November 2024.

Kennedy, Tammie M., et al. "The Matter of Whiteness: Or, Why Whiteness Studies Is Important to Rhetoric and Composition Studies." *Rhetoric Review*, vol. 24, no. 4, 2005, pp. 359–373. *JSTOR*, https://www.jstor.org/stable/20176676. Accessed 31 July 2024.

Morrison, Toni. *Playing in the Dark: Whiteness and the Literary Imagination*. New York: Vintage Books, 1993.

Morrison, Toni. *The Bluest Eye*. 1970. New York: Vintage Books, 2007.

Morrison, Toni. "Nobel Lecture, 7 December 1993." *The Georgia Review*, vol. 49, no. 1, 1995, pp. 318–323. *JSTOR*, https://www.jstor.org/stable/41401645. Accessed 31 July 2024.

Orwell, George. *1984*. New York: Signet Classic, 1961.

Roşca, Dumitru D. *L'influence de Hegel sur Taine, Théoricien de la Connaissance et de l'Art*. 1928. Library of Congress, https://catalog.loc.gov/vwebv/holdingsInfo?searchId=21004&recCount=25&recPointer=0&bibId=1218732. Accessed 31 July 2024.

Shulman, George. "Thinking Authority Democratically: Prophetic Practices, White Supremacy, and Democratic Politics." *Political Theory*, vol. 36, no. 5, 2008, pp. 708–734. *JSTOR*, https://www.jstor.org/stable/20452662. Accessed 14 February 2024.

Vankin, Jonathan. "Gun Control: How Ronald Reagan and the Black Panthers Started a Movement." *California Local*, 13 April 2022, https://californialocal.com/localnews/statewide/ca/article/show/4412-california-gun-control-reagan-black-panthers/. Accessed 25 November 2024.

Wellek, René. "Hippolyte Taine's Literary Theory and Criticism." *Criticism* vol. 1, no. 1, 1959, pp. 1–18. *JSTOR*, www.jstor.org/stable/23091097. Accessed 14 Feb. 2024.

Wolfsfeld, Gadi, et al. "Social Media and the Arab Spring: Politics Comes First." *The International Journal of Press/Politics*, vol 18, no. 2, April 2013, pp. 115–137. https://doi.org/10.1177/1940161212471716. Accessed 25 November 2024.

Zumas, Leni. *Red Clocks*. New York: Little, Brown and Company, 2018.

Map Before Territory: Cartography and Ecology in Erik Granström's *Svavelvinter*

Svante Landgraf

O NE DISTINGUISHING FEATURE OF FANTASY literature is the inclusion of a map at the beginning of a book, detailing the secondary world where the story is taking place (Ekman, "Map and Text" 71; Ekman, *Here Be Dragons* 11). The map sets the stage for the forthcoming action; being the first thing the reader encounters, after the cover but before any characters or other linguistic descriptions, it establishes the significance of the fantastic space. Thus, the map represents a fusion of space and language, and of text and image, serving as a manifestation of the fundamental multimodality of the fantastic text; a space is described with words and images, two-dimensionally taking up space on the page. While other literary genres, such as Bibles or children's books, occasionally feature maps (Ekman, *Here Be Dragons* 14), the fantastic affords unique forms of interplay between map, text and textworld. The map can itself function as an artifact within the text, for example, the map in J. R. R. Tolkien's *The Hobbit* being a representation of the actual map used by the characters in the narrative to find their way. By enticing the reader to follow along on the map, the reader takes on a more active role. Furthermore, in the fantastic, it is possible for the same map to magically affect the setting, creating a metafictional loop not unlike the one in *The Lord of the Rings*, where Sam and Frodo are discussing being part of a fairy-tale or problematizing earlier versions of the text (Israelson 135, 126). In the fantasy novels of the *Fifth Conflux* series by Swedish author Erik Granström, which are reworked from table-top role-playing game adventures, this happens when space represents and is dependent upon the map, not the other way around, so that a change in the divine, magical map changes the depicted part of the world. The novels contain fantasy maps detailing the country where the action takes place. This essay analyzes these features in Granström's work, including how the multimodality of incorporating maps as images in the text activates the reader and makes the reader more akin to a gameplayer, how the fantastic can allow for a reversal of the usual relationship between a map and the space depicted, and how a story is transformed from RPG adventure to novels, well suited to be studied through the lens of general ecology. This does not mean ecology in the sense of pertaining to nature, but a kind of generalized media ecology, meaning the importance of networks, systems and feedback, aiming to dissolve the division between nature and culture, between life and technology (Hörl 2). It is possible to problematize the anthropocentrism of the Anthropocene, study the nonhuman as monstrous assemblages akin to Donna Haraway's cyborgs, and accentuate the fundamental materiality of media (cf. Parikka, Fuller, Haraway). These perspectives are useful for the following analysis.

This essay aims to demonstrate ways in which the fantastic not only allows for, but is intimately and fundamentally connected to, a transgression of material boundaries, including between reader and textworld as the reader interprets maps in the books. There is a transgression between map and territory in the textworld when the map magically affects the world, and a transgression between narrative levels in the text. This analysis answers questions such as how the maps in the different texts are depicted, how this is affected by printing processes, and in turn how the maps affect the reader. The fantastic allows for a blurring of metaphor, theme, and form, especially in the usage of maps. This usage is tied to the game-like nature of the text, making the reader take on the role of game-player. Through analyzing this mapping, the current essay explores how the fantastic is intimately tied to today's shifting media landscape and continuing renegotiations of space.

Firstly, I compare maps in the *Svavelvinter* novels, clarifying their various roles in the narrative and in the reading process. Then, I study the cases in which maps magically affect the narrative, and I continue by tracing ecological themes throughout the novels and game books, arriving at the interplay between novels and role-playing games.

The *Fifth Conflux* series of novels (2004–2016) by Erik Granström (b. 1956) is well suited for discussing issues of fantasy mapping. Granström wrote the adventure *Svavelvinter* (*Sulphur Winter*; none of Granström's works are translated in more than fragments, so these titles are translated by the author of this essay) in 1987 for Sweden's largest tabletop role-playing game, *Drakar och Demoner*. It was followed by the adventures *Oraklets fyra ögon* (*Four Eyes of the Oracle*, 1990), *Kristalltjuren* (*The Crystal Bull*, 1992) and *Den femte konfluxen* (*The Fifth Conflux*, 1994), collectively forming the *Fifth Conflux* series, along with the companion geographical volume *Trakorien* (*Trachoria*, 1988). In 2004, Granström then published the novel adaptation *Svavelvinter*, followed by *Slaktare små* (*Little Butchers*, 2011), *Vredesverk* (*Deeds of Wrath*, 2014) and *Vanderland* (*Wanderland*, 2016). Together, the four novels are adaptations of the adventure series, the plot and the setting being roughly the same but with several facts and characters added or significantly changed.

The novels and the adventures are constructed around the concept of a conflux—a point in space and time at which the future of the world will be decided—and the ensuing battle among different factions for domination. The story starts in the northern glacial island of Marjura, where an ancient king is awakened into undeath along with his armies. The king is advised by the wizard Shagul, the main antagonist, who wants to dominate the conflux in order to wrench his name from the gods and master his own destiny. Through a set of prophecies uttered by a talking mountain in the island kingdom of Trakorien a month's sailing distance to the south, of which Marjura is a colony, the protagonists learn about the upcoming conflux and the need to stop Shagul and the undead. After various adventures in Trakorien politics and maneuvering for various resources, including a trip to another world to retrieve a powerful magic item, all factions eventually converge upon Marjura for the finale where the conflux will take place. Due to various schemes, the continental drift of Marjura was magically stopped, forcing it to stay in the north when it should have been situated in Trakorien to the south, where the conflux should be located. The protagonists must resolve this situation so that the map of the gods once again aligns with reality. In the end, in the novels, Shagul is stopped, and a new world is born. In the game, there are several possible endings, based on who dominates the conflux.

Just as Swedish literature scholar Per Israelson shows that the presence of parodies of *The Lord of the Rings* highlights the materiality of the media ecology of Tolkien's work (Israelson 156), Granström's novels and adventures are parts of a much larger media-ecological system. This system includes not only the novels and the original adventures written by Granström, but also his blog about writing the novels, the comments on the blog, and thus

Granström's dialogue with his most dedicated readers. Additionally, the system includes the role-playing game set in his world but written mostly by other people, and even the music by the band Svavelvinter, to which Granström has written lyrics (*Svavelvinter - Encyclopaedia Metallum: The Metal Archives*; Granström, "About Mörkrets Tid"). The storyworld expands beyond what is directly perceived by the reader, both into different media and geographically, as Jeff Vance Martin and Gretchen Sneegas have mentioned in the context of worldbuilding in speculative fiction (15). This multimodality is important for the genre, both in the inclusion of maps in the books and also as one part of—using Israelson's term—the especially participatory aesthetics of the fantastic, as for example Gunther Kress has pointed out in comparing multimodal texts to more traditional ones (37).

One very central part of the convergence of image and text in the fantastic concerns maps. The presence of printed maps of the secondary worlds is a defining feature of fantasy literature, as fantasy scholar Stefan Ekman has noted ("Map and Text" 71); literary geographer Robert Tally has also made the connection between the fantasy genre and the importance of maps, bringing up the example of how the map in *The Hobbit* is both a part of the story and a way to understand the text (*Topophrenia* 132; *Spatiality* 148). While Ekman's survey of fantasy literature shows that maps are not as ubiquitous as one might have imagined, considering the monumental influence of Tolkien on the genre, maps are nevertheless frequently present. Maps do play an important role in Granström's fantasy, where novels and adventures all contain multiple maps. Therefore, these maps are the first object of analysis in this essay.

The maps in the *Fifth Conflux* novels are usually found on the inside of the front cover and are thus the first thing encountered by the reader after the cover and its title. Some of these maps have a double existence both inside the fictional world and outside of it; but the map exists here as in any other map in a fantasy novel. The map is a representation of space, just like the text can be, but the map affords different ways of interacting with the reader, based on different material components. What, then, can be said about the map in this sense?

Here, I analyze several properties of the *Svavelvinter* maps: their artistic style, the typography of the text used in the maps, which symbols are present and which of them are explained in a legend, and the symbols's apparent age. Through this analysis, I attempt to answer questions such as how the maps relate to the reader and to the fictional world, how the maps change over time and between forms of media, which kind of information about the fictional world the maps can and cannot convey, what can be said about diegetic artistic style and printing processes of the maps, and how the maps relate to conventions of genre and media. Most significantly of all, I address how the *Svavelvinter* maps work to bring the relationship between text and reader to the forefront.

The maps in question mainly depict two areas: the remote northern glacial island of Marjura, and the archipelago kingdom of Trakorien. All the novels and adventures contain multiple maps. The maps of Trakorien and Marjura in the novel *Svavelvinter* give the impression of a diegetic artifact: they are hand-painted and supplemented by hand-written text. The mountains and forests are painted in a style reminiscent of medieval maps; the forests are marked by groups of single trees, and the mountain ranges are built from individual mountains. The hand-written text is irregular and adorned. This diegetic quality is further enhanced by the presence of monsters, both giants on the ice shelf and typical medieval-looking fish beasts in the seas. There is a frame, consisting of an alternating pattern of light and dark bands with further embellished corners, around each page of the map, even alongside the inner margins of the spread, breaking up the view of the island into two parts. The first map, of Trakorien, takes up only a single page.

Notably, there is no legend explaining any of the symbols in use. There is, however, a scale, in what are called "Trakorian miles." But the symbols deployed cover coastlines, settlements, mountains and hills, forests, the inland ice shelf, and the icebergs where the glaciers reach the sea. All these are painted representatively, without abstractions other than the synecdoche of buildings meaning cities and trees meaning forests. Roads are present, shown as fine, almost invisible dotted lines. Place names on the map denote settlements, mountain ranges and the ice shelf itself. The Trakorien map also contains names of the different islands of the archipelago, as well as political entities, in addition to cities, seas, and ocean bays.

The maps are printed in greyscale but give the impression of having originally been painted in color, due to the low contrast, the light variations in light grey on large areas, and artefacts of digital noise, probably appearing out of bad scanning or too-high file compression. They are also not found on the inside covers as in the other novels, but in between the title page and the text proper. In the second novel of the series, *Slaktare små*, the maps are vastly different. Their objects are the same: one map depicts Trakorien, and one Marjura, though the former covers the entire nation and not just a small portion of it, as in *Svavelvinter*. However, the maps are printed on the inside covers, which means they can be printed in color. Color is used sparingly: one base color for water, one for land, one for mountains (or, in the Marjura case, one for land, one for ice); it might be printed in three colors only (black, teal, beige). Mountains are denoted by painted mountains, and forests by tiny painted trees. But settlements are represented as black squares here, not by buildings as in *Svavelvinter*. No roads or any kind of political subdivisions are visible. The textual labels are typeset, not hand-written, all in the same font but with differing sizes, denoting mountain ranges, marshlands, plains, lakes, oceans, and also cities and political entities. The text has clearly been added after the maps were painted, because several denotations are quite hard to read—for instance, printed with thin black against a background of dark brown mountains. Again, there is no legend, but also no scale, no frame and no monsters. It is hard to say what impression the map is meant to convey. While the map is clearly hand-painted, the modern computer typography and the uniform black squares marking settlements contrast harshly with that.

Moving forward to *Vredesverk*, color maps are on the inside covers, this time in full color: first, a map of Trakorien, and at the end, a map of the capital city of Tricilve. As the subject matter of the Tricilve map is different from the others, however, I exclude it from the current analysis. The Trakorien map is very different from the one in the preceding novel, *Slaktare små*. The Trakorien map is incredibly detailed, featuring computer-set text, some of which is impossible to read without the help of a magnifying glass: the names of small settlements, islands, straits, and rivers. The style of mountains and trees denoting forests is very similar to the map in *Slaktare små*. There are also a number of monsters and ships painted at sea, but they are less integrated with the style than on the map in *Svavelvinter*. Again, there is no legend, but there is a scale, both in kilometers and "Trakorian miles"[2] (with the additional note of "100 miles = 24 h sailing"), as well as no less than three compass roses and accompanying rhumb lines (the lines originating from a compass rose). There is also faux wear near the edges of the map, giving the map the appearance of a fictional artifact. That way, the Trakorien map is fundamentally different from the map in *Slaktare små*.

Finally, in the concluding novel in the series, *Vanderland*, the maps depict first Marjura, then the small part of that island called Clusta Noba where the ending takes place. Here is another drastic shift in artistic style, back to one more like a drawing. The first map, of Clusta Noba, is painted, but naturalistically, without stylized mountains but instead in the style of satellite photography. The text is typeset in the same uniform, deprecated antique typeface as in the maps in *Slaktare små*. There is no legend, no scale and no monsters, or any other kind of elements indicating it could be a fictional artifact. The concluding map of Marjura is different: more hand-drawn in style, with mountains and trees, and settlements consisting of drawn buildings, but the sea has the same featureless colored stretches of water as on the Clusta Noba map; there are still no monsters. It is also more detailed than any other map of Marjura, showing more features such as individual place names of small mountains and fjords. However, there are no roads marked. Of note is that regions of the land are denoted by text on an off-white strip. The typography is otherwise identical to the Clusta Noba map.

To compare, then, from the corresponding role-playing game adventures: in *Svavelvinter*, the map is separate from the books, a fold-out spread in A3 size. The map is hand-painted, in full color, with different hues denoting ocean, ice, forest, heath, and moss forest. The mountains and settlements are both drawn as shapes in a simplistic style. Paths and roads are marked out. This is clear because the map is supplemented with a legend and a scale, denoting most terrain features except for the ocean and, oddly, the mountains, but including road and path which only occur once each. There is also a compass rose exterior to the map itself, as part of an elaborate border, as well as a heraldic weapon. There are a few monsters shown, none of which are featured in the story.

In *Trakorien*, the map is made in a similar style, by the same artist and in the same size. The legend is slightly more elaborate, explaining the difference between smaller and larger cities and distinguishing between a larger number of types of terrain. Mountains still don't get an explanation. The glossy paper partially ruins the feeling of an in-game artifact. There are also several smaller maps in the book. One of them does depict the same area as the larger color map, the main four Trakorien islands, but this time in black and white. That same map is also reprinted unchanged in the coming two adventure books, *Oraklets fyra ögon* and *Kristalltjuren*. The map only contains text, no symbols, besides the drawn contours of the land masses, not mountains. There is a scale, and a compass rose with eight rhumb lines. The text describes both geographical and political features, making it hard to decode at first glance. The text is hand-written in a few differing weights.

In the concluding adventure in the series, *Den femte konfluxen*, there is a similar small black and white map of Marjura, covering half of a G5 page. This only depicts the major features of the island: some settlements, the coastlines and the ice, a lot of mountains, and a few other places central to the game. There is a scale and a compass rose but no legend. Things such as forests and roads are absent, and the artistic style is more abstract. Finally, a fold-out game board in the shape of a map of the island of Clusta Noba is included, where the ending of the story is played out, as the story ends there in *Vanderland*. This map is different from any other, covered in hexagonal tiles to facilitate the playing of a war game, with one symbol in each hexagon, described by a legend, distinguishing between different heights of mountains and hills. This map has a more abstracted feel.

To compare all these maps, one dividing line is between the hand-painted ones and the ones which are computer-generated and typeset. This division is connected to how much the map takes the shape of an in-world artifact. But while several of the maps are fully hand-painted, and most of the other ones lie closer to that end of the spectrum, none are fully made to appear as part of the diegetic world. Contrast this with, for example, the map in *The*

Hobbit (Ekman, *Here Be Dragons* 21), which is a representation of the map the characters in the novel are using.

A legend is only present on the earliest maps from the role-playing game. One could think that the legend has a constraining function on the reader's imagination and their use of the map. The map could be seen as didactic and denotative, pointing out what can be read from the map. But as Stefan Ekman claims, the legend can be a sign in its own right ("Map and Text" 74), and as such it adds information instead of limiting comprehension of the map, indicating which features are present, and which ones are important or, perhaps, which ones are non-obvious, new, or strange. The missing legends leave the maps more open, less defined, and vaguer.

The set of symbols is nevertheless very similar throughout the maps. The outliers are the map in *Slaktare små* with its abstracted squares marking settlements, and the one in *Vanderland* with its completely new artistic style. The symbols show which information is important on the map (Ekman, *Here Be Dragons* 33), but, similarly, what is missing also conveys important information. The lack of roads on the maps of Middle-earth in Tolkien's works show the land as unpaved and wild (Ekman, *Here Be Dragons* 59), and roads are also often lacking from the *Svavelvinter* maps. The subject matter is quite consistent throughout the maps: mountains, hills, coastlines, settlements, forests, ice shelves. The lack of roads could be regarded as simultaneously limiting movement, because a road by its very nature is used to facilitate movement between two places, and opening up the possibility of movement, since no clear direction is thereby pointed out. If viewed as a gameboard, the map conveys the image of a world offering a multitude of potential moves. This is corroborated by many of the maps showing more place-names than are mentioned in the texts. The depicted world appears larger than what is described as the backdrop of the fiction.

Regarding modernity, the maps give off somewhat conflicting impressions. The *Vanderland* map of Clusta Noba is again an outlier, since its painted mountains resemble satellite photography. The way hills and mountains look on a map—what cartographers call hill signs—are an important way to chronologically situate map styles (Ekman, *Here Be Dragons* 41). The same can be said for forests. Here, those are marked by groups of individual trees, just as the symbol for settlements— except in *Slaktare små*—is groups of miniature houses. These map signs are a sort of metonymy. The presence of painted monsters and faux-medieval borders contributes to making the maps skeuomorphic, resembling a medieval manuscript. However, there are features that give the opposite impression. The text in many of the maps is obviously computer-typeset, even when a decorative antique-style font is used. And, perhaps more importantly, north is always pointed upwards, something that is not a given in older maps (Ekman, *Here Be Dragons* 25). It might be relevant to note that the cardinal directions mean different things in the fictional world of the novels and games, since, though the world is spherical, its north pole is eternally cold while the south pole is eternally scorching hot. The scale, frequently present, conveys a more modern, scientific look, even though it is labeled in Trakorian miles.

Some of these differences can be explained by the technological development of methods of production. Typography of a map is much easier in the 2000s than in the 1980s. Also, the great difference in map style between *Svavelvinter* and *Slaktare små* could be attributed to a change in publisher and the accompanying role-playing game being released before the second novel, letting the novel use the map created for the game. The map is reproduced in shrunken size, which does explain the scale of details and the miniaturization. Many place-names on the map are never mentioned in the novels, as the game needs to provide a larger world for the players to explore than can be described in the novels.

The monsters depicted on the maps are rarely the ones present in the stories: a giant on the ice does occur in the fiction and is depicted on the *Svavelvinter* map of Marjura, but there is nothing resembling the whale-like sea monsters that are so common on the maps. In fact, the monsters on the map in the first *Svavelvinter* novel appear to be copied from a map of Iceland from 1570, the *Theatrum Orbis Terrarum* by Abraham Ortelius.[1]

The presence of these monsters, together with the place-names that never occur in the text, could be said to mean that the maps expand the world of the text. The maps resemble archetypal maps, with their compass roses, scales, and elaborate borders. No matter if they are hand-painted or more obviously computer-generated, the maps depict an abstract world; they are material artifacts representing an ideal map, making the reader look at the map as a fantasy map. This creates a disconnection between the map and the text; the map is no longer a representation of the same space as the text when it describes the fictional world; instead, the map represents the concept of a fantasy map, being a second-order sign denoting the concept of a map, thereby activating the reader to jump between map and text to try to discern their differences, adapting different stances of reading and interpretation. The map is a tool in the creation of the fantasy space (cf. Siegert), transforming the reader into a player of a game, further strengthening the game-adjacent aspect of the novels.

To continue the parallels to Tolkien, the situation is not unlike that of a reader who follows along on the map in *The Lord of the Rings*, especially in the early editions in which the map was a separate, fold-out sheet, highlighting its materiality, as Per Israelson writes, when "the foreign-sounding names and strange places of Middle-earth obtain a geographical presence, triangulating reader, book and map in a distributed perception"

(183). The runes appearing on a tomb in the storyworld are depicted in an illustration in the novel, being the same runes as in the fiction (168). The images draw the reader into the fictional world, creating a participatory breach in the narrative levels.

A physical map can serve to increase the engagement of the reader. But going further, in one particular case in the novels, the map is also used as a figure of narrative metalepsis, creating a breach in the continuity of the storyworld. Because this is best understood through the lens of general ecology, there follows a study of general ecological themes in the novels and games, like the destabilization of human primacy, or the dissolution of delineation between living/nonliving.

Maps are metafictional devices. In the fictional world, the gods have created the world through the use of maps as blueprints, a sort of Platonic ideal of what the world should be like. When anything is changed on such a map, a corresponding change takes place in the world. This could be seen as a literal case of fantastic worldbuilding. In the novels, a piece of just such a divine map has gone missing and been tampered with, resulting in a part of the continental shelf getting stuck in the wrong place, since the titanic fire-creature carrying the crust on its back has gotten lost. Through manipulating the map, the protagonists solve puzzles in the narrative. Samuel R. Delany has pointed out in *Silent Interviews* that one characteristic of the fantastic is that metaphors can be understood literally—for example, the statement "her world exploded"—and this is what occurs here (27). The map is usually a representation of space; a fantasy map here is a representation of fictional space in text and image (Ekman, *Here Be Dragons* 20); the map can be seen as a metaphor for real or fictional space. In Granström's novels, the metaphorical step is broken, with the metaphor instead being read literally.

The reader can look at a representation of the same map printed in the book, while the protagonists in the narrative solve puzzles through manipulating the map; the boundary between reader and character is blurred or breached. When the map supersedes the actual territory, the reader and character converge with the author. Compare how the German media philosopher Bernhard Siegert states "the map is not the territory" in the sense that a map is more like an instrument and a tool than a representation of space. In fact, the map can be said to produce territory in a historically determined process, in a physical medium, creating the space it is depicting (13–14). Maps can bestow a more active role on the reader.

As Granström has a character exclaim: "No, no, the holy weave is no map. It is no reproduction at all. It *is* the reality" ["Nej, nej, den heliga väven är ingen karta. Den är alls ingen avbildning. Den *är* verkligheten"] (Granström, *Vredesverk* 520, italics in the original). In the text-world, the map is said to be real and not a reproduction or representation. This is shown through how minor changes to the map-weave affect the world. A blue thread in the weave can be removed to drain the water blocking the path forward, because then it has never existed (Granström, *Vanderland* 378). In another place, a drop of sweat falling upon the map causes a flood in the world. So, the map both exists in the world and is an image of the world. The map becomes not just a representation of space, but space itself: not a metaphoric statement, but a literal one. One could say, as does literary scholar Andrew Thacker, that the barrier between social and material space becomes blurred or breaks down. Even, at one point, while discussing the divine book of creation in the novel, there is a spread in *Vanderland* that is completely empty, save for the single sentence "I can hear pages turn" ["Jag kan höra blad vändas"] (Granström, *Vanderland* 452). This brings to mind concrete poetry, where the placement of words on the page is of utmost importance and can be seen as a case of what Thacker describes as textual space having impact on literary style. Within the language and typography of the book, space is represented (Thacker 63).

The characters in the novel solve the puzzle by comparing maps from different time periods and realizing that the island of Marjura has slowly been spinning in place around a certain point, instead of moving slowly southwards as was the wish of the gods. This is due to halted continental drift, caused by the primordial fire creature on whose back the continental shelf rests having been pinned into place by someone manipulating the gods's map of the world (Granström, *Vredesverk* 480–81; Granström, *Vanderland* 210). This is taken one step further in the games, where two conflicting maps can be found in the game, then presented as in-game artifacts to the players to solve the riddle. The maps are thus a crucial part in activating the players and letting them move the story forward. Puzzles are common in role-playing games, but this one is unusually materially anchored, as it relies on the players handling physical maps, engaging them not just through the characters they control or inhabit.

There is also a second map-based puzzle in one of the adventures, *Kristalltjuren*, the part of the story where novel and game diverge the most. It is a classic treasure map where the players have to navigate through a set of rebus-like instructions to find the entrance to an underground chamber (Granström, *Kristalltjuren* 15). There is in *Kristalltjuren* another map-based transgression of narrative levels. In a very Gnostic tale, the characters become imprisoned in a small, failing world created by an incompetent demiurge, a lower creation deity. Once they finally escape, they realize they have been living inside a rolled-up scroll on the demiurge's workbench: the dark sea they saw was made of spilled wine, the glacier was a piece of cheese, and the giant monsters they have been fighting are mites spreading from a moldy part of the parchment. The scroll is the map of the world, and at the same time it is the world itself; hereby map and world become one.

These metafictional maps, both in the games and the novels, form a clear case of the importance of generally ecological themes throughout Granström's work. As media theorist Bruce Clarke has outlined, the self-reflexivity and recursive elements of a narrative metalepsis means metafiction is a cybernetic process, best understood through feedback systems (Clarke, passim), an important part of the general ecological theory complex (cf. Burton 256). There are many such cases.

Several of these cases are connected to the dissolution of the difference between living and unliving matter. In the fictional world, objects frequently act and speak, similarly to people (cf. Bennett). The mountain of Ranz has a voice but speaks so slowly that only specially trained monks can understand its speech. This recalls how the philosopher Timothy Morton, in the treatise of "ecological thought," has pointed out that there are nonhuman entities in the real world, not only animals, possessing language, imagination, and reason (Morton 71); this concept also ties into Morton's observation on vast timescales, such as how fossils connect the true age of the Earth to the contemporary world (Morton 42). Furthermore, the very continental shelves are attached to the backs of living fire-creatures; a magical fortress of stone grows organically from a seed; a magical dagger speaks to its bearer; and a demon materializes in the form of a statue, a sword or a plague.

The antagonist Shagul is one mind in several cloned bodies, breaking up the anthropocentrism and the humanistic mind-body complex. The Kaklun is an amoeba-like but intelligent entity that absorbs any new organism it encounters, existing as a collective consisting of parts of hundreds of creatures—a literal embodiment of the concept of assemblage, the idea that agency does not primarily belong to humans but to networks of nonhuman beings and objects, with the network of objects having primacy over the objects themselves (cf. Latour). The theoretical metaphor of assemblage is here literalized. A monstrosity such as this thus serves to break down human/non-human distinction, as Nikita Mazurov details in "Monster" in the *Posthuman Glossary* (262).

An especially important case of metafictionality in the novels is that one character, superficially human, turns out to be the physical manifestation of a book, one of the gods's creation books made flesh (Granström, *Vanderland* 534). The true gods in the setting are called narrators, and this confluence between divine and narratorial power takes on other forms. The villain Shagul wishes to break free of the tyranny of the narrators, using the titular conflux—the point in spacetime at which the world can change its course—to take full ownership of his own name and break out of the story.

> Shagul felt free. He was strong. Still, he was struck by doubt. Was he after all only the written one and the read one? Were there beyond the world of his own imagination another scene on which he was a marionette among others, a scene where his defiance became but a spicy play? ["Shagul kände sig fri. Han var stark. Ändå drabbades han av tvivel. Var han trots allt bara den skrivne och den läste? Fanns bortom hans egen föreställnings värld ytterligare en scen på vilken han var en marionett bland andra, en scen där hans trots endast blev ett pikant utspel?" (Granström, *Slaktare små* 614)]

As in classic romantic irony, the reader and the author are drawn into the storyworld. British cultural theorist James Burton has pointed out that metafictional loops are essentially ecological, through the cybernetic nature of feedback connecting reader, writer and storyworld: that "worldmaking [...] is already akin to metafiction" (267). The fantastic is intimately tied to the practice of worldmaking or worldbuilding (Martin and Sneegas 15), which is here made manifest on the level of the textworld.

One female character having been male in an earlier version of the story is an in-joke referring to how Granström changed the character when writing (Granström, *Svavelvinter* 383; Granström, "Språkets roll i Trakorien - Metafysik 1"). This is not unlike how, as Israelson points out, in *The Lord of the Rings* Frodo refers to "the other tale," meaning a first edition of *The Hobbit* which later was partly rewritten (126), and how Frodo and Sam refer to themselves as part of a fairy-tale (Israelson 135). Even in that seminal fantasy novel, the metafictional is present. Another metafictional loop is opened and closed in the penultimate chapter of the last novel, *Vanderland*, in an epilogue summarizing the resolution of the story. The chronicler there makes remarks about not only how the geography seems to have changed, the island of Marjura no longer where it should be according to the maps; but also that "the chronicle is divided and bound into four separate volumes, mirroring the phases of the story" ["att krönikan delas och binds i fyra separate volymer som speglar berättelsens faser"] (Granström, *Vanderland* 589). The *Conflux* series itself does consist of four volumes.

Finally, a quite different ecological aspect of the novels is the media-ecological system created by the novels along with the role-playing games and adventures. But this ecology, too, contributes to engage the reader and strengthen the participatory aesthetic of the text.

In the introduction, I describe the overall story of the *Fifth Conflux* transformed from role-playing game adventures into novels. This process is chronicled by Granström on his blog, starting in 2008 with the work on *Slaktare små*, the second novel in the series (Granström, "Om Tankar från Trakorien"). There, the author engages in a dialogue with new readers and old players, drawing the presumptive reader into the creative process. Many of the overt and covert references in the texts are explained.

This process forms a parallel with parodies and fan-fiction continuations of Tolkien's stories. Israelson maps the similarities between unauthorized parodies, Tolkien's own revisions, and the large number of new editions of backstories compiled by Tolkien's son Christopher Tolkien, showing the importance of co-creation in the aesthetic of the fantastic (150–62). In Granström's work, the expansion of the text into different media and throughout different publishing channels and communities is part of a feedback loop, as the game's adventures tie into the novels, which are then turned into role-playing games. Between the publication of the first and second novels in the series, in 2012, the publisher Fria Ligan released a role-playing game based on both the novels and the old adventures, also called *Svavelvinter*. By playing the game, readers of Granström's novels can participate in their own expansion of the fictional world. As Dimitra Nikolaidou writes, "[w]hile the game book is created by game designers, published, and sold to the players, its setting will only come alive when players narrate their own stories within" (222). Role-playing games engage players as co-creators, and in established fictional worlds, allow for expanding an already-existing narrative.

This also foregrounds the affective part of collaborative creation, as Israelson points out in an argument based on David Punday's writing, highlighting that it is "not merely a matter of adapting a literary text into a game format; the adaptation is also provoked by and highlights the presence of an ergodic and participatory textuality in the source text" (Israelson 162). Erik van Ooijen has also remarked that a gameworld forces the player to use affective capabilities to create meaning out of their environment, building upon how Jakob von Uexküll claims that every world has to be a world for someone (30). Similarly, Jonas Linderoth points out that a game forces the player to work more for immersion than a reader of text (Linderoth 1).

The interaction between Granström and presumptive readers on his blog bestows a more active role upon the reader. Analyzing the maps above, I show how both the map-based puzzles and the act of following along on the map transform the reader into a game-player. Together, these aspects serve to highlight a game-like quality of the novels, further strengthened by how they interact with the role-playing games. Games also occur as a motif in the text; for example, one character describes ordinary people as "pieces in the great boardgame of the gods" ["spelpjäser i gudarnas stora smickelbräde" (smickelbräde being the name of a popular boardgame in Trakorien)] whereas "the dragons are, so to say, part of the very board" [drakarna är så att säga en del av själva brädet"] (Granström, *Svavelvinter* 262). In the game, the player is a co-creator. Something similar is at work in the novels: the reader takes an active role due to the game-like qualities of the text, and in the media-ecological system of Granström's writing; furthermore, the novels employ games as a theme.

In general, a player has no privileged position relative to the game being played. He or she is a part of it, connected to the game through its systems, rules and procedures, having been drawn into the game-world, no longer being able to stand outside. Thus, one could claim that the game is more suited than the text as the model of cultural interaction in a time where the anthropocentric nature of the Anthropocene is increasingly being questioned. Taken all together, this highlights what Israelson has called the participatory aesthetics of the fantastic: "The fantastic object is in this sense a quasi-object, a thing in movement and a thing with agency, magically disrupting any clear and oppositional distinction between nature and culture, form and content, meaning and presence" (355). This further shows how these texts transgress the material boundary of the format of the classical novel.

In this article, I have studied a few cases highlighting the transgression of material boundaries in the fantastic aesthetic object: between reader and textworld as the reader interprets maps in the book, between map and textworld territory as the map can magically affect the space it depicts, and between narrative levels in the text by metafictional leaps. This has been done by employing tools and strategies connected to the field of general ecology, encompassing themes such as the dissolution of boundaries between human and nonhuman actors, between living and nonliving matter, between nature and culture, and decentralizing the place of humanity in the world at large. I have shown how the fantastic mode affords specific methods for blurring form and content, for example, when the map occurs as metaphor, theme and form. The hybrid nature of this fantastic aesthetic object reveals ecological themes in the texts, and also contributes to making the reader a co-creator of the aesthetic experience.

This transgressive property of the fantastic shows the importance of studying that form of literature in this age of increasing ecologization of space, of reconfigurations and renegotiations: migration and globalization simultaneously transcend and highlight issues of physical borders and of places blending into each other; technological developments in augmented reality and online communications blur the lines between virtual and actual space; the concept of the Anthropocene highlights how humanity is reshaping the physical world; AI is rapidly increasing in complexity and power. In the fantastic, these aspects of the world are made especially visible; the metaphors can take on literal meanings, as has been argued by Samuel R. Delany, bringing light to how nature and technology, science and culture, human and non-human interact and intertwine: in short, the importance of ecology. As Rebecca Evans has put it, the world is science fiction now (2); therefore, scholars need to study the fantastic to understand the world.

Notes

1. Many thanks to Stefan Ekman for alerting me of this observation in personal correspondence.
2. Trakorien is the territory; "Trakorian" is the adjectival version.

Works Cited

Bennett, Jane. *Vibrant Matter: A Political Ecology of Things*. Duke University Press, 2010.

Burton, James. "Metafiction and General Ecology: Making Worlds with Words." *General Ecology: The New Ecological Paradigm*, edited by Erich Hörl and James Burton, Bloomsbury Academic, 2017, 253–284.

Clarke, Bruce. *Neocybernetics and Narrative*. University of Minnesota Press, 2014.

Delany, Samuel R. *Silent Interviews: On Language, Race, Sex, Science Fiction, and Some Comics: A Collection of Written Interviews*. Wesleyan University Press, 1994.

Ekman, Stefan. *Here Be Dragons: Exploring Fantasy Maps and Settings*. Wesleyan University Press, 2013.

---. "Map and Text: World-Architecture and the Case of Miéville's Perdido Street Station." *Literary Geographies*, vol. 4, no. 1, February 2018, 66–83.

Evans, Rebecca. "Nomenclature, Narrative, and Novum: 'The Anthropocene' and/as Science Fiction." *Science Fiction Studies*, vol. 45, no. 3, 2018, 484–499. *JSTOR*, https://doi.org/10.5621/sciefictstud.45.3.0484.

Fuller, Matthew. *Media Ecologies: Materialist Energies in Art and Technoculture*. MIT Press, 2005.

Granström, Erik. "About Mörkrets Tid." *Tankar från Trakorien*, 15 Apr. 2018, http://erik-granstrom.blogspot.com/2018/04/about-morkrets-tid.html.

---. *Kristalltjuren*. Target Games, 1992.

---. "Om Tankar från Trakorien." *Tankar från Trakorien*, 9 Dec. 2008, http://erik-granstrom.blogspot.com/2008/12/om-tankar-frn-trakorien.html.

---. *Slaktare små: Andra delen av krönikan om den Femte Konfluxen.* Coltso, 2011.

---. "Språkets roll i Trakorien - Metafysik 1." *Tankar Från Trakorien*, 9 Dec. 2008, https://erik-granstrom.blogspot.com/2008/12/sprkets-roll-i-trakorien-1.html.

---. *Svavelvinter: Första delen av krönikan om den Femte Konfluxen.* Svensk fantasy, 2004.

---. *Vanderland: Fjärde delen av krönikan om den Femte Konfluxen.* Coltso, 2017.

---. *Vredesverk: Tredje delen av krönikan om den Femte Konfluxen.* Coltso, 2014.

Haraway, Donna Jeanne. *Simians, Cyborgs, and Women: The Reinvention of Nature.* Free Association Books, 1991.

Hörl, Erich, and James Burton. *General Ecology: The New Ecological Paradigm.* Bloomsbury Academic, 2017.

Israelson, Per. *Ecologies of the Imagination: Theorizing the Participatory Aesthetics of the Fantastic.* Department of Culture and Aesthetics, Stockholm University, 2017.

Kress, Gunther R. *Multimodality: A Social Semiotic Approach to Contemporary Communication.* Routledge, 2010.

Latour, Bruno. *Reassembling the Social: An Introduction to Actor-Network-Theory.* Oxford University Press, 2005, http://hdl.handle.net/2027/heb.32135.

Lilja, Mattias et al. *Svavelvinter: Rollspel i Erik Granströms Trakorien.* Fria ligan, 2012.

Linderoth, Jonas. "The Effort of Being in a Fictional World: Upkeyings and Laminated Frames in MMORPGs." *Symbolic Interaction*, vol. 35, no. 4, 2012, 474–492. *Wiley Online Library*, https://doi.org/10.1002/symb.39.

Martin, Jeff Vance, and Gretchen Sneegas. "Critical Worldbuilding: Toward a Geographical Engagement with Imagined Worlds." *Literary Geographies*, vol. 6, no. 1, June 2020, 15–23.

Mazurov, Nikita. "Monster/The Unhuman." *Posthuman Glossary*, edited by Rosi Braidotti and Maria Hlavajova, Bloomsbury Academic, 2018, 261–264.

Morton, Timothy. *The Ecological Thought*. Harvard University Press, 2010.

Nikolaidou, Dimitra. "The Evolution of Fantastical Storyworlds: A Study of Tabletop Role-Playing Settings." *Ex-Centric Narratives: Journal of Anglophone Literature, Culture and Media*, vol. 1, no. 2, Dec. 2018, 218–229. *ejournals.lib.auth.gr*, https://doi.org/10.26262/exna.v1i2.6741.

Ooijen, Erik van. "Att äta digitala djur: Spel, våld och ideologi." *Tidskrift för Litteraturvetenskap*, vol. 45, no. 4, Jan. 2015, 29–41. *publicera.kb.se*, https://doi.org/10.54797/tfl.v45i4.8944.

Ortelius, Abraham. *Theatrum Orbis Terrarum*. 1570.

Parikka, Jussi. "Deep Times and Media Mines: A Descent into Ecological Materiality of Technology." *General Ecology. The New Ecological Paradigm*, edited by Erich Hörl and James Burton, Bloomsbury Academic, 2017, pp. 169–192.

Siegert, Bernhard. "The Map Is the Territory: Dossier: What Is German Media Philosophy?" *Radical Philosophy*, no. 169, 2011. *www.radicalphilosophy.com*, https://www.radicalphilosophy.com/article/the-map-is-the-territory.

Svavelvinter - Encyclopaedia Metallum: The Metal Archives, https://www.metal-archives.com/bands/Svavelvinter/3540388779. Accessed 19 May 2023.

Tally, Robert T. *Spatiality*. Routledge, 2012.

---. *Topophrenia: Place, Narrative, and the Spatial Imagination*. Indiana University Press, 2019.

Thacker, Andrew. "The Idea of a Critical Literary Geography." *New Formations*, vol. 2005, no. 57, December 2005, *journals.lwbooks.co.uk*, https://journals.lwbooks.co.uk/newformations/vol-2005-issue-57/abstract-8321/.

Reviews

Anastasio, Matteo, Margot Brink, Lisa Dauth, Andrew Erickson, Isabelle Leitloff, Jan Rhein, Editors. *Transnationale Literaturen und Literaturtransfer im 20. und 21. Jarhrhundert: Plurilinguale und interdisziplinare Perspektiven.* [transcript], 2023. 240 pp. ISBN: 978-3-8376-6471-3 (pbk.) ISBN: 978-3-8394-6471-7 (pdf)

The English version of the "Presentation" or introduction to *Transnational Literatures and Literary Transfer in the 20th and 21st Century* asks "in which ways do concepts such as *transnationalism, world literature(s), creolization* and *diachronic interculturalism* contribute to understanding contemporary literature [emphases in the original text]?" as well as querying "To what extent do postcolonial perspectives inaugurate futures beyond (literary) nationalisms and (cultural) hegemonies?" The "Presentation" explains that its "contributions indicate a spectrum of transnational literatures, with their aporias, borders and concepts of freedom as well as the concepts and theories that accompany them" (frontispiece).

This deeply thoughtful assemblage of essays on the above topics originates from lectures delivered in German, English, French, and Spanish at the Europa-Universität in Flensburg, Germany, assembled in three sections in the collection. The first section offers "considerations of literary studies as it is shaped by transnational and transcultural or intercultural perspectives" (frontispiece). The second section, titled "Traveling Concepts: Book Markets, Education and Political Discourse," is summarized as engaging "with aspects of cultural and theoretical transmission" (ibid). The third section, titled "Transnational and Transcultural Crossings," is described as the "most comprehensive" and credited with focusing "on postcolonial perspectives and related topics, such as migration and exile" (ibid). This review discusses the essays in English, French and Spanish, three of the languages I read. I found each of the four essays in the languages I do read fascinating, detailed, classically thorough in each essay's presentation of a critical contribution advancing established scholarship, and original in their research. In fact, I found the essays I was able to read in their entirety so promisingly thought-provoking that I could not help but come away from this impressive collection regretting, perhaps for the first time in my scholarly career, that I do not also read German and therefore could not enjoy those chapters in their entirety.

"'La créolisation est l'avenir de l'humanité': Créolisation et migration de Glissant à Mélenchon" ["'Creolization is the future of humanity': Creolization and migration (as theorized) by Glissant and (adapted by) Mélenchon," my translation]
   -Martina Kopf

In "'La créolisation est l'avenir de l'humanité': Créolisation et migration de Glissant à Mélenchon" ["'Creolization is the future of humanity': Creolization and migration (as theorized) by Glissant and (adapted by) Mélenchon," my translation], Martina Kopf analyzes how to make a practical political application of a poetic vision of unification in a disparate society. "La créolisation" opens with the French electoral campaign's 2022 left-wing leader, Jean-Luc Mélenchon, positioning present-day French society and the future of the world as becoming creolized, borrowing a concept put forth by Édouard Glissant, a philosophical cultural theoretician from Martinique. The Abstract in English summarizes, "Creolization is not limited to a postcolonial Caribbean context but must be seen as a global movement that also raises questions about nation, migration, and integration" (84), but situates politician Mélenchon's argument specifically as "an idealizing description of a diverse French society, in which there is no distinction between French and migrants and in which no one dominates the other" (84), while troubling the concordance of Mélenchon's conclusions with Glissant's theories. Mélenchon is quoted in a 2021 speech pointing out that the French favor couscous, pizza and rap music, leading to Kopf's study of Mélenchon's choice to centralize the Caribbean philosopher's postcolonial concept as a unifying political vision for France. Kopf points out that, in centering a postcolonial Caribbean theory as fundamental to French self-conceptualization, Mélenchon has enacted a noteworthy equalizing revolutionary approach to French political discourse.

Glissant, styled as "poet of a future world" (<< poète d'un monde à venir >>) in a 2020 broadcast of France Culture, has proposed a vision of creolization that Kopf explains as an alchemy intended for the entire world, envisaging human relations characterized by enrichment, variability and sharing, evolving into an unforeseeable multiple identity characterized by diversity (87). Kopf thereby argues that Glissant's concept of creolization is not solely intended to be viewed in a postcolonial Caribbean context but instead visualized as a worldwide movement in which cultural identity is neither an essence nor immutable, but a dynamic response to an individual's choices of diverse self-expressions. Based on Glissant and Chamoiseau's call for French recognition of an interpenetration of cultures brought on by not only contact but ongoing migration (89), Kopf develops a series of arguments in which racism and nationalism cede to a larger wholistic concept of humanity being in a constant trans-mutational process of creolization in which human contact across such boundary descriptions continually renews and enriches relations (90).

Mélenchon is quoted as taking up Glissant's concept of creolization as a way to continually self-transform without losing oneself, and even as a space where what has been shattered, disordered, and disharmonized can reassemble itself, absorbing the disparate hostilities of even the most recent political disruptions into a positive and creative future (91). In this way, Kopf concludes, Mélenchon poses the concept of creolization as counter to conservative national identity hierarchical politics. Mélenchon distinguishes France as a nation that has already undertaken foundational creolization in the precepts of the French Revolution (92), thereby distancing his adaptation of the concept of creolization from Glissant's own: Kopf summarizes that creolization (Glissant) and Republican universalism (Mélenchon) are difficult concepts to reconcile (93).

However, as Kopf quotes Laetitia Riss, if Glissant's concept of creolization is one of "a reachable utopia and an unstoppable process" (93), then perhaps Mélenchon has offered what Kopf calls a "traveling concept" of that theory, transposing on French identity the process of migration and the inclusion of immigrants as integral to French identity, still insisting that neither peoples dominate the other and embracing the creolization concept's capacity to admit change and interaction, rejecting what is static, conservative and immovable (93).

"Transiciones entre <nacional> y <mundial>: La exhibición de países y literaturas en ferias internacionales del libro" ["Transitions between 'national' and 'global': The exhibition of countries and literatures in international book fairs," my translation]
   -Matteo Anastasio

In "Transiciones entre <nacional> y <mundial> : La exhibición de países y literaturas en ferias internacionales del libro" ["Transitions between 'national' and 'global': The exhibition of countries and literatures in international book fairs," my translation], Matteo Anastasio argues that expositions and programs with Guests of Honor at book fairs do not limit themselves to reproducing traditional cultural canons but propose provisional canons that are relative and circumstantial to fair attendants (102). Anastasio explains that, if the function of a canon is to indicate common references in a society or culture, as argued by Pozuelo Yvancos, then the book fair, with its Guest of Honor, produces a separation between a culture and its society, to reuse elements and references that the Guest of Honor puts into dialogue as points of contact in common between international communities (102-3). Anastasio summarizes that such events redefine a non-canonical transnational literary space (<espacios literarios> 104) in which it is within the power of Guests of Honor to highlight a specific global dimension of their literature and open avenues of global "bibliomigration," referencing Venkat B. Mani's definition of "the physical and virtual migration of literature" (104). This displacement or relocation of literary products and activities between places, languages, customary values, and differing intertextual relations reconfigures differing global systems, illustrating the plurality of forces and directions interacting in each space under consideration (105). In this context, Anastasio discourses on the problematization of Goethe's Eurocentric concept of a potential world literature and displaces this with Pascale Casanova's vision of a world literature built intentionally upon the political and economic separations and rivalries between nations, not the valorizations recognized within them (106-7). These polar approaches to the building of a world literature or literatures of the world lead to Gesine Müller's proposal of consideration of, firstly, the undeniable importance of

204 • Reviews

a work of literature, and secondarily the consideration of a text or author from an underrecognized world region. Anastasio concludes with recognition of the impact of Guests of Honor in intervening in interstitial spaces and transversal movements that break national and global dialectics of canonization, deconstructing both (108). This essay thereby succeeds in focusing and intensifying academic awareness of the ethical issues implicit in offering and accepting the distinguished role of Guest of Honor or Distinguished Scholar, given these honored roles' implicit empowerment to step forward as intercultural ambassadors and selectors of the materials and theories driving development of an international literary canon.

"Sowing the Black Atlantic in Octavia E. Butler's *Parables*: Transnational African Knowledge Transfer in Black American Speculative Fiction"
   -Andrew Erickson

Andrew Erickson's "Sowing the Black Atlantic in Octavia E. Butler's *Parables*: Transnational African Knowledge Transfer in Black American Speculative Fiction" opens with his assessment that "amid the apocalyptic violence of the Middle Passage, ideas and identities were forged anew, blending worlds and ways of knowing and being" and his theoretical argument that, "This is perhaps nowhere more evident than in the imagination and materialization of Black American Speculative Fiction (SF) and its Afrofuturism" (139). Erickson begins his study acknowledging that, "Butler, like many Afrofuturist and Black SF makers, understands the generational aftermath of enslavement as a space of violent destruction and dystopia" that nevertheless "continues to carve out spaces for renewal and recovery of Black American and/as Afrodiasporic visions of the future" (140).

In this way, it is Erickson's thesis that "transnational Black Atlantic cultural productions speak to the heterogeneity of Black experiences and their many movements throughout the spaces of the Black Diaspora, all the while continually carrying with them ways of knowing and being that (re)situate and/or (re)imagine African origins" (141), arguing that Butler's *Parables* "develop a heterogenous plurality of African and/as Black American knowledges in response to the despair of world destruction" (142).

Erickson highlights Deborah Wood Holton's recognition of Oya, the middle name of the *Parables'* central character Lauren Olamina, as a Yoruba and West African goddess of disruption, literally centered as Lauren discovers her religious dicta centered on the power of embracing change. In light of this religious connection signaled by Butler, Erickson concludes that "African knowledge and ongoing right relation with ancestors remain essential to the survival of [Butler's] characters and the (Afro)futures they work to bring about" (143). Erickson recognizes and pays tribute to the apparent prescience of Butler's *Parables* having been written in the 1990s about the apocalyptic world inexorably approaching but not globally recognized until the earliest 2020s, noting that Lauren's actions as a teenaged child are "strategies for surviving the apocalyptic conditions of twenty-first century America [that] arise out of knowledges from another world-ending period—namely, the European colonization and enslavement of African peoples and places" (143). Clarifying the historical relevance of Lauren Oya Olamina's mimicking of her ancestresses' actions in the saving and hoarding of seeds for transmission to and rebuilding in a safer space, Erickson specifically identifies "Seed-keeping, a particular relationship to land and movements on it, and ongoing resistance to external forms of oppression," as evidence of the "transfer of knowledge from one generation to another, sometimes across significant genealogical and geographical leaps of time and space [that] indicates the Black Atlantic at work in Butler's Black American speculative fiction" (143).

Erickson cites Leah Penniman's study that "the collected seeds moved along with the kidnapped women across the Middle Passage to the Americas" (Erickson 144), proving that Lauren, similarly "removed from her home by the violence of world-destruction," pursues the establishment of Earthseed as a lifestyle built on that joint faith in change and personal perseverance. In this way, Erickson argues, Butler's protagonist "recalls the home of her youth alongside a longer generational awareness of African origins and her place among the Back Diaspora" (144), establishing "something more akin to a controlled dystopia" (145). Erickson points out that "Planting trees among the dead remembers them in the community," and will "provide sustaining nourishment for the living, body and soul" (145); thus, Lauren's carefully planned, protected and planted new trees become "the embodiment of transitioned ancestors" (146). Establishing fitting terminology for this process of positivizing forced and violent relocation as a hopeful and faith-based project, Erickson concludes that it is Lauren's prescient "Reworlding a future amid a ruined past" that "foregrounds the restored balance in the relationship among Black farmers, ancestors, and land" (146).

Erickson's detailed and irrefutable establishment of the link between Butler's depiction of apocalyptic violence and displacement and her teenage protagonist's determination to rebuild community among like-minded strangers by carrying literal and figurative seeds of hope, community and futurity proves that Butler's *Parables* "thus functions as a primary vehicle for driving the transfer of restored and/or reimagined African knowledges toward Afrofutures among the Diaspora" (147). Erickson's study is thus established as a significant contribution to and imperative reading for students and scholars of Butler Studies, of her *Parables*, and of the implications of African and

Diaspora traditionality as evidenced in Speculative Fiction, SF, and, specifically, in the growing field of Afrofuturism.

"The 'Eastern' and 'Irish' Questions: Bram Stoker's *Dracula* in the Periodicals"
   -Michelle Witen

In "The 'Eastern' and 'Irish' Questions: Bram Stoker's *Dracula* in the Periodicals," Michelle Witen examines the intersections of British periodical culture at the end of the nineteenth century—the time of the publication of *Dracula*—with what were known as the Eastern and Irish Questions. The Eastern Question regarded "the importance of Turkey to the European Great Powers" (213), while the Irish Question was "to determine Ireland's place within the British Empire" (213); Witen's approach to these overlaid Questions takes into consideration as well "the effect of periodical culture on the dissemination of news" (213). Witen reviews how Britain's "repeal of the taxes on knowledge" (214) removed "additional taxes for advertisements (1853), stamps (1855), and the weight of paper (1861)" (214), thus permitting a rapid increase in both the frequency of output due to increasing demand for periodicals, so that they became available daily, and the range of classes and social standing of people who bought and read them as often as they were printed, "giving rise to a mass media environment" (215). Conflating Ireland's fight for self-governance with Britain's suspicious sense of superiority to Eastern Europe though it suspected that it might need alliance with Turkey, Witen describes John Tenniel's illustration in *Punch* of 4 February, 1893 that depicts Gladstone as a genie rising from a bottle labeled "Session," and "telling tales of Irish geographic and economic independence" in contrast to the *Arabian Nights/1,001 Nights* storyteller, "Scheherezade, who tells stories every night to amuse the monarch and keep him from raping and beheading her" (218), graphically drawing attention to the contemporary reader's sense of the manipulation, high stakes and trickery involved in the political Questions debated at the end of the nineteenth century in Parliament. The next Tenniel illustration of that period depicts "The Temptation of Good St. Gladstone" (223) dressed as a hooded monk and beset by Home Rule as a crone disguised as a young woman, in the company of a bevy of flying and creeping bat-winged politicians who foreshadow Tenniel's 24 October 1885 depiction of a man-sized "Irish Vampire" with National League across its chest. The "Irish Vampire" hovers with its bat wings outstretched lasciviously over a sleeping Hibernia/Erin who, while representing Ireland, has dark hair, headdress and ankle-gathered trousers that make her appear remarkably reminiscent of Sheherezade (224).

Witen likens British Othering of the Irish to that of the Eastern European, pointing out that, "It is interesting to note how the wolf, bat, and supernatural caricatures that are used to represent and vilify Irish people in the periodicals of the time are similarly used as demonizing markers for Dracula in Stoker's text" (228), concluding that "Stoker uses these images to represent Dracula as Other, at a time when Irish people are being similarly Othered" (228). That Tenniel's genie, wolves, illusory virgin, and bats as "animals and supernatural images that are used as tools of demonization for the Eastern and Irish Other alike" (231) bear a striking similarity to the seductive and terrifying denizens of the castle of Stoker's Dracula is further complicated by Witen's pointing out that the fictional Jonathan Harker discovers a collection of British periodicals in Dracula's library.

Bram Stoker's *Dracula*'s pause in the library to reference the Eastern European Count's substantial collection thereby suggests that the vampire has benefited from the popular and affordably available British periodicals to educate himself to English cultural fluency, if not societal correctness or assimilation. In this way,

Witen's very engaging study makes it clear that both the Eastern Other and his remarkably similar Irish Other are simultaneously being seen as threatening the British Empire (229-230) through their manipulation of information that has been readily and regularly supplied to them by the very periodicals that caricature their cultures.

ALEXIS BROOKS DE VITA is a Regular Graduate Faculty member and Full Professor at Texas Southern University, a historically African American university founded as Texas state's concession to losing Thurgood Marshall's Supreme Court presentation of *Sweatt versus Painter,* the lawsuit that preceded Marshall's *Brown versus Board of Regents.* Dr. Brooks de Vita serves as the Accessibility and Sensitivity Coordinator and Submissions and Reviews Editor for Africa and the African Diaspora for the *Journal of the Fantastic in the Arts.*

Kimberly Cleveland, *Africanfuturism: African Imaginings of Other Times, Spaces, and Worlds.* Ohio: Ohio University Press, 2024. 200 pp.

Around the late 19th and early 20th centuries, and shortly after most of the African countries gained their independence, the struggle to break free from ever-invasive Eurocentric proclivities of Whitewashing almost all African literary, historical, and creative productions ushered in the era of decolonization characterizing the works of W.E.B. Du Bois, Aime Cesaire, Kwame Nkrumah, Leopold Sedar Senghor, Ngugi wa Thiong'o, Walter Rodney, Amilcar Cabral, Frantz Fanon, and a host of other prominent scholars. The ember of this bequeathed legacy, looking forward into the future, is what scholars and artists such as Alondra Nelson, Ytasha Womack, Sun Ra, Octavia Estelle Butler, Djwali Kumalo, Nkisi Crutchfield, Reynaldo Anderson, Samuel Delany, and others kept fanning until the term "Afrofuturism" was coined by "Mark Dery, in his 1993 seminal essay on science fiction literature, 'Black to the Future'" (Cleveland 1), wherein he proposes the need to carve a niche for Afrocentric speculative narratives about the future that addresses African American concerns in the context of twentieth-century techno-culture. But with the release of Ryan Coogler's *Black Panther* twenty-five years later, the scholarly and discursive scope of Afrofuturism has grown to encompass African-based futurist works from multiple sites across the Diaspora and the African continent. This practice has engulfed cross-cultural, Diaspora, and intercontinental African speculative fictions from diverse disciplines and periods, triggering reactions from Africanists and African creatives on the continent against "the extension of the Afrofuturist label to African creative work without distinction" (Cleveland 2). This reaction has led to the emergence of "African Futurism" as a phrase employed by Phatsimo Sunstrum "for African productions in different mediums characterized by a number of common themes" (Suntrum 114), followed by the term "Africanfuturism" popularized by Nnedi Okorafor in 2019, as an intellectual lens more suited for the continent-centered future-related speculative expressions of Africans. The nuances, divergence, and points of convergence of Africanfuturism vis-à-vis Afrofuturism imbued with analysis of African speculative works from the continent are the preoccupation of Kimberly Cleveland's *Africanfuturism: African Imaginings of Other Times, Spaces, and Worlds*.

Cleveland deconstructs the uniqueness of Africanfuturism "as a body of African speculative expression that is distinguishable from, albeit unquestionably related to 'Afrofuturism'" (Cleveland 2) by engaging the roots of African speculative thoughts and imaginings via the meta-critical analysis of the productions of African creatives from diverse locations and mediums in Africa. The relational valences that characterize Afrofuturism and Africanfuturism are systematically engaged and clarified via this expository project by the way Cleveland harnesses the debates around Africanfuturism with surveys of key African texts, media, and productions that resonate with rich African mythological, spiritual, historical, and digital culture tropes, trends in African science fiction, and African concepts of time and space. Thus, Cleveland contextualizes the significance of "African" in "the perspective of the interests, concerns, and tendencies of contemporary African cultural producers [of speculative fictions] related to an African yet to come" (Cleveland 10). The text resolves the fluidity of "African" in "Africanfuturism" and clarifies that the interpretation of Africanfuturism as an African-centered intellectual lens for identifying and analyzing African creative expressions to foreground African perspectives, strategies, and concepts is not to outline a rigidly narrow category for the purpose of exclusion but "to use it to connect the contemporary contributions of African creatives across forms of expression and geographic spaces to the larger body of speculative production" (Cleveland 9). This clarification aligns with Wole Talabi's (8) standpoint on the distinction between the two terms maintained while quoting Okorafor's 2019 blog:

> Africanfuturism is similar to 'Afrofuturism' in the way that Blacks on the continent and in the Black Diaspora are all connected by blood, spirit, history, and future. The difference is that Africanfuturism is specifically and more directly rooted in African culture, history, mythology, and point-of-view as it then branches into the Black Diaspora, and it does not privilege or center the West. (Talabi 8)

In Chapter One, Cleveland, via the lens of John Reider's 2008 study (Reider 4-6), establishes how Africa's relationship to Eurocentric speculative expression, including Afrofuturism, is historically linked to colonial projects on the continent. She submits that African Americans became interested in featuring African themes and tropes in their speculative fiction towards the second half of the twentieth century, based on their Diaspora concerns and equal rights struggles to establish a deeper connection with Africa and work against the interests of a Whitewashed future in the United States. While Cleveland elucidates the positive and negative effects of Afrofuturism on the works of African producer, she interprets the obvious disruption of Eurocentric dominant influences on the continent by Afrofuturists and Africanfuturists as being due to the impetus of decolonization.

In Chapter Two, Cleveland graphically conceptualizes space and time exploration as culturally significant sites to African creatives from an African perspective, through analyses of diverse works such as Frances Bodomo's short film, *Afronauts,* Gerald Machona's sculpture *Ndiri Afronaut (I am Afronaut)*, Jacque Njeri's digital collages from the series of *Maasci,* and photographs from Masiyaleti Mbewe's multimedia installation *The Afrofuturist*

213 • Reviews

Village. In Chapter Three, Cleveland investigates the tropes of otherworld creation, ranging from explorations of imaginative alternative surroundings to the abstract inner worlds of the human mind by creative producers to affirm Ekow Eshun's standpoint on Africans' proclivity for the fantastic in reaction to Eurocentric dominant history. Cleveland does this through the analysis of Abdourahman Waberi's novel *In the United States of Africa*, Wanuri Kahiu's *Pumzi*, and Isek Kingelez's *Ville Fantome* to elucidate how Africans might navigate imagined environments and existence. This is closely followed by an examination of technology and the concept of the digital divide in Chapter Four, to foreground that technology in Africa is not a new development, outdated or limited to urban areas. The focus of Chapter Five is on "Akan's principle of Sankofa" (107), which conceptualizes drawing from an Indigenous past and Indigenous traditions in moving the continent toward a better future. The final chapter presents the act of mythmaking and the dynamics of its application to fit imaginings of African presents and futures.

Cleveland's painstaking commitment to the principle of balanced arguments, substantiated with specific and verifiable evidence laced with examples throughout her book, validates her arguments and claims. Her effort is not limited to discussing African speculative productions; she also articulates how the circulating thoughts, opinions, and standpoints reflect the preoccupation of Africanfuturism, making the book a project that forms the bedrock for the growth of Africanfuturism. Cleveland organizes the chapters of the book in a way that hones the common themes and characteristic features of Africanfuturism while she engages the analysis of each work and compares it with other examples in the chapter. All the creative works she deals with are carefully selected to manifest multiple themes, and can therefore be discussed across multiple chapters.

Africanfuturism: African Imaginings of Other Times, Spaces, and Worlds represents a quintessential handbook of Africanfuturism useful for students, scholars, writers, artists, and Africanfuturism/Afrofuturism enthusiasts who are not only interested in African-centered futurisms but also interested in the intersections between African Cultural Studies, Diaspora Studies, and African Postcolonial Studies. Quite striking too is its use of language: it is generally accessible to a wide range of readers devoid of abstract terminologies, jargon, and linguistic and structural density. The quality of the paper used for the pages of this book matches the quality of its scholarly content, and it is enclosed in an unprovocative but alluring and glossy cover that resonates with the dream of a better future for the continent.

As a handbook of critical studies of African creative expressions and their intersection with technology, this wide-ranging and well researched book on Africanfuturism is undeniably a great addition to existing scholarship in the field of science fiction, and most fittingly, in the scholarly niche of Africanfuturism. Its scope and relevance to twenty-first-century endeavors in African critical creativity and imaginings is *sine qua non* to the furthering and expansion of the frontiers of African productions in this category, as it furthers the legacy of Pan-Africanist and decolonialist struggles for a truly free and decolonial Africa yet to come.

Works Cited

Cleveland, Kimberly. *Africanfuturism: African Imaginings of Other Times, Spaces, and Worlds*. Ohio: Ohio University Press, 2024.

Okorafor, Nnedimma Nkemdili. "nnedi OKORAFOR." 19 October 2019. *Nnedi's Blog Page*. 04 June 2024. <https://nnedi.blogspot.com/2019/10/africanfuturism-defined.html>. Accessed July 1, 2024.

Reider, John. *Colonialism and the Emergence of Science Fiction*. Connecticut: Wesleyan University Press, 2008.

Suntrum, Pamela Phatsimo. "Afro-Mythology and African Futurism: The Politics of Imagining and Methodologies for Contemporary Creative Research Practices." *Africa SF*, special issue of *Paradoxa*, edited by Mark Bould, vol. 25, 2013, pp. 113-130.

Talabi, Wole, ed. *Africanfuturism: An Anthology*. www.brittlepaper.com: Brittle Paper, 2020. Accessed July 1, 2024

Taylor, J. Taryne, et al. *The Routledge Handbook of CoFuturism*. New York: Routledge, 2024.

OLAWALE OLADOKUN is affiliated with Florida Atlantic University.

Córdoba, Antonio and Emily A. Maguire, Editors. *Posthumanism and Latin(x) American Science Fiction*. New York: Palgrave Macmillan, 2022.

Studies of posthumanism have recently taken preeminence within literary studies as concerns of human extinction have been in the forefront of the climate crisis (Córdoba and Maguire 4). Antonio Córdoba and Emily A. Maguire's *Posthumanism and Latin(x) American Science Fiction* examines speculative fiction and posthumanist studies within Latin American and Latinx communities. The collection of essays by various scholars works to underline the relationships of posthumanism, or the "entanglements of human materialities and agencies and non-human ones" within Latin American works to question Eurocentric ideology (Córdoba and Maguire 5). While many works have focused on the posthuman as an invention from the Global North, Córdoba and Maguire frame posthumanism as already found within Latin American and Latinx media. Highlighting different aspects of the posthuman, this collection brings to light prostheses, zombies, aliens, mutants, and cyborgs as posthuman subjects. The work engages with tropes and motifs that are typically overlooked in posthumanist science fiction such as the creation of the zombie in Haiti and "the anxiety of racial infection that can turn all island dwellers (and the rest of the Americas) 'Black' through the disease" (Córdoba and Maguire 95). The collection is broken up into three parts: "Posthuman Subjects," "Slow Violence and Posthuman Environments," and "Posthuman Others," containing a total of twelve chapters, the last chapter being an afterword. The organization of the chapters is broken up into three parts to center "a different aspect of posthuman subjectivity or environment" and to characterize each chapter's configuration of the posthuman (Córdoba and Maguire 12).

Editors Córdoba and Maguire innovatively introduce science fiction from both Latin America and the Latinx Diaspora. The editors clearly mention that the collection will not include analysis of works from Central America, Colombia, Peru, or Chile, because "it is simply not possible in one volume to do justice to the wealth of perspectives that the different Latin American countries and Latinx communities have to offer in a wide range of media" (Córdoba and Maguire 12). This book challenges hegemonic rhetoric that science fiction is a Eurocentric product by utilizing many different forms of media to debunk such ideology while analyzing the different motifs and tropes found within such works. The book comprehensively covers many works, for example, *Sobre los nerds y otras criaturas mitológicas* and the different ways prosthetics are used to represent nerds and weirdos. Córdoba and Maguire analyze Maielis González's work and the prosthetics that are used to create "normality" within the "nerd"; yet, the editors critique the utilization of such prosthetics because it denotes the disabled body. More specifically, the connection of Cuba to prosthetics is clear as "Cuba [...] manifests as the timeless and partially counterfeit promised land for the displaced" (Córdoba and Maguire 39). In Part One, Chapter Two, "Prosthetic Futures: Disability and Genre Self-consciousness in Maielis González Fernández's *Sobre los nerds y otras criaturas mitológicas*," Ana Ugarte looks more deeply into the tropes that have influenced González's stories and argues that "prosthesis – artificial body parts – " denotes the disabled body; however, González Fernández's nerd-monsters's consciousness and self-consciousness utilize such entities to "create an intimate knowledge about fictionalization processes that include the construction of otherness, disability, gender, and genre, as well as Cuba's exceptional status" (Ugarte in Córdoba and Maguire 47).

Moving to the posthuman subject, in Chapter Three, "We Have Always Been Posthuman: Eve Gil's *Virtus* and the Reconfiguration of the Lettered Subject," Miguel García focuses on critical posthumanism which serves to reject "the human as a universal given and has pointed out how this supposed universal human has been deployed to hide the white, European, male, upper-class subject" (García in Córdoba and Maguire 51). The neo-lettered cyborg identity in *Virtus* works to emphasize the crossroad between humanism and posthumanism, while adding value and authenticity to the posthuman subject. The collection's fourth chapter, Stephen C. Tobin's "Does Posthuman *Actually* Exist in Mexico? A Critique of the Essayistic Production on Posthumanist Discourse Written by Mexicans (2001-2007)," considers the long neglect of Mexican speculative fiction by underlining the "Eurocentric way of conceptualizing the posthuman" (Tobin in Córdoba and Maguire 81). Tobin claims this exclusion is a "hegemonic essentialism" or, as Francesca Ferranda coins the term, "'the widespread habit of only referring to thinkers, artists or theorists who belong to the cultural hegemony'" (Tobin in Córdoba and Maguire 83).

In Part Two, Chapter Five, Maia Gil'Adí's "Fukú, Postapocalyptic Haunting and Science-Fictional Embodiment in Junot Díaz's 'Monstro'" discusses the fear of racial infection in Haiti and the Dominican Republic shown through the original zombies. Such fear then spreads to "other foreign 'brown' nations such as Cambodia, Cuba, and other Caribbean islands" (Gil' Adí in Córdoba and Maguire 103). The monstro Junot Díaz creates collides with the capitalist system by registering the violence of chattel slavery and focusing on the collective of the posthuman subject rather than on the individual. Gil'Adí's focus is to transition the term "negrura," which means blackness or darkness, to the term "los negreados" or the blackened ones, to highlight the horrid histories of colonization and racism (Gil' Adí in Córdoba and Maguire 113). In Chapter Six, Jonathan Risner's "Villa Epecuén: Slow Violence and the Posthuman Film Set," describes a town in Argentina, Villa Epecuén, transformed into a posthuman space due to violence against the environment. The three movies made in this area "offer something not through the narratives or actors per se, but rather through their landscapes" (Risner in Córdoba and Maguire 140). In Chapter Seven, Samuel Ginsburg's "Catfish and Nanobots: Invasive Species and Eco-critical Futures in Alejandro Rojas Medina's *Chunga Maya*" analyzes the rhetoric of invasive species, bringing forth the ideology of humans controlling nature. "The comparison with invasive species also highlights the role of economic impact in the labeling of invasive technologies as dangerous" (Ginsburg in Córdoba and Maguire 155). In *Chunga Maya*, humans stop attempting to control nature and decide on agreements between the human and non-human, offering kinship with their surroundings.

In Chapter Eight, Córdoba and Maguire show how the cyborg in *El Cementerio de Elefantes* "is used to explore the figure of the Indian in contact with the forces of the capitalist market" (Córdoba and Maguire 169). In Part Three, Chapter Eight, Liliana Colanzi's "Andean Cyborgs: Market and Indigeneity in Miguel Esquirol's *El Cementerio de Elefantes*" discusses the posthuman as a product of violence within Latin America. Cyborgs are used to characterize the Indian in *El Cementerio de Elefantes* while imagining a futuristic world "from the margins" (Colanzi in Córdoba and Maguire 175). Colanzi claims the Indian in *El Cementerio de Elefantes* to be a displacement who is used to disrupt modernization. However, I cannot help but wonder if the Indian is also used to represent exploitation of the poor. It seems the Indian in Esquirol's work is written as a displacement that will eventually join the resistance movement; however, this character seems to be purposefully depicted to object to the capitalist market. Rather than being analyzed as a rejection of Eurocentric society, the Indian is not an Other but a perfect fit within the resistance, and therefore a product of his environment. Thus, these essays open space for further work on these topics, such as that which discusses the individual exploitation of each character within his, her or their society.

In Chapter Nine, M. Elizabeth Ginway's "The Politics of Resistance in Brazil's Dystopian Thriller *3%*" analyzes the Netflix series *3%* and argues that the two Black women characters are used to estrange "viewers from social norms" as the series' way of resisting normative modernity (Ginway in Córdoba and Maguire 190). In Chapter Ten, William Orchard's "Bruja Theory: Latinidad Without Latinos in Popular Narratives of Brujería" examines bruja narratives as a response to White supremacy. The chapter introduces the TV series *Brujos* and its push towards revolution. In Chapter Eleven, Antonio Córdoba's "'A Mutant Faith': Science Fiction, Posthumanism, and Queer Futurity in Area's *KiCK* Album Pentalogy" discusses the popular album utilization of cyborg imagery and tropes to fully articulate Arca's work as "productive disorientation, re-creation, and cognitive and affective estrangement" to open doors to a "limitless future" (Orchard in Córdoba and Maguire 223).

Overall, this book is a great choice for academics as many theorists introduce a topic in an area not typically discussed: science fiction in Latin American countries and the Latinx Diaspora. The collection covers many forms of media from TV series to tropes found within Latinx communities. This book offers a deep immersion in Latin(x) American Science Fiction, encouraging the reader to explore more about this topic.

CAILEY POIRIER

www.ingramcontent.com/pod-product-compliance
Lightning Source LLC
LaVergne TN
LVHW030635080426
835510LV00022B/3372